S O V E R E I G N

SOVEREIGN AMITY

FIGURES OF FRIENDSHIP
IN SHAKESPEAREAN
CONTEXTS

Laurie Shannon

THE UNIVERSITY OF CHICAGO PRESS

Chicago & London

LAURIE SHANNON is assistant professor of English at Duke University. Her articles and essays have appeared in *Modern Philology, Shakespeare Studies, American Literature, ELH,* and *English Literary Renaissance.* This is her first book.

The University of Chicago Press, Chicago 60637
The University of Chicago Press, Ltd., London
© 2002 by The University of Chicago
All rights reserved. Published 2002
Printed in the United States of America

11 10 09 08 07 06 05 04 03 02   1 2 3 4 5
ISBN: 0-226-74966-5   (cloth)
ISBN: 0-226-74967-3   (paper)

Library of Congress Cataloging-in-Publication Data

Shannon, Laurie.
  Sovereign amity : figures of friendship in Shakespearean contexts /
Laurie Shannon.
     p.   cm.
Includes bibliographic references and index.
  ISBN 0-226-74966-5 (cloth : alk. paper) — ISBN 0-226-74967-3
(paper : alk. paper)
  1. English literature—Early modern—1500–1700—History and
criticism. 2. Friendship in literature—England—Early modern.
3. Kingship in literature—England—1500–1700. 4. Shakespeare,
William, 1564–1616—Views on friendship. 5. Renaissance—
England—Political thought. 6. Renaissance—England—
Treatment of gender and sexuality. I. Title.

  PR3069.F73 S48 2002
  822.3′3—dc21

2001001936

For thy sweet love rememb'red such wealth brings
That then I scorn to change my state with kings.
                                    —Shakespeare, Sonnet 29

CONTENTS

᷒

ILLUSTRATIONS

ACKNOWLEDGMENTS

A scholar of friendship experiences, perhaps, too much pleasure in the chance to reckon her debts. I'm grateful for the ways that mine range among teachers, colleagues, students, friends, and family; grateful too that most of them belong to some multiple of these categories.

First and foremost, I thank Janel Mueller, who supervised this book's beginnings at the University of Chicago. In addition to her keenness and candor, I have also benefited from her way of reading. The kinds of things she sees in historically distant texts and the precise way she focuses the lens of reading to adjust to them were then—and still are—an inspiration. Josh Scodel consistently helped me to ground my thinking; Lauren Berlant always prompted me to uproot it. I am also glad to be able to thank Jim Chandler, Paul Hunter, Beth Helsinger, David Bevington, Wendy Olmstead, Jay Schleusener, Richard Strier, Isaac and Janine Barchas, Tom Krise, Paula McQuade, Glenn Clark, Barbara Crawford, Meiling Hazelton, Tom Thuerer, and Tim Child for the many kinds of help and friendship they gave me. I owe a special debt to fellow Hyde Parkers Maurine Stein and Isabel, Harold, and Steve Gabel and to Maryla Nienhuis, whose friendship and camaraderie helped me toward the question of friendship—and distracted me from it. Leny Jansen generously coped with this book's earliest formulations, and I thank her, especially, for much more beyond that kindness.

At Duke and beyond, I have enjoyed a wonderful array of colleagues and friends, who diversely supported both this book and its author. I thank Jonathan Goldberg most particularly for his friendship and for his grand questions and particular readings (of my work and of texts we've read together); Michael Moon, for his profound goodwill (what Cicero calls "the very name of friendship"); Cathy Davidson and Ken Wissoker, for their irrepressible optimism (what Burton calls friendly "confabulation"); and Marianna Torgovnick, Nahum Chandler, Catherine Beaver, Chris Newfield, Karla Holloway, Avery Gordon, Kate Radway, Lara Bovilsky, Stanley Fish, Eve Sedgwick, Barbara Herrnstein Smith, Tyler Curtain, Maureen Quilligan, Annie Jones, Cathy Gruber, Leigh DeNeef, Jim Siedow, Irene Tucker, and Irene Silverblatt, for many cumulative hours spent deliberating subjects both monumental and ephemeral—as Bacon says, it's a bad thing to allow one's thoughts "to passe in smother." Peter Stallybrass has cheerfully afforded me new angles from which to chart the book's completion. At the University of Chicago Press, I thank Alan Thomas, Leah Marcus, and Bruce Smith for their generous engagements with the manuscript, and Doug Mitchell, Randy Petilos, and Sandy Hazel for their crucial support.

My family, Sue, Pearl, and Bill Shannon, have been "friends" in the most vigorous early modern sense of the word: through so much, and for so long, they have been backers and partisans, and their backing made the path leading to this book possible. Nabil Abu-Assal has been my true counselor under all conditions—in such a counselor, Bacon says, one has, "as it were, two Lives in one's desires." My partner, Jan Radway, has seen me through to the completion of *Sovereign Amity* and affected its course by energizing the link between friendship and readership. With a darting verve that is hers alone, she also brings the sweeping rhetorical hopes of "Renaissance friendship" to life. As Montaigne writes, the parties "to this amitie I speake of . . . can no more finde the seame that hath conjoyned them together."

I have presented parts of this book at the University of Pennsylvania History of the Material Text seminar, the John Donne Society open session and the "Formulations of Friendship" panel at the San Francisco MLA meeting in 1998, and the Renaissance Workshop at Chicago; the questions I received on these occasions have been contributions. I am also grateful indeed to the Mellon Foundation, the National Endowment for the Humanities, the Newberry Library (where John Powell was especially helpful in gathering illustrations), and Duke University for fellowships enabling my research and archival efforts.

My thanks to *English Literary Renaissance, ELH,* and *South Atlantic Quarterly* for their permission to reproduce versions of arguments that first appeared in their pages. An earlier version of portions of chapter 2 appeared as "*The Tragedie of Mariam*: Cary's Critique of the Terms of Founding Discourses" in *English Literary Renaissance* 24, no. 1 (winter 1994): 135–53; a shorter version of chapter 3 appeared as "Emilia's Argument: Friendship and 'Human Title' in *The Two Noble Kinsmen*" in *ELH* 64, no. 3 (September 1997): 657–82; and portions of chapters 4 and 5 appeared as "Monarchs, Minions, and 'Soveraigne' Friendship" in *South Atlantic Quarterly* 97, no. 21 (winter 1998): 91–112.

Finally, I thank the students at Chicago and at Duke who spent time thinking about the history of friendship with me. I dedicate this book to the memory of Claude J. Falcone (1932–2000), an extraordinary high school art teacher and the sporadic deliverer of a truly Shakespearean rendition of Sonnet 29.

"Soveraigne Amitie"

❧

In any history of friendship and its formulations, the early modern period commands particular attention. On the one hand, friendship's history seems to defy historical particularity. The conceits reckoning the friend *another self* predate Aristotle, and they remain proverbial even now; a small, tightly knit friendship canon extends from Plato to Derrida, and its detailed cross-referencings suggest a conversation that takes place outside of time.[1] But against this perennialism stands the virtual chorus of Renaissance writers who celebrated friendship in a very specific form. In fact, these writers so extensively engaged the tropes of amity that the expression "Renaissance friendship" now routinely names the entire discursive phenomenon. As we shall see, this discourse not only poeticized likeness, but also created a unit *(e pluribus unum)* with its own experimental relations to agency and polity.

The phrase "Renaissance friendship" does more than invoke the terms of a literary-historical period; it also periodizes affect, setting an era of affectivity and its representations apart from its historical others. Indeed, Renaissance friendship's repeated privileging of (erotic and non-erotic) same-sex bonds over (presumptively erotic) heterosexual relations marks the gaping distance between early modern "homonormative" affects and contemporary heterosexual, erotic normativity. Describing a text from

---

1. Aristotle, though often credited with first reckoning the friend "another self," described variant phrasings as already common sayings: "all the proverbs agree in this; for example, 'Friends have one soul between them' [and] 'Amity is equality.'" Aristotle, *Nicomachean Ethics,* trans. Horace Rackham (Cambridge, Mass.: Harvard University Press, 1926), p. 535 (bk. 9, pt. 4, sec. 5) and pp. 549–51 (bk. 9, pt. 8, sec. 2). Plato's *Lysis* (ca. 370 B.C.) and Jacques Derrida's *Politics of Friendship,* trans. George Collins (London: Verso, 1997) may serve here as bookends for this canonical and philosophical conversation.

1630, Jeffrey Masten says it comes "comparatively late in the history of Renaissance friendship."[2] This history is a history of the early modern rhetorical practice of "soveraigne amitie," and it remains to be told.

Against the philosophizing tendency to read friendship for truths that cross the limits of time and material determinations (a tendency in the friendship canon itself and among its commentators as well), this book places friendship discourses historically in order to assess the more local cultural work they do. Addressing the friend in Sonnet 29, Shakespeare avows that his "sweet love rememb'red such wealth brings / That then I scorn to change my state with kings." Taking its cue from the reversible "states" suggested here between amity and kingship, *Sovereign Amity* contextualizes early modern interest in friendship and its tropes of likeness to propose a historical account of their broader implications for English culture, subjects, and political thought. Renaissance writers explore friendship's figures with a vigorous attention, and we shall see how the resulting dispensations of gender, chastity, agency, sexuality, counsel, responsibility, and lawfulness can be surprisingly mobile.

Scholars have long observed the special emphasis on likeness between friends, noting its rhetorical flourish as a poetic conceit.[3] But this conceit is not merely ornamental. The radical likeness of sex and station that friendship doctrines require singly enables a vision of parity, a virtually civic parity not modeled anywhere else in contemporary social structures. Further, the insistent emphasis on sexual and social sameness is a systematic response to that most acute form of early modern difference: the hierarchical difference of degree, especially the categorical difference between rulers and the ruled (which, in friendship, becomes a difference in "kind"). A discourse of degree separates sovereign and subject through a quasi-legal differentiation of "private persons" from those of "public estate," and complex dispensations of agency and powers result. While for the subject the exalted discourses of amity radically figure a fantasy of agency that I term private sovereignty, the monarch's situation is sharply distinguished. The precondition of the king's function as an emblem of public sovereignty is his emphatic and comprehensive preclusion from exercising the very ges-

---

2. Jeffrey Masten, *Textual Intercourse: Collaboration, Authorship, and Sexualities in Renaissance Drama* (Cambridge: Cambridge University Press, 1997), p. 30 (describing Richard Brathwait's 1630 *The English Gentleman*).

3. See Laurens Mills's encyclopedic account of ideal friendship's literary appearances, *One Soul in Bodies Twain: Friendship in Tudor and Stuart Literature* (Bloomington, Ind.: The Principia Press, 1937).

tures and capacities friendship celebrates. Heroic, "true" friends, flatterers, counselors, monarchs, tyrants and their minions, and the tales of consent and counsel they enact all join to embody a mythography of the political institution before liberalism. Their early modern life enables these friendship figures to become familiars of the political imagination.

The Sovereign Subject

Classically derived figures of friendship at the center of the humanist curriculum held out a discourse of more than self-fashioning to readers when they cast the friend as "another self" and merged a pair of friends as "one soul in two bodies." Referencing an insistently same-sex friendship with complex relations to eroticism, these two phrasings appear across a remarkable range of cultural locations in the English Renaissance. Together, the two notions enable a sixteenth-century inquiry into the hypothetical workings of what must have seemed implausible on its face: volitional polity. Likeness in both sex and status *is* (the only) political equality in period terms; on the basis of this likeness, writers stress the making of a consensual social bond or body that is not inherently subordinating.[4] In the first English translation of Cicero's *De amicitia* (an incunable from William Caxton's press), humanist John Tiptoft terms the friend "another . . . the same" and recommends to his reader in 1481 "that of tho[se] tweyne he shold make wel nygh one."[5]

Through the sixteenth century, friendship's phrases make their way across increasingly popular materials. Erasmus's *Adagia* (1536) offers as economical a formulation as one could hope to find: "Amicitia aequalitas. Amicus alter ipse" ("friendship is equality" and "the friend is another self"). This adage appears as the second entry in a collection of more than four thousand adages (the first is "between friends all is common").[6] Thomas Elyot improvises on the *alter ipse* notion, informing readers of

4. For a discussion of "voluntary submission," see François Rigolot, "Reviving Harmodius and Aristogiton in the Renaissance: Friendship and Tyranny as Voluntary Servitude," *Montaigne Studies* 11 (1999): 107–19.

5. Cicero, *De amicitia,* trans. John Tiptoft (London: William Caxton, 1481), fols. 22r–22v. Subsequent references to this work are to either this translation or the one in the Loeb Classical Library series (*De senectute, De amicitia, De divinatione,* with an English translation by William Armistead Falconer [Cambridge, Mass.: Harvard University Press, 1923]), unless otherwise indicated, and will be referenced as "Tiptoft" and "Falconer," respectively.

6. Erasmus of Rotterdam, *Adagia,* trans. Margaret Mann Phillips, in *The Collected Works of Erasmus* (Toronto: University of Toronto Press, 1982), 31:31 (bk. 1, sec. 1, adage 2).

The Boke Named the Governour (1531) that "a frende is properly named of Philosophers the other I."[7] Richard Taverner's gathering of "proper wytty and quycke sayenges," *The Garden of Wysdom* (1539), asserts that when Aristotle was "demau[n]ded, what a frend is, One soule, [quothe] he, in two bodyes."[8] Translating Erasmus's popular *Apophthegmes* through the 1540s and 1550s, Nicolas Udall further trades on these phrasings by referring to one of the most famous pairs of exemplary friends in friendship's archive: "Alexander estemed Hephestion a second Alexander, according to the prouerbe *amicus alter ipse* that is, two frendes are one soul and one [sic] body."[9] The errors here, glossing one proverb as the other and substituting "one" body for "two bodies," make no mistake: two equal corporeal bodies bound in friendship constitute a single corporate or juridical body, a legal fiction creating an operative unity.

From this basis in the broadly pedagogical texts of diverse social strata, the tropes of friendship make their way into even wider contexts in the latter part of the century. The poem "Of Frendship" appears in *Tottel's Miscellany,* condensing the much-circulated sentiments in a couplet: "Behold thy frend, and of thy self the pattern see: / One soull, a wonder shall it seem, in bodies twain to be."[10] Michel de Montaigne, in an essay plundered by English writers, affirms that such friends constitute "no other than one soule in two bodies, according to the fit definition of *Aristotle.*"[11] Shakespearean instances abound: in *As You Like It,* for example, Celia chides Rosalind for not realizing that any misfortune is a shared one, say-

7. Thomas Elyot, *The Boke Named the Governour,* ed. Foster Watson (New York: Everyman, 1907), p. 164.

8. Richard Taverner, *The Garden of Wysdom* (London: Richard Bankes, 1539), no pagination; quotations are from the second page of the section on Aristotelian sayings.

9. *Apophthegmes, that is to saie, prompte, quicke, wittie and sentencious sayinges, of certain emperours, kynges, capitaines, philosophiers and orators . . . First gathered and compiled in Latin by the ryght famous clerke Maister Erasmus of Roterodame,* trans. Nicolas Udall (London: Richard Grafton, 1542; John Kingston, 1564; reprint, ed. Robert Roberts, Boston: Lincolnshire, 1877), p. 233.

10. *Tottel's Miscellany (1557–1587),* ed. Hyder Edward Rollins (Cambridge, Mass.: Harvard University Press, 1965), p. 106. The poem is attributed to Nicolas Grimald.

11. Michel de Montaigne, *The Essayes of Montaigne: John Florio's Translation,* ed. J. I. M. Stewart (New York: Modern Library, 1933), pp. 150–51. Subsequent English quotations from Montaigne's essays are to this edition, which was entered in the Stationer's Register in 1600 and published in 1603. The *Essais* were first published in 1580, with revised editions appearing in 1588 and, after Montaigne's death, in 1595; the essay "De l'amitié" shows some modifications, mostly additions. Florio's text follows the fullest, 1595 edition.

ing she lacks "the love / That teaches thee that thou and I *am* one." [12] The
plural subject attaches to a singular verb, according to a friendship doctrine that schools its pupil-subjects about themselves and the specific rules
governing their engaged unity, their assembled condition as they become
"one." Friendship discourses invariably link the mirroring of selves with
this making of (quasi-civic) bodies. There are selves, to vary Stephen
Greenblatt's phrasing, and a sense that they can be doubled. [13] Such doubling is an instance of political formation, and it finds repeated valorization
in the texts of Renaissance self-fashioning.

Throughout these materials, we see friendship granted a doctrinal status, one eliciting ongoing acts of interpretation and by which specific conduct may be judged. Readers are envisioned as active; they are called to
apply what they read. Elyot proposes that his friendship tale be "studiousely radde"; the Newberry Library copy of Tiptoft's Cicero is strewn
with marginal nota benes as numerous markings of "nota" and "nota de
vera amicitia" record one early reader's attention to friendship's precepts. [14]
This doctrinal cast is literally evident in an extraordinary book, *A Tipe or
Figure of Friendship. Wherein is liuelie, and compendiouslie expressed, the
right nature and propertie of a perfect and true friend.* Written by Walter
Dorke and published in 1589, it literally enumerates twenty points of
friendship's law: "I have set downe certaine Articles, precepts, or statutes
of the lawe of Amitie . . . the whiche, whosoeuer dooth not obserue and
performe, cannot obtaine the name of a sincere friend." [15] Dorke's friendship checklist offers an equation for virtuous selfhood. The reader is asked
to compare himself to its itemized strictures.

12. Shakespeare, *As You Like It,* in *The Complete Works of Shakespeare,* ed. David
Bevington (New York: Longman, 1997), 1.3.92–93, emphasis mine. All subsequent quotations to Shakespeare are from this edition unless otherwise noted.

13. "There were both selves and a sense that they could be fashioned." Stephen Greenblatt, *Renaissance Self-Fashioning from More to Shakespeare* (Chicago: University of Chicago
Press, 1980), p. 1.

14. Elyot, *The Boke named the Governour,* p. 166; Cicero, *De amicitia,* trans. Tiptoft,
fols. 7r, 7v, 8r, 15r, and passim (see also figure 1 in the present text).

15. Walter Dorke, *A Tipe or Figure of Friendship. Wherein is liuelie, and compendious-
lie expressed, the right nature and propertie of a perfect and true friend* (London: Thomas
Orwin and Henry Kirkham, 1589). For other occasional publications, see also Thomas
Churchyard, *A sparke of frendship and warme goodwill, that shewest the effect of true affec-
tion and unfoldes the finenesse of this world* (London: Thomas Orwin, 1588); and Thomas
Breme, *The mirrour of friendship: both how to knowe a perfect friend, and how to choose him*
(London: Abel Jeffes [and William Dickenson], 1584).

Shakespeare's Falstaff will instruct Prince Hal on such a finer "point of friendship"; Angel Day's guidebook to gentlemanly conduct will propound that "The limits of *Friendshippe* . . . are streight, and there can be no *Friend* where an inequality remayneth."[16] John Donne will designate friendship "my second religion" and, with the casuistry ensuing from any body of law, play out the question of orthodoxy by considering whether letter-writing is among "the *precepts* of friendship" or only "of the *counsels*."[17] Statutes, precepts, counsels, limits, points: friendship registers as a set of laws, a doctrine by which to live, a prevailing code on which the behavior of individual subjects may be modeled and by which their condition may be measured. Ironically, while the books of friendship register as a discourse of interpellative force, they draw on Stoicism to propose the reader's freedom to shape himself. It is an external directive to self-mastery, here signifying "self-rule" in the most literal way. Friendship takes shape, then, as a law of the subject—but not of his subordination.

For the political and affective contexts within which these representations circulated show how renovated classical tropes served specific local purposes. Pronouncing the friendship doctrines of antiquity in the vocabularies of their own time, Renaissance writers called this friendship *sovereign*. John Tiptoft translates the description of Cicero's speaker, Laelius, as "excelle[n]t in the soverayn fame of frendship"; he translates the unmodified Latin *benevolentia,* by adjectival addition, into idiomatic English as "souerayne benyuolence."[18] Tiptoft proselytizes "the thynge of moost souerayne plesaunce," and John Lydgate praises "frenship" as "the moost sovereyn blys."[19] Celebrating the special candor that pertains between friends, Philemon Holland, translating Plutarch, calls it a "soveraign remedie."[20] Francis Bacon describes such friendship counsel as "Healthfull

16. William Shakespeare, *Henry IV, Part One* (5.1.122); Angel Day, *The English Secretorie* (London: P. Short, 1599), p. 118.

17. John Donne, *Letters to Severall Persons of Honour* (London: J. Flesher, 1651), p. 87, emphasis mine. The letter is to Henry Goodyere and probably dates to 1607.

18. Laelius is described as "amicitiae gloria excellens" ["distinguished by a glorious friendship"]. Cicero, *De amicitia,* trans. Falconer, pp. 112, 122; trans. Tiptoft, fols. 2r, 6v.

19. Ibid., trans. Tiptoft, fol. 24r; John Lydgate, *Fabula duorum mercatorum,* cited in Laurens Mills, "The Meaning of *Edward II*," *Modern Philology* 32 (1934–35):11–31, 16.

20. Plutarch, *The philosophie commonlie called, the morals, written by the learned philosopher Plutarch of Chaeronea. Translated out of Greeke into English, and conferred with the Latine translations and the French, by Philemon Holland* (London: Arnold Hatfield, 1603), p. 94.

and Soveraigne for the Understanding."[21] Walter Dorke's pamphlet casts the "sweete communication" of a friend as a "soveraigne consolation" and "most cordiall medicine."[22] Montaigne simply termed this perfect friendship "souveraine maitresse amitié," which his translator Englishes in 1600 as "soveraigne mistris amitie" and Donald Frame casts as "sovereign and masterful friendship" in 1943.[23] In *The Merchant of Venice,* Shakespeare only exponentializes this sense, raising the phrase to the power of "godlike amity."[24] A nineteenth-century U.S. title encapsulates the oxymoronic sense of sway and submission sovereign amity entails: *Friendship: the Master-Passion.*[25]

What made friendship "sovereign" for these writers? "Efficacious or potent in a superlative degree," according to the *Oxford English Dictionary, sovereign* as a qualifier marks a greatest good. As the quasi-medical examples from Dorke, Holland, and Bacon show, a sovereign remedy is not just any cure, but the best cure; what is sovereign is maximally "Healthfull." But sovereign, of course, has another, more obvious meaning. It names both the form of a nation (sovereign autonomy) and a form of personage (a king himself). It also refers to power over others, hierarchical sway; Tiptoft translates *superiores* as "soverayns."[26] Insofar as friendship arrived from classical models as a fully consensual image of participation, it offered Renaissance readers a world in which there are, so to speak, *two sovereigns.* As a sharp counterpoint to the terms understood to hold within the hierarchical relations of monarchical society, friendship tropes comprise the era's most poetically powerful imagining of parity within a social form that is consensual. *Consent* is a key pun, as we shall see. It serves as a terminological switching point, carrying the weight of both a condition of likeness ("agreement" in its grammatical sense; correspondence) and the

21. Francis Bacon, *The Essayes or Counsels, Civill and Morall,* ed. Michael Kiernan (Cambridge, Mass.: Harvard University Press, 1985), p. 84. Subsequent references to Bacon are to this collated edition (which is based on Bacon's final edition of 1625).

22. Dorke, *A Tipe or Figure of Friendship,* sig. A3.

23. Michel de Montaigne, "De l'amitié," in *Essais,* ed. Pierre Villey (Paris: Presses Universitaires de France, 1988), pp. 184–90, 190 (subsequent French references are to this edition, which annotates the variations among Montaigne's editions); "Of Friendship," in *The Essayes of Montaigne,* p. 150; *Selected Essays,* trans. Donald Frame (New York: Walter Black, 1943), p. 65.

24. Shakespeare, *The Merchant of Venice,* 3.4.3.

25. H. Clay Trumbull, *Friendship: the Master-Passion* (Philadelphia: John Wattles, 1894).

26. Cicero, *De amicitia,* trans. Falconer, p. 180; trans. Tiptoft, fol. 20r.

actions of assent or contract ("to agree"). Montaigne's phrase "agreement of wils" confounds any determination of which of these senses is entailed. Instead of expressing dissent as such, friendship models configure an image of political consent, offering a counterpoint to prevailing types of polity. These political valences are central to "sovereign" friendship's rhetorical, affective, and political dispensations.

The Subjected Sovereign

Representations of friendship rarely fail to include a monarch in the wings; this is Renaissance friendship's early modern signature. Strewn across friendship materials one finds countless juxtapositionings of the befriended subject and the sovereign. These appearances never indicate an easy equivalence, but the benchmark of sovereign kingship does provide the convoluted measure of friendship's meanings. The much-retold stories of Damon and Pythias and Orestes and Pylades both include a tyrant figure who is reformed by friendship's spectacular example, presenting a humanist fantasy of the highest order and suggesting friendship's political sights. The notion of a friend as something more valuable than a kingdom was proverbial. Montaigne, for example, recounts the anecdote of a soldier who would not swap his horse for a kingdom, but would "willingly forgoe him to gaine a true friend." [27] In Elyot's extended friendship tale, Titus describes having foregone political sway for the sake of his friend Gysippus: "I chosynge rather to lyve with hym as his companyon and felowe, ye, and as his seruaunt, rather than to be Consull of Rome." [28] As these examples show, friendship and sovereignty are at once the same (exchangeable alternatives) and different (relativized or reversible values).

Even Shakespeare's sonnets, circulated among his "private friends" and so much considered for the historical balance they strike between heterosexual and homosocial forms, raise this question of sovereignty. In one of Shakespeare's many variants, the phrase "my friend and I are one" arises as a tongue-in-cheek instance of friendship casuistry, where the poet sardonically cancels a woman's betrayal if it transpires with his friend: "Sweet flattery! then she loves but me alone." [29] Eve Sedgwick's work has definitively traced fundamental, homosocial structures in the sonnets, showing how relations "between men" govern avowedly heterosexual configura-

27. Montaigne, *The Essayes of Montaigne,* p. 152.
28. Elyot, *The Boke Named the Governour,* p. 176.
29. Shakespeare, Sonnet 42, lines 13–14.

tions.[30] During the Renaissance itself, however, as Sedgwick notes, relations between men enjoyed the kind of privilege marking heterosexual relations in later eras; Renaissance homosociality is explicit rather than implicit. In Elyot's recounting of the Titus and Gysippus story, for example, one friend gives away his betrothed without deliberation, "more estemynge true frendship than the loue of a woman."[31] Triangulation remains critical. But the third term triangulating Renaissance male friendship (female friendship, too, as we shall see), is not necessarily a heterosexual love interest. It is most likely to be a king.

This haunting royal presence begins to suggest how friendship's affective dispensations connect to broader political questions and metaphors of rule. Lost friendship retrospectively casts its possession as somehow delusory and kingly at the same time: Shakespeare's Sonnet 87 concludes, "Thus have I had thee as a dream doth flatter, / In sleep a king, but waking no such matter."[32] In raising the specter of the flatterer again here, Shakespeare taps the rich vein of advice-to-princes texts, in which the friend's evil twin presents immediately recognizable, classically political dangers. Celebrating one friend's comprehensive redemption of the other, the already noted final couplet of Sonnet 29 offers a distilled example of this comparative measure: "For thy sweet love rememb'red such wealth brings / That then I scorn to change my state with kings." Such "states" are exchangeable, but ranked conditions; the subject-in-friendship is more sovereign than a sovereign. The trajectory of this sense of *sovereignty* is perhaps taken furthest in the vocabularies of American politics. As Mark Twain glosses it, "I am a free-born sovereign, sir, an American."[33] Here we see a fantasy of private agency (its reference is transferred to a nationalist frame), and it is calibrated through a figure of regal political power.

But if this constellation of powers "sovereigns" the subject, what are its interpellative effects for the sovereign himself? Translations of Greek and Roman friendship formulas are adaptations; they appropriate classical conventions to distinct contemporary functions. While the subject of monarchy is accorded the powers that private sovereignty assembles, the logics of Renaissance friendship also constrain the agency of "public" persons or

---

30. Eve Kosofsky Sedgwick, *Between Men: English Literature and Male Homosocial Desire* (New York: Columbia University Press, 1985), pp. 28–29.

31. Elyot, *The Boke Named the Governour,* p. 177.

32. Shakespeare, Sonnet 87, lines 13–14.

33. Mark Twain [Samuel Clemens], *The Innocents Abroad* (Hartford, Conn.: American Publishing, 1869), chap. 11, p.110.

bodies. As friendship protocols will make especially clear, an early modern idiom of public and private largely concerns a categorical difference in "personage." As the foot soldier Williams in Shakespeare's *Henry V* sarcastically frames this incommensurability, "That's perilous shot of an eldergun that a poor and a private displeasure can do against a monarch!"[34]

The office-holding "public person" (archetypically but not necessarily a monarch) maintains a governmental function that distinguishes him from the status of a merely private subject. Elyot, for example, offers to "declare howe suche personages may be prepared" for their receipt of "any great dignity, charge, or governaunce of the publike weale."[35] This status takes various names: honor, worship, office, greatness, "room," or place. The subtitle of Barnabe Barnes's 1606 *Foure Bookes of Offices* offers another condensation of the split: it describes the text as "enabling privat persons for the speciall service of all good princes and policies."[36] The differentiation of *personage* effects a distribution of what we might more familiarly call capacities, by both conferring specified forms of agency and limiting the scope of their use, as we will see. Friendship discourses consistently highlight this bifurcation as a foundational political gesture, offering a chapter in the history of public and private divisions. But they also strangely reverse the distribution of power and agency implied by the distinction—by constituting an arena in which the private person has more power than a king.

As a pre-liberal utopian discourse, one imagining what a politics of consent might look like, friendship reverses expectations about this differentiation by switching who is sovereign and who is subjected with its own allocation of capacities and deprivations. Friendship expresses both the height of a subject's power and the depths of a monarch's weakness, to the point that a king's entrance into such an absolute friendship brings about his demise as a public person, a status theorized (in an uncanny echo of friendship's "one soul in two bodies") as "one Person in Two Bodies." The rules of *amicitia* run afoul of the rules ideologically prescribing proper monarchy. Those precepts construct a king who is "peerless"; whose public function is to represent polity in generic, not particular or personal, terms; and whose duties include the sublimation of his affective interests to the good of the realm. The sense of autonomy and self-disposition cen-

---

34. Shakespeare, *Henry V,* 4.1.196–98.
35. Elyot, *The Boke Named the Governour,* pp. 18, 116.
36. Barnabe Barnes, *Foure Bookes of Offices: enabling privat persons for the speciall service of all good princes and policies* (London: A. Islip, 1606).

tral to friendship, then, forms a precise counterpoint to the processes interpellating kings in the protobureaucratic theorization of a "neutral" public power without affective interests of its own.

Sovereign Amity so contributes to an archeology of the perennial division of public from private. But it describes a moment in this history that is partly disjunctive with the forms this divide has taken in its modern iterations. We are familiar with casting this split as a matter of separate spheres between which any given person may or may not move, or as modes of operation (personal, political, professional) that one person may exercise in different contexts, or, more sharply, as fragmentations within a given self. By the twenty-first century, the fissures that "office-holding" entails have become a daily matter for all of us in corporatized or bureaucratized milieus. Renaissance discourses of friendship reveal a preliminary and different experiment in this allocation of capacities and agency. Instead, the English Renaissance calibration of a public and private divide establishes separate ontologies for the mutually exclusive states of personage—the public figure versus the private person—that appear as the dramatis personae of early modern polity.

The Range of Chapters

Sovereign Amity establishes a broad discursive context and ranges widely across the generically mixed, networked array of Tudor and Jacobean texts construing friendship's political and affective dispensations. Chapter 1 establishes the cultural scope of friendship ideas, examining classical texts and their Renaissance dissemination through pedagogy and translation, redactions, popular pamphlets, commonplace books, and emblem collections. It then explores the complex effects generated by the principles of likeness (homonormativity) in Renaissance translations of Cicero, humanist advice-to-princes texts, Elyot, Ascham, Montaigne's "Of Friendship," and Donne's "Sir, more than kisses." Likeness, parity, equality, and consent present a thoroughgoing antidote to hierarchies and tyrannies now (seemingly) obsolete; the likeness between friends radically cancels vertical difference. Self-rule, self-possession, and consensual self-disposition add up to a private sovereignty that is first calibrated in affective terms. The chapter then pairs these claims of likeness with friendship texts' treatment of differences in opinion and power, relations assessed under the guise of counsel. In these instances, instead of a pair of affectively linked twinned souls, one finds, contrarily, a cautious mode of address to a superior power, a mode in which the "private" register of friendship voices the "public" issue of the prince's need of counsel. Friendship's celebration of the uses of candor takes on a special force here; its sixteenth-century formulations enshrine liberty of speech as an extraordinary personal duty, one familiar now as a general right. Friendship thus marshals whatever there is of a specifically private subject's powers.

Chapter 2 multiplies the historical meanings of chastity to assess the ways gender difference inflects friendship discourses. It considers marriage and friendship as alternative modes of rule (over the self and over others) to frame readings of Elizabeth Cary's play, *The Tragedy of Mariam* (the first original English play published by a female writer), and also Donne's elegies and verse letters to Lady Bedford. These texts and others use gender to investigate the paradoxical terms of a "subject's independence." They invoke friendship, as Montaigne had, to figure a utopian "counterpolity" composed of two private persons. In diverse ways, however, they contest the exclusive masculinity of both classical and Renaissance friendship models; by gendering friendship female, they acutely focus the way amity figures "human title" as a prerogative of self-disposition. *Mariam* draws an analogy between female chastity and male friendship (as homonormative discourses that both oppose tyranny) and protests female friendship's impossibility under Herod's regime; Donne casts the bias against female friendship as "heresy" and imagines an identification across gender lines. These texts thus suggest ways that cross-gendered *analogies* become possible, even though cross-gendered *contacts* are otherwise invariably eroticized, and thus (in period terms) debased. Gendering friendship female links principles of chastity with the (male) Stoic doctrines of integrity so favored by Renaissance writers. The actual or implied threat of tyrannical incursions into the self's terrain, a standard feature of friendship texts, forges these analogies and enables a perspective from which gender difference is secondary to an overriding political difference of "degree."

Chapter 3 raises the stakes of this analogy between female friendship and what we might call male political chastity by considering John Fletcher and William Shakespeare's play, *The Two Noble Kinsmen,* and Donne's verse epistle "Sapho to Philaenis." The drama pluralizes chastity into a comprehensive form of female friendship advocated, strikingly, by an Amazon who serves as friendship's partisan in a political struggle with an unreasoning ruler over affective autonomy. Not only are women reckoned capable of friendship in the play, but this Amazon also revises the orthodoxies against sexuality within friendship's terrain. The play thus extends the implications of recent work on Donne's astonishing poem in the voice of Sappho: the stakes of female friendship and lesbian sexuality are made virtually identical to the more abstractly political question of a subject's threatened prerogative under monarchy. What these texts show is that the even the strongest conventions regarding gender and sexuality could rewrite themselves when governed by a stronger urgency: the frightening blend of powers embodied in Renaissance conceptions of political authority.

While friendship may figure a subject's sovereign aspiration, however, the public being that is the king cannot embark upon that exclusive relation without risk to his sovereign status. Indeed, the iterations of private and public power both offer "sovereign" figures in a double-bodied form. Hinging on permutations of the king's two-bodies theory, friendship discourses raise questions about the monarch's interiority and the regulation of his "private" self. The tensions between a potentially seditious utopian counterpolity and the ideological requirements of a state expressed in terms of royal personage generate an entire field of friendship theory problems.

Chapter 4 constructs *mignonnerie* as both a friendship paradigm in conflict with classical models and an improper mode of rule. *Mignonnerie* entails a friendship crossing the boundaries of degree, most particularly one captivating a king. In charting the cultural history of a transition in which the figure of the king's "minion" gathers increasing opprobrium (in part through explicit eroticization), the chapter incorporates materials from law cases, Edward Hall's chronicles, Elizabeth I's public speeches, and Sir Thomas Smith's treatise on governance, *De Republica Anglorum*. At stake in the early modern theorization of kingship is the formulation of a doctrine still evident in Anglophone juridical and cultural contexts: the public figure. The monarch's person, in this at once legal and popular understanding, is public property. Lacking title to himself, the king's personal dedication to one subject above all others subordinates the principle of commonweal it was his function to embody.

Chapter 5 takes up friendship's place in the reversed processes of kinging and unkinging as exemplary moments displaying conceptions of the civic condition and its institutions. Christopher Marlowe's *Edward II* directly takes up the clash between the discourses of ideal friendship and those of ethical monarchy. In an irresolvable dilemma of identity, Edward uses an exalted and classical friendship idiom; his nobles speak only of his improper *mignonnerie*. In theoretical terms, royal estate pre-empts the king's self-disposition in friendship, the precise power represented as the apex of private agency. The chapter then reads Shakespeare's *Henry IV* (parts 1 and 2) as, in effect, a friendship play, one in which the unkinging process of Marlowe's tragedy is reversed. Specifically, the becoming of a king proceeds by a disavowal of the *mignonnerie* that the prince's association with Falstaff had threatened. In an ironic inversion of the norms of true friendship and false flattery, here we find a dissembling prince and, in Falstaff, a self-designated "friend *and* a true subject." Hal's repudiation of his old companion exiles private friendship from court as he leaves personal affectivity behind in a gesture instituting proper governance. His "friends," now more abstract counselors like the Chief Justice, are not a matter of private affection, but of public office; the play thus affords a friendship allegory for government's founding moment.

Chapter 6 shifts from the ontological questions that so absorbed Renaissance writers and focuses instead on treatments of friendship's performative work. By assessing Plutarch's discourse, "How to Tell a Flatterer from a Friend" (a much-translated text throughout the sixteenth century), a model of friendly speech appears, one that is associated with a mode of acerbic rebuke that ultimately grounds not only the test of true friendship, but also the political speech of the humanist counselor. This speech mode and its essential relation to the preservation of both the self and the state comprise a practice of antibiological reproduction, a kind of regeneration. An analysis of Francis Bacon's essays on counsel and friendship launches a reading of Shakespeare's *The Winter's Tale,* one that challenges the heteronormative readings this play typically generates to emphasize instead the enormous and central shaping power of friendship forms. Turning sharply away from the processes of biological reproduction, this late Shakespearean romance reckons friendship practice ("the offices of friendship") as the ultimate frame of both individual and political life, here operating across the familiar Renaissance analogy between the self and the state.

Many of the principles that the phenomenon of Renaissance friendship made familiar in "personal," affective, or embodied terms persist, in senses now more commonly abstracted in the idioms of political ideology: consent, "liberty of speech," self-determination, affective autonomy, "public" institutions, "public" figures, and "bureaucratic" (neutral and impersonal) justice. Linking the historical development of ideas about "public" bodies (especially their establishment and the "disinterestedness" they should reflect) to the histories of reading, agency, sexuality, and affect, *Sovereign Amity* thus advocates the richly intersubjective paradigm of friendship as an indispensable vein for historical—and contemporary—critical analyses of affectivity and the political imagination.

PART ONE

THE SOVEREIGN SUBJECT

ONE

The Early Modern Politics of Likeness: Sovereign Reader-Subjects and Listening Kings

As symylytude ioyned frendshippes, so dissimylytude disseuerith them.[1]
—Cicero, *De amicitia* (1481 translation)

In the amitie I speake of; they entermixe and confound themselves one in the other, with so universall a commixture, that they . . . can no more finde the seame that hath conjoyned them together.[2]
—Montaigne, "De l'amitié" (1600 translation)

The critical reputation of *likeness* has probably never been lower, associated, as it now is, with practices ranging from narcissism to political exclusion. But to specify the uses made of classical friendship theory in early modern contexts, we must read its rhetoric of likeness in historical and political terms. Localization of its tropes of similitude reveals them to be engaged in the experimental generation of bodies, at one time both refiguring the bodies of individual subjects and forming a "corporate" body or micropoly with complex relations to the state. The enabling relation between states of "symylytude" and these acts of "commixture" in English Renaissance texts will suggest the politically generative role of likeness in friendship discourses. Friendship works as a powerful and persuasive kind of political imagination, and its figures traverse an array of forums, from humanist and courtly contexts to popular literature. Its imaginative acts are of two quite different kinds: one entails a utopian vision of human engagement (a vision of consent), and the other ultimately offers a pragmatic strategy for differences of opinion and stature (a vehicle for counsel). One

1. Cicero, *De amicitia,* trans. John Tiptoft (London: William Caxton, 1481), fol. 21r.
2. Michel de Montaigne, "Of Friendship," in *The Essayes of Montaigne: John Florio's Translation,* ed. J. I. M. Stewart (New York: Modern Library, 1933) [1603], pp. 144–54, 149. All subsequent references to Montaigne are to this edition and will appear in the text.

step shy of explicit political theory, the protocols generated by friendship's conceit of likeness may have had even broader quotidian effects than the direct theorization of similar but more systematic concepts like political "rights" could then have had.[3] Indeed, in Renaissance friendship we see certain forms of agency and capacity imagined that would only later be justified by more abstract arguments entitling political subjects to exercise them.

Neither democratic nor republican—and not even directly civic—sixteenth-century friendship does not bespeak larger social or national formations in microcosm, as it would later do in rhetorics surrounding modern democracies.[4] For Montaigne and other writers, while friendship pairing magnifies the self, the mere step toward tripling fragments it and subjects it to intolerable conflicts of interest. "This amitie which posesseth the soule and swaies in it all soveraigntie," Montaigne declaims, "it is impossible it should be double. If two at one instant should . . . crave contrary offices of you, what order would you follow? . . . A singular and principall friendship dissolveth all other duties and freeth all other obligations" (pp. 151–52). As Thomas Breme writes in *The Mirrour of Friendship* in 1584, "the number of friends causeth great importunity, the which causeth *perfect amity* to diminish, for considering well the liberty of our hearte, it is impossible that one man shoulde, or can, conforme or dispose his nature and condition to the will and liking of many."[5] So for all its markedly political terminologies (*soveraigntie* and *liberty*), this friendship discourse offers no comportment or affect to be generalized beyond the pair, no pattern to link all political subjects *to one another*. Instead, its preliminary forum is intimate: a couple, complicated in the ways I shall suggest here.

3. For a listing of historical liberal ideals and their grounding in a "rights" discourse, see Annabel Patterson, *Early Modern Liberalism* (Cambridge: Cambridge University Press, 1997), pp. 1–2. Patterson dates the emergence of liberal ideologies to the midseventeenth century. Quentin Skinner similarly considers the reemergence of Roman ideals in mid- and latter-seventeenth century political thought in *Liberty before Liberalism* (Cambridge: Cambridge University Press, 1998).

4. Jacques Derrida reads friendship discourses in the contexts of gestural and early democracy in "The Politics of Friendship," *The Journal of Philosophy* 85, no. 11 (November 1998): 632–44. Renaissance formulations, however, invariably resist generalizing the form beyond the particularized pair, separating ideal friendship from a generalizable affect such as, for example, *caritas*.

5. Thomas Breme, *The Mirrour of Friendship: both how to knowe a perfect friend, and how to choose him* (London, Abel Jeffes, 1584), sig. B.iii.r (emphasis mine).

Before a conception of rights, it grounds itself instead in a virtually Stoic emphasis on self-possession and acts of will. In this, it is rather a performative practice than a theory of entitlement. Offering no image—in itself—of a larger politics of equality, friendship operates instead as a distinguishing interpellative discourse, one that maintains the differentiated roles of sovereign and subject, but subtly begins to recalibrate their powers.

Friendship's dramatis personae invariably include a specific cast of characters: a sovereign, or agentive subject; good counselors and the flatterers who disable them; proper kings attentive to friendship virtues; and the tyrants who ignore them. Navigating by the lights of likeness, its scripts enact fundamental mythographies about the diverse members of early modern polity, their constraints, powers, and jurisdictions. I will term the perspective it articulates one of private sovereignty, crafted as it is from the position of nonparticipation in direct forms of institutional governance (office). The Latin *privatus* ("not in public office") suggests the non-office-holding condition so critical to friendship's articulation. These figures of friendship and the rhetorical tropes of likeness around which they cluster thus offer a distant prehistory to what has become the "liberal" subject. But in this story we can see a road not taken in the abandoned intersubjective roots of a narrowed modern individualism. A twisting trajectory from ancient and early modern valorizations of "liberality" (magnanimity) toward a modern "liberated" self as an unrestrained actor marks this later disjunctive history. It did not unfold inevitably.

The Homonormativity of "Wonderfull Lykeness"

Renaissance friendship's intersubjective condition founds itself on emphatic principles of sameness; its most consistent impulse is homonormative. Using the word *normative* in this way, I mean to evoke the strange blend of ordinariness, idealization, and ideology entailed in this rhetorical regime. Homonormativity, as we shall see, suggests both an affective regime and a political one. If offered as a microcosmic figure for the nation-as-democracy, this requirement of likeness, or even friendliness for that matter, would generate a wholly regressive politics. Deconstructive analysis has taught us to locate implicit logics of sameness and their political, epistemological, and philosophical effects in discourses of various kinds, stressing the resulting status of difference (its eradication or subordination as whatever is not like a given first term). Friendship's internal logics, evident in Cicero's densely paradoxical reckoning of the friend in *De amicitia* as an *alter idem* ("the/an other the same"),[6] are not immune to this analysis, but its grammars and the ramifications of its historical work also far exceed it.

Within a deconstructive perspective, critics have variously assessed the workings of likeness in Renaissance friendship, ranging its effects on a spectrum from the totalizing to the impossible. Even here, all samenesses are not the same. In an essay subtitled "Jonson's Community of the Same," Stanley Fish shows that Ben Jonson establishes himself as "the proprietor of an internal kingdom" through an exclusion of difference that, in turn, renders that kingdom "empty"; Jonson constructs an emptied community to resist, deeply, the intersubjective workings that situate him as a supplicant speaker.[7] Conversely, considering Edmund Spenser's *Shepheardes Calender,* Jonathan Goldberg pursues those "differences that refuse . . . identifications within the self-same and proper" and thus exceed the "specular relationship of similarity and simulation" in friendship's idiom.[8] In either case, whatever is "the same" replicates a prior order or singularity. These logics suggest that friendship's emphasis on likeness creates so powerful a singularity that both difference and multiplicity are made either impossible or improbable within it. On the other hand, in a recent essay on likeness and its effects in John Donne's poetry, Paula Blank stresses the sheer impossibility not of difference, but of identity itself. Poetic comparison ("homopoetics," the likening of two things) invariably falls short, she argues, and "difference emerges as the only inviolable, invariable feature of . . . experience with an other."[9] Whether sameness is empty, inevitable, reactionary, or impossible, each of these accounts—for diverse good reasons—casts likeness in negative terms.

6. Cicero, *De senectute, De amicitia, De divinatione,* trans. W. A. Falconer (Cambridge, Mass.: Harvard University Press, 1923), pp. 188–89. All references to Cicero's Latin are to this edition, as are quotations in English unless otherwise noted, and will appear in the text.

7. Stanley Fish, "Authors-Readers: Jonson's Community of the Same," *Representations* 7 (summer 1984): 26–58, 33, 34, 57. I agree with the "emptiness" Fish describes in Jonson's rhetorically-established "kingdom," but attribute it to a Jonsonian misanthropy that does not characterize friendship arguments generally.

8. Jonathan Goldberg, *Sodometries: Renaissance Texts, Modern Sexualities* (Stanford, Calif.: Stanford University Press, 1992), pp. 66, 79. See also Jeffrey Masten, *Textual Intercourse: Collaboration, Authorship, and Sexualities in Renaissance Drama* (Cambridge: Cambridge University Press, 1997), where Masten traces the authorial effects of friendship discourses as "identical homo/geneous gentlemen engaged in a homoerotic self-duplication" (p. 36).

9. Paula Blank, "Comparing Sappho to Philaenis: John Donne's 'Homopoetics,'" *PMLA* 10, no. 3 (spring 1995): 358–68, 359.

The species of likeness-as-identity invoked in these analyses emerges from contemporary philosophical discourses, especially those addressing the fallout of prevailing models of the liberal subject, where the production of equals has entailed a concomitant disenfranchisement of others. The liberal individual, in this regard, is only intersubjective in the most aggressive and negating way. But since samenesses differ, what other readings of likeness pertain before the ascendancy (and demise) of the liberal subject and its technologies? Instead of judging early modern likeness from a post-liberal perspective, this chapter tracks its rhetorical patternings to assess them for the specific opportunities they afforded sixteenth-century subjects and selves.

Friendship discourses themselves depend upon such likeness being rare, even anomalous and bizarre, celebrating it as a wonder or a marvel. In Thomas Elyot's exemplary tale of Titus and Gysippus, the longest embedded story in *The Boke Named the Governour* (1531), the two friends are classed as "wonderfull lyke." [10] Nicolas Grimald's poem "Of Frendship" in *Tottel's Miscellany* (1557) confirms "one soull, a wonder shall it seem, in bodies twain to be." [11] Thomas Churchyard's *A Sparke of Frendship and Warme Goodwill* (1588) calls friendly affect "a wonder of nature" and "a merveilous motion." [12] Such friendships, Montaigne proclaims, are so unusual that "amongst our moderne men no signe of any such is seene . . . it may be counted a wonder, if fortune once in three ages contract the like" (p. 145). At the same time, phrasings of this wondrous likeness appear to be rather flexible: friends are "lyke and semblable," "the same or semblable," or "semblable or moche like." [13] Sameness, then, is not a matter of philosophical identity, as we will see, and the texts of friendship carefully track Cicero's modifiers in the nuanced and suppositional phrase, "the friend is, *as it were*, another the same [est enim is qui est tamquam alter idem]" (pp. 188–89). Metaphorical, approximated, comparative, and, as it were, virtual: likeness remains an imaginative process or poesis.

What, then, are the meanings and cultural work of this particular

10. Thomas Elyot, *The Boke Named the Governour,* ed. Foster Watson (New York: Everyman, 1907), p. 164. References to Elyot are to this edition and will appear in the text.

11. Hyder Edward Rollins, ed., *Tottel's Miscellany (1557–1587)* (Cambridge, Mass.: Harvard University Press, 1956), p. 106.

12. Thomas Churchyard, *A Sparke of Frendship and Warme Goodwill, that Shewest the Effect of True Affection and Unfoldes the Finenesse of this World* (London: T. Orwin, 1588), sig. Cr.

13. Cicero, *De amicitia,* trans. Tiptoft, fol. 15r; Elyot, *The Boke Named the Governour,* pp.161, 162.

species of sameness as a figure in the texts and imaginings of the English Renaissance? The remarkable energy of the likeness topos in Renaissance friendship derives from its virtue as a way of envisioning a secular enfranchisement of a preliberal sort for the "private" subject, that is, anyone not occupying a place or room in the architecture of offices understood to embody government. A thought experiment generating new positions and modalities for both the formation of persons and the public institution of government, friendship operates rhetorically to construct agentive subjects and respondent kings. The most specific, local contexts suggest that its "politics of likeness"[14] voices—in radical ways for the sixteenth century— an alternative politics in which the sovereignty of the private self was speculative, rather than orthodox or normative. The sense of an equally matched pair in which such a sovereignty might be expressed was not evident anywhere else in Renaissance social structures.

Reading likeness historically in this chapter, I will consider the ways friendship languages were introduced, focusing first on the trajectory of Cicero's *De amicitia* and its advocates, the scope and formats of its dissemination, and the demographies of its readerships. The tropes and norms of this classically based model enjoyed widespread attention, and *De amicitia* and Plutarch's "How to Tell a Flatterer from a Friend" must be counted among the most resoundingly successful elements of the humanist educational program. Evidence of their curricular afterlives, too, marks friendship as a crucial, nonheteronormative model in the early modern self-fashioning repertoire. Rhetorics of friendship likeness take up residence at the very heart of the interpellating structures of Tudor culture, but its effects diverge strikingly from any simple ideological replication. Renaissance readers took up its ideas with astonishing interest. We will not find a passive readership here.

What we do find is that the political logics of sameness in Elyot, Montaigne, Shakespeare, Donne, Bacon, and myriad lesser-known writers figure an explicit mode of self-construction that proves enabling to a detailed scheme of sovereignty for the self. This intersubjective scheme suggests the terms of a radically alternative polity that celebrates ideals of autonomous consent. *Consensio* will work to signify both being alike and making an agreement. By figuring parity in this way, friendship enables, in turn, a kind of critical speech, what Montaigne calls "the admonitions and corrections (which are the chiefest offices of friendship)" (p. 145). A friend's

---

14. My phrase varies Masten's "erotics of similitude" (*Textual Intercourse,* p. 35) and the common phrase "the politics of difference."

honest counsel, crucial to texts emphasizing the discernment of true friends, must sometimes take the form of harsh or admonishing corrective speech. So embedded within the fabric of a likeness discourse (consent) we find the germ of protopolitical dissent. Circulations of Plutarch's "How to Tell a Flatterer from a Friend" link these friendly acts of truth-speaking with a sharply different relation: the emerging one between early modern monarchs and their professional counselors. For readers in contemporary constitutional democracies, Philemon Holland's 1603 translation of Plutarch employs a retrospectively rich phrase for this practice: "liberty of speech."

Together, these two dramatically different friendship arguments—an alternative, consensual polity that maximizes autonomy, and a form of subordinate speech to a sovereign power—comprise a strategy of private sovereignty, formed as they are from a (royal) subject's point of view. Better-disseminated than political theory (indeed a popular discourse), friendship discourses take up a key place not only in the vocabularies of self-fashioning, but also in political mythography. Under friendship's colors, self-determination is embodied; bonds without subordination and (doubled) selves without bounds take shape. Across the ordinary reading habits of the sixteenth century, friendship discourses establish the Ciceronian-Stoic self and its enhancement in the pair, Plutarchan counselors, and listening Kings.

"Out of Latin into English": Circulating Cicero

In the midst of Roger Ascham's *The Scholemaster* (1570), the Tudor pedagogue swerves from his discourse on Latin teaching methods to tell a personal story. The tale recalls an encounter with one John Whitney, whom Ascham names "a deare frende" and a "bedfeloe"; together, they served in Elizabeth's retinue before she became queen.[15] Ascham persuaded Whitney to learn Latin by the method advertised in his book. The shared text of Cicero's *De amicitia* structures their friendship—literally. "We began after Christmas," Ascham recounts; "I read unto him *Tullie de Amicitia,* which he did every day twise translate, out of Latin into English, and out of English into Latin agayne." The incident illustrates Ascham's celebrated "double translation" technique, richly compounding the book's doubled-self content; it also attests to a quotidian presence for Cicero's text. *De*

---

15. Roger Ascham, *The Scholemaster, Or plaine and perfit way of teachyng children, to understand, write, and speake, in Latin tong* (London: John Day, 1570), pp. 90–91. All Ascham quotations are to this passage unless otherwise noted.

amicitia appears, enmeshed with the material conditions of household life and shaping an event in two biographies in the courtly self-fashioning milieu of Princess Elizabeth's house.

Ascham does not stop with the mere narration of this Ciceronian exchange. John Whitney died young, "to the great lamentation of that whole house, and specially to that most noble Ladie, now Queene Elizabeth her selfe." Just as service to Elizabeth triangulated the two friends' coming together, the queen provides a sovereign cognizance of Whitney's virtue that frames Ascham's own lamentation. (As we will see, royal attention to friendship virtues and virtuous friends shows the prince to be no tyrant). The lament proceeds as a page-long memorializing poem he calls a "kinde of misorderlie meter," erupting from the teacher's prose "though I had never Poeticall head, to make any verse, in any tong." Seized by friendly affect, Ascham digresses from his pedagogical mission and even suspends his own "misliking of Ryming" to voice a highly sentimental friendship poem.[16] Ascham's crisis in narrative voice traces one literal exchange of the Ciceronian text and two transactions in selfhood. The exchange leads a promising young courtier into Latin and is an act of pedagogy that changes the teacher. The passage pivots from textual attention to *De amicitia* (shared and double-translated) to an attestation to Whitney's irreplaceability and to a display of the "private" Ascham, inspired to poetic expression, all presided over by "Queene Elizabeth her selfe."

Ascham's episode instances how the peregrinations of *De amicitia* make available a discourse of (doubled) self-formation by taking friendship tropes "out of Latin into English." *De amicitia,* translated in 1481 by the early humanist John Tiptoft, was among those texts printed by William Caxton. The preface to Tiptoft's translation of Cicero's "lityl treatys" introduces "Tullius de Amicicia [sic] translated in to our maternall Englisshe tongue."[17] Tiptoft emerges from a medieval monastic engagement with friendship doctrines, one that had struggled with the apparent worldliness

---

16. Ibid., p. 146; T. W. Baldwin, with good reason, calls this a "fearful paroxysm of meter" in *William Shakspere's Smalle Latine & Lesse Greeke* (Urbana: University of Illinois Press, 1944), 2:591 n. 29.

17. Cicero, *De amicitia,* trans. Tiptoft, fol. 1r. Relaying Cicero's etymology for amity, Tiptoft writes that it "is love of whome amytee hath his name / ffor of Amor comyth Amicicia [sic]" (fol. 8v). Tiptoft not only refers to amity and friendship, but also uses the word *frendlyhode* (i.e., fol. 10v). Elyot's later redactions extend Cicero's commentary to English, referencing the "latin *Amor,* whereof *Amicitia* cometh, named in englisshe frendshippe or amitie" (*The Boke Named the Governour,* p. 162).

of an attachment to a particular friend.[18] Caxton's publication of *De amicitia* begins a process that will distribute its tropes farther afield and locate it at the heart of a secular public culture.[19] This dissemination hinges on an expanding readership deemed to be actively interested in consuming classical examples by putting them to use to detect and to practice "true" friendship.

As Lorna Hutson has described it, a new pattern of subjectivity resulted from humanist strategies of teaching through *copia,* and it entailed the practice of what she terms "the husbandry of exempla," a rhetorical and prudential mastery in marshaling tropes and examples proper to an occasion.[20] Friendship texts prove no exception to this reading practice. The Newberry Library copy of Tiptoft's translation of *De amicitia* is strewn

18. Aelred of Rievaulx, a Yorkshire Cistercian (d. 1167), composed *De Spirituali Amicitia* deeply impressed by *De amicitia;* the opening sentence of his dialogue on friendship suggests the stakes of a Christian perspective: "Aelred: Here we are, you and I, and I hope a third, Christ, is in our midst." *Spiritual Friendship,* trans. Eugenia Laker, S.S.N.D. (Kalamazoo, Mich.: Cistercian Publications, 1974). See also Thomas à Kempis, *Imitation of Christ,* trans. Leo Shirley-Price (London: Penguin, 1952): "If you have dwelt in [your cell] and kept it well, it will later become a dear friend"; he calls the relation to Christ "a Friendship exceeding all expectation," saying "Love him, . . . and keep Him as your friend" (pp. 51, 67, 75). Medieval *ars moriendi* frequently cast friends as potential obstacles to dying well, generating "ouer-much occupacion & besynesse about outward temporall [th]ingis . . . loued inordinatly" (*The Book of the Craft of Dying,* quoted and discussed in Christina von Nolcken, "'O, why ne had y lerned for to die?': *Lerne for to Die* and the Author's Death in Thomas Hoccleve's *Series,*" in *Essays in Medieval Studies* 10 (1993): 27–51, 37). Each of these instances problematizes the primacy of the exclusively coupled and earthly pair.

19. Baldwin suggests that this translation was widely used until John Harington's *The boke of frendshippe* (1550), which is based on a French version, and then Thomas Newton's *Of Frendshippe* (1577) arrived on the scene (Baldwin, *William Shakspere's Small Latine & Lesse Greeke,* p. 590 n. 27). On the influence of Cicero in the wider European context, see Barry Weller, "The Rhetoric of Friendship in Montaigne's *Essais,*" *New Literary History* 9 (spring 1978): 503–23, 504.

20. Lorna Hutson, *The Usurer's Daughter: Male Friendship and Fictions of Women in Sixteenth-Century England* (London: Routledge, 1994). Richard Halpern argues that the humanist emphasis on *copia* as a pure form had the effect of minimizing the specific content of classical materials; the weird irreducibility of friendship tropes seems an exception to this neutralization. See *The Poetics of Primitive Accumulation: English Renaissance Culture and the Genealogy of Capital* (Ithaca, N.Y.: Cornell University Press, 1991), p. 45–56. For the sprawling meanings of the term *copia* for riches and plenty, see Terence Cave, *The Cornucopian Text: Problems of Writing in the French Renaissance* (Oxford: Clarendon Press, 1979).

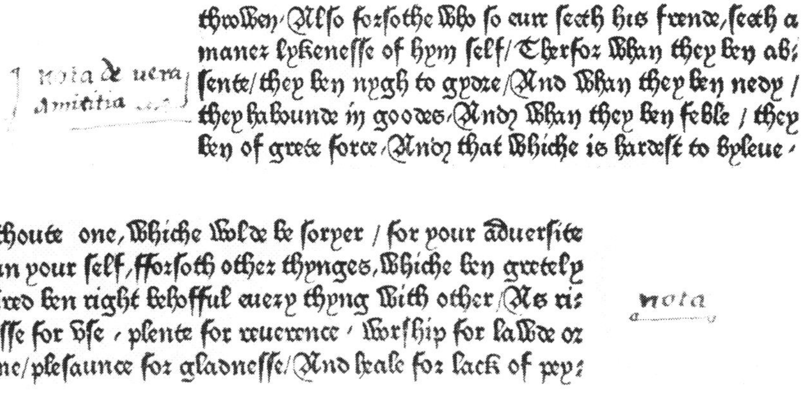

¶ nota de uera
amicitia

thewißen/Alßo forfothe Wßo fo eur feeth his frende/feeth a
maner lykeneffe of hym felf/Therfor Whan they ben ab-
fente/they ben nygh to gydre/And Whan they ben nedy/
they haßounde in goodes/And Whan they ben feble/they
ben of grete force/Andß that Whiche is fardeft to byleue·

Withoute one/Whiche Wolde be foryer/for pour aduerfite
than pour felf/fforfoth other thynges/Whiche ben gretely
defired ben right beßoffuß euery thyng With other/As ri-
cheffe for bfe · plente for reuerence · Worßhip for laße or
fame/plefaunce for gladneffe/And skale for lack of pep-

nota

FIGURE 1. Annotated passages from Cicero, *De amicitia*, translated by John Tiptoft (London: Caxton, 1481), fols. 7v and 7r. Photo courtesy of The Newberry Library, Chicago.

with inked markings of "nota" and other Latin highlightings (see fig. 1). The reader has ornamented one of the most key definitional passages for sixteenth-century appropriations of Cicero ("forsothe who so evir seeth his frende, seeth a maner lykenesse of hym self / Therefor whan they ben absente / they ben nygh to gydre"), glossing it with "nota de vera amicitia" (fol. 7v). A programmatic drive to harvest useful textual fragments reflects, as Walter Ong has shown, both the "humanist desire to expedite *inventio* by having at hand massive stores of material" as well as the "habit" of collecting commonplaces.[21] It also, it is worth recalling, entails a conviction of the relevance of classical exempla to contemporary practice. Friendship texts not only instance these transactions in phrases and subjectivity; they are at once uniquely central in Latin learning contexts and singularly successful beyond them, in English modes of reading, writing, and oral culture.[22]

De amicitia plays an astonishingly key role in the school curricula for-

21. Walter Ong, "Tudor Writings on Rhetoric, Poetic, and Literary Theory," in *Rhetoric, Romance, and Technology: Studies in the Interaction of Expression and Culture* (Ithaca: Cornell University Press, 1971), p. 76. Halpern details the economistic motivations of this habit (*The Poetics of Primitive Accumulation*, pp. 19–60).

22. The Caxton preface even addresses "al them that shall here or rede" the treatise, a reminder of the importance of aural textual experience among both the literate and nonliterate. See also Roger Chartier, "Reading Matter and 'Popular' Reading: From the Renaissance to the Seventeenth Century," in *A History of Reading in the West*, ed. Guglielmo Cavallo and Roger Chartier (Amherst: University of Massachusetts Press, 1999), pp. 269–83, 270.

mulated by humanist and education writers, where it appears as a gateway text in Latin learning. Its special place derived from its double service as a model for both grammatical and "moral" imitation. Referencing the Continental milieu, Kristian Jensen cites an anonymous German textbook writer (from the mid-1480s) who propounds the virtues of Italian methods: "as soon as [the boys] have learned the most elementary grammar they . . . study the *Epistulae ad familiares, De amicitia, De senectute, Paradoxa Stoicorum* and other works by Cicero."[23] English treatise writers confirm this phased curriculum. Richard Mulcaster, author of *Positions concerning the Training Up of Children* (1581) and the first schoolmaster at the largest school in London at the time, the Merchant Taylors' School, implemented such a curriculum during his twenty-five-year tenure.[24] We have seen *De amicitia*'s place in Ascham's personal repertoire, but he, too, prescribes its curricular place. After the scholar has mastered double translation, he moves to a stage where reading for "content" is emphasized more strongly, and here Ascham recommends "some booke of Tullie, as the third booke of Epistles chosen out by [Johan] Sturmius, *de Amicitia, de Senectute,* or that excellent Epistle conteinyng almost the whole first booke *ad Q. fra.*"[25] The progression here moves directly from grammatical imitation to moral self-formation.

T. W. Baldwin's comprehensive survey of classical pedagogy confirms widespread implementation of this basic curriculum, one in which *De amicitia* functioned as the pivotal entry into moral philosophy on the completion of grammatical training. Detailing the definitive Forms established under Edward VI and examining curricula at Eton, Winchester, Paul's, and other smaller schools, Baldwin's information shows Cicero's friendship treatise normally being read in the earliest period of upper school (Fifth Form), sometimes complemented by *De senectute* (Of old age).[26] In fact, by at least 1574, Latin textbooks gathering Ciceronian material were being printed in England, and they included not only these two works along with the more advanced *De officiis,* but also *Paradoxa, De somnio Scipionis*

---

23. Anonymous, *Exercitium puerorum grammaticale per dietas distributum* (Hagenau: n.p., 1491), sig. A1v–2r, cited in Kristian Jensen, "The Humanist Reform of Latin and Latin Teaching," in *The Cambridge Companion to Renaissance Humanism,* ed. Jill Kraye (Cambridge: Cambridge University Press, 1996), pp. 63–81, 67.

24. Richard Mulcaster, *Positions concerning the Training Up of Children,* ed. William Barker (Toronto: University of Toronto Press, 1994), pp. xiii, lx, lxiii.

25. Ascham, *The Scholemaster,* p. 87.

26. Baldwin, *William Shakspere's Small Latine & Lesse Greek,* 1:316, 341, 348, 354, 433, 583; 2:541.

(neither of which Baldwin finds mentioned in curricular use), and prefatory annotations by Erasmus and Philip Melancthon.[27] In the grammar school use of this volume, *De amicitia* normally preceded the penultimate text in moral philosophy, *De officiis;* Baldwin describes many of these used grammar school copies as having seen "hard service" and being scarred by "scribbles and other boyish devices." [28] Ong has characterized Latin learning, for better or worse, as a "puberty rite" for English boys.[29] For any schoolboy completing grammar school (and any not quite finishing), exposure to *De amicitia,* in Latin, could hardly have been avoided; it must be counted among the most commonly learned Latin texts in the Tudor era.

In the contexts of childhood Latin learning, one can easily imagine the commonsense appeal of *De amicitia* to schoolmasters trying to keep the attention of their pupils. By 1577, the treatises gathered in the Cicero textbook were also bound together in Thomas Newton's single-volume English translation, *Fowre Seuerall Treatises of M. Tullius Cicero,* and the grouping remained a favorite in both languages.[30] Beyond these actual editions of Cicero, *De amicitia* cycles through an array of publishing formats for diverse English-language readerships, in commonplace books like Richard Taverner's *Garden of Wysdom;* collections of apothegms and adages like Nicolas Udall's translations of Erasmus; redactions such as Elyot's or Montaigne's; small books such as those of Walter Dorke, Thomas Breme, and Thomas Churchyard;[31] emblem book imageries; and

27. Cicero, *De Officiis M.T. Ciceroni Libri Tres. Item, De Amicitia: De Senectute: Paradoxa: & de Somnio Scipionis. Cum D. Erasmi Roterodami, Phillipi Melancthonis, ac Bartholomaei Latomi Annotationes* (London: John Kingston, 1574), listed in Baldwin as unrecorded (*William Shakspere's Small Latine & Lesse Greek,* 2:581). Publication of this textbook accrued to the Society of Stationers in the early seventeenth century monopoly on schoolbooks (1:506).

28. Baldwin, *William Shakspere's Small Latine & Lesse Greek,* 2:590–91, 581–82.

29. Walter Ong, "Latin Language Study as a Renaissance Puberty Rite," in Ong, *Rhetoric, Romance, and Technology,* pp. 113–41.

30. Cicero, *Fowre Seuerall Treatises of M. Tullius Cicero, Conteyninge his most learned and Eloquente Discourses of Frendshippe: Oldage: Paradoxes: and Scipio his Dreame,* trans. Thomas Newton (London: Thomas Marshe, 1577); Baldwin, *William Shakspere's Small Latine & Lesse Greek,* 2:590.

31. Walter Dorke, *A Tipe or Figure of Friendship. Wherein is liuelie, and compendiouslie expressed, the right nature and propertie of a perfect and true friend* (London: Thomas Orwin and Henry Kirkham, 1589). For other occasional publications, see also Thomas Churchyard, *A sparke of frendship and warme goodwill, that shewest the effect of true affection and unfoldes the finenesse of this world* (London: Thomas Orwin, 1588); and Thomas Breme, *The mirrour of friendship: both how to knowe a perfect friend, and how to choose him* (London: Abel Jeffes [and William Dickenson], 1584).

headings in the personal commonplace books all Renaissance readers (Latined and un-Latined alike) were taught to compose. As Roger Chartier has argued, "rigid divisions and cultural distinctions" inappropriately freeze Renaissance reading practices, since "the same texts and the same books often circulated in all social milieus."[32] While formatting and modes of consumption vary sharply, the strong element of recycling across these divides connects the content of materially divergent texts.

Friendship matter, in its crisscrossing of social and print categories, confirms this view of textual circulation. As Chartier describes, diverse publishing strategies "led to the diffusion, among 'popular' readers, of texts that had already had a more limited circulation in another print form" among those of higher social status or more learned orientation.[33] As a result, friendship discourses that had been brought to Tudor culture through a humanist program in Latin learning made their way to the widest demographic reaches. As the epigraph to a 1562 versification of Elyot's version of the Titus and Gisippus story boldly claims (blithely attributing this democratizing view to "Aristotell"), "Frendshyppe is a vertue, / For *all* men to take holde."[34] While this does not mean that we will see idealized friendship recommended to span gaps of various kinds (i.e., gender or social status), nevertheless its discourses are taken up as if they address all persons, regardless of condition, urging each to find a corresponding equal with whom they may, in Elyot's phrase, "practise amitie."

Elyot himself provides an analysis justifying *De amicitia*'s special educational suitability as well as its popularity from a humanist viewpoint, whether in a Latin, English, or even pictorial version. Friendship calls up a limited set of undisputed models (Damon and Pythias, Orestes and Pylades, and sometimes Harmodious and Aristogiton, Theseus and Pirithous, or Alexander and Hephaestion), and it enjoys a flatly presumed desirability (Tiptoft's Cicero exemplifies this certainty: "alle men acorde in thoppinyon [sic] of frendship").[35] In these two respects, friendship espe-

---

32. Chartier, "Reading Matter and 'Popular' Reading," p. 270. See also Louis B. Wright, *Middle Class Culture in Elizabethan England* (Chapel Hill: University of North Carolina Press, 1935), which argues, somewhat askew of Chartier here, that collections of commonplaces, adages, emblems, etc. formed, according to Ong, "the staple of the ordinary man's reading" ("Latin Language Study," p. 48).

33. Chartier, "Reading Matter and "Popular" Reading," p. 272.

34. Edwarde Lewicke, *The most Wonderful and pleasaunt History of Titus and Gisippus, whereby is fully declared the figure of perfect frendshyp, drawen into English metre* (London: n.p., 1562), emphasis mine.

35. Cicero, *De amicitia*, trans. Tiptoft, fol. 23r.

cially rewards the humanist's familiar faith in the use of examples and his advocacy of pleasure and sweetness as spurs to learning. Friendship discourses seem perfectly cast to serve the reader as such pedagogical writers theorized him.

Elyot announces he "will declare some what by way of very and true friendship," hoping that it "perchaunce may be an *allectife* [incitement or enticement] to good men to seeke for their semblable" and to "practise amitie" (p. 161, emphasis mine). Assuming a searching-and-gathering readership, Elyot focuses on declaration, even display, rather than argumentation, assured that the mere image of friendship works to allure and incite readers to take up its practices. Thus he relies on both the affective power of examples and the utility of readerly pleasure as mechanisms for interpellating and recalibrating that reader—in ways understood to magnify his agency. Lest his reader become "fatigate with longe preceptes," in the very midst of *The Boke of the Governour* Elyot proposes "some newe pleasaunt fable or historie" to address readers' desire for "varietie of mater" (p. 166). "The Wonderfull History of Titus and Gisippus . . . whereby is fully declared the figure of perfet amitie" ensues (a story of the proper dispensation when a pair of friends fall in love with the same woman). It retells a story already recycled in Boccaccio's *Decameron* and explored in Chaucer's *The Knight's Tale* (Shakespeare will rework it in *Two Gentlemen of Verona* and *The Two Noble Kinsmen*). For Elyot, the tale's didactic leverage (its "allectife" capacity) derives from its power to produce a transformative state of wonder. He sets out to "reherce a right goodly example of frendship," promising "whiche example, studiousely radde, shall minister to the redar's singular pleasure and also incredible comforte to practise amitie" (p. 166). A rehearsed example, by means of pleasure and a readerly construing of cases, will generate new practices. Holding up a single, "wonder-full" example, Elyot anticipates "declar[ing] the figure of perfet amitie" by its means.

Singular Figures: "An Alectiue to Our Anglians"

Doctrinally speaking, friendship's first figure is the self. Before it can be doubled it is required to be single, that is, autonomous and integral. Locating the appropriate friend, then, starts with being a certain kind of self, and Renaissance disseminations of Cicero are deeply engaged in providing the tools of this self-fashioning. "First of all," Cicero's speaker Laelius argues, "be a good man yourself and then . . . seek another like yourself" (p. 189). This prerequisite self follows a Stoic pattern. He is emphatically independent: "to the extent that a man relies upon himself and is so fortified by virtue and wisdom that he is dependent on no one and considers all his possessions to be within himself, in that degree is he most conspicuous for seeking out and cherishing friendships."[36] We see the success of these ideas when Hamlet will say of Horatio, "Give me that man / That is not passion's slave, and I will wear him / In my heart's core, ay, in my heart's heart" (*Hamlet,* 3.2.68–70). Such radical self-sufficiency liberates a given friendship from any inference that it might stem from "slavery" to weakness or need. Cicero's Laelius is understood to be the ideal voice of friendship in having embodied this hyperadequacy. In a concentrated reduction of Stoic philosophy, Fannius (an interlocutor in the dialogue) describes Laelius as "wise" in this way because "you *consider* all your possessions to be within yourself and *believe* human fortune of less account than virtue."[37] Subsequent variations of the notion maintain its propositional quality; the predicate of wisdom is an act of supposing.

Tiptoft's rendering of this passage especially highlights the sense of preliminary self-governance the model entails. His language is instructive for the early modern sense of "soveraigne amitie" as an apex of individual or "private" sovereignty: "Ye suppose hou you haue nothing but suche as is your *plenare power.* And therewith every fortune happe or chaunge be *subget* to *vertu.*"[38] The subjection of chance to virtue (with all its valences, from manliness or strength to moral condition) depends on the invocation of a suppositional and performative "plenare" power.[39] Normally, the term *plenary* suggests completeness or fullness in institutional proceedings or assemblies of various kinds, corporate bodies that can act (and perhaps can only act *if*) in a "plenary" state. Indeed, the opening shot in Henry VIII's legal separation from papal jurisdiction (nothing less than The Act in Restraint of Appeals, 1532–33) articulates political sovereignty in just these terms, avowing an England with "one supreme head and kynge . . . institute and furnisshed . . . with plenari, whole, and entier

36. "Ut enim quisque sibi plurimum confidet et ut quisque maxime virtute et sapientia sic munitus est, ut nullo egeat suaque omnia in se ipso posita iudicet, ita in amicitiis expetendis colendisque maxime excellit" (Cicero, trans. Falconer, pp. 140–43).

37. "Omnia tua in te posita esse ducas humanosque casus virtute inferiores putes" (Ibid., trans. Falconer, p. 115, emphases mine).

38. Cicero, trans. Tiptoft, fol. 3r (emphasis mine).

39. The other phrasing of this self-sufficiency similarly references it suppositional aspect: "ffor als so moche more as a man is most asured . . . so that he hath no nede of ony outward helpe / but thynketh that in hym self is / alle that he hath nede of, so moche more is he excellent in frendshippes to be atteyned" (Ibid., trans. Tiptoft, fol. 9r).

power."[40] Thomas Newton's translation describes this self who will enter friendship as "with vertue and wisedome . . . *singularlye* furnished."[41]

It is this kind of sovereign, maximal power, inscribed in the individual, that inheres in Montaigne's phrase "soveraigne . . . amitie." Distinguishing true friendship from the lesser forms generated by weakness, need, profit, or the mere commands of "the law and duty of nature," Montaigne goes on to associate amity with the purest concept of sovereignty as unfettered private agency: "our genuine libertie hath no production more properly her owne, than that of affection and amitie" (p. 146). Thomas Breme, too, in *The Mirrour of Friendship,* frames this freedom affectively, as "the liberty of our hearte."[42] Shakespeare also voices this idiom in Hamlet's assertion to Horatio that "[s]ince my dear soul was mistress of her choice / And could of men distinguish her election, / S'hath sealed thee for herself" (3.2.60–62). For Montaigne, trust in another's will begins with certainty of one's own: "I am not in doubt of my will, and as little of such a friend's will" (p. 150) (we will see in moment, however, the ultimately qualified status of this will). Thomas Churchyard's language in *A Sparke of Frendship* similarly indexes a political sense of self-determination or "liberty." One chooses friends "by election and privie liking," with "privie" linking the will not to "inwardness" necessarily, but to a liking "proper" to the self rather than imposed on it by external (re)direction.[43] For Montaigne, this autonomous condition is the signature basis for an "amitie" that is "soveraigne" (p. 150); for Churchyard, such friendship is "princely and noble of condition."[44] He who is most eligible for friendship holds plenary power over himself; he is (a) sovereign over himself by being slave to nothing; "liberty," "choice," "election," and "sealing" go forward on this basis alone.

The doctrine of a self-possessed, agentive, single actor is mirrored in its iconographic disseminations. Elyot's example-based technique typifies a practice of launching singular figures, a formula in which amity's perfection will be shown in a declaratory figure and which envisions a "sovereign" reader navigating examples and cases in order to incorporate them into practices. Taking the notion of exemplarity to its farthest reaches, Church-

40. Act 24 Henry VIII, c.12 s.1. The text of the Act of Restraint of Appeals is reprinted in G. R. Elton, *The Tudor Constitution* (Cambridge: Cambridge University Press, 1982), p. 353.
41. Cicero, *Fowre Seuerall Treatises of M. Tullius Cicero,* trans. Newton, fol. 14v (emphasis mine).
42. Breme, *The Mirrour of Friendship,* sig. B.iii.r.
43. Churchyard, *A Sparke of Frendship,* sig. Cv.
44. Ibid., sig. C2r.

yard goes so far as to propose that the "bare and naked name" of friendship "is sweet and most acceptable . . . and of . . . sufficience to set out at the full, the fulnesse of so flourishing a vertue."[45] Breme's full 1584 title tells the rest of the story, as *The Mirrour of Friendship: both how to know a perfect friend, and how to choose him.* In 1589, Walter Dorke's title, *A Tipe or Figure of Friendship. Wherein is liuelie, and compendiouslie expressed, the right nature and propertie of a perfect and true friend,* echoes Elyot's language, too, and it richly suggests its own mixture of elucidation and celebration.

The approach across these texts is to stress discernment, explicitly engaging in the shaping of subjects by shaping their practices. Montaigne himself, despite the ostensible errancy of the *Essayes,* follows a checklist strategy, and he enumerates relations that are emphatically not friendship (heterosexuality, pederasty, commercial relations, and biological relatedness) before proceeding to state what true ("unspotted") friendship is. Walter Dorke follows the same procedure. He even drafts "Articles of Amitie" to aid in the accurate determination of "true" friendship "because no man should be deceived, as the Painter who supposed light colours to be linnen cloath."[46] Professing himself too poor to erect a temple to friendship in the middle of the city, Dorke hopes to have "according to my slender facultie framed a *Figure* . . . which . . . yet . . . may be suffered in the corners and Suburbes . . . in honour of *Amicitia.*"[47] Here he evidences the demographic extent of friendship's domain as he names his goal as the modeling of subjects.

Like Elyot, Dorke hopes that by means of a "Figure," "some men may bee perhaps the sooner moued to Amitie, Friendship, and gratefulnes"; indeed, he echoes Elyot's term in wishing "this present *Figure* may be an *alectiue* to our *Anglians* to entertaine and imbrace *Friendship.*"[48] Similarly, Churchyard's little book proposes to "utter and revive matter . . . knowne and talked of long agoe" on the same logic of incitement, hoping in *A Sparke of Friendship* that "by small sparkes . . . great fire is made . . . this true friendshippe . . . burnes with a quenchlesse flame, like a blazing Beakon, or sparkling Torche."[49] Allectives, incentives, beacons, and icons that move readers to new modes of agency: this is the work these texts set

45. Ibid., sig. B4r.
46. Dorke, *A Tipe or Figure of Friendship,* sig. A5.
47. Ibid., sig. A2.
48. Ibid., sig. A2r, A2v.
49. Churchyard, *A Sparke of Frendship,* sig. Bv, B4r.

FIGURE 2. Cesare Ripa, *Amicitia,* from *Nova Iconologia* (Padua: Pietro Tozzi, 1618), p. 17. Photo courtesy of the Department of Special Collections, University of Chicago Library.

out for themselves. Composing the *Religio Medici* in the 1630s, Thomas Browne testifies to the efficacy of these writers' hopes to incite readers to a mode of self-fashioning: "I have often thought those Noble . . . examples of friendship not so truly Histories of what had beene, as fictions of what should be," and he goes onto conclude, "I now percieve nothing in them . . . which mee thinks . . . I could not performe within the narrow compasse of my selfe."[50] Here we see friendship's doctrines held applicable to the self, itself, as if their ultimate reference were to the self in its single state. The discourses of amity address this sovereign self—in order to produce it.

More popular modes like commonplace books and emblem collections similarly enshrine singular icons of a sovereign self. In *The Anatomy of Melancholy* (1621), Robert Burton testifies to their impact in conveying

50. Thomas Browne, *Religio Medici,* in *The Major Works,* ed. C. A. Patrides (London: Penguin, 1977), p. 142.

FIGURE 3. Henry Peacham, *Amicitiae effigies,* from *Minerva Britanna or A garden of heroical devises* (London: W. Dight, 1612), p. 181. Photo courtesy of The Newberry Library, Chicago.

friendship love, considering a point of friendship to have been "well illustrated in an Emblem."[51] Cesare Ripa's *Nova Iconologia* figures friendship by a single human form, one with a more graphic sense of the shapes of "plenare" power (fig. 2). A female figure, alone, signifies *Amicitia.* Her powers flow from her, enumerated on ribbons: one at her hem ("mors et vita") and the other ("longe et prop") rippling outward like a banner from the heart image held in her hand. The stretch of friendship's domain — across near and far, life and death — magnifies her competence, extending the reach of her plenary powers. English readership consumed numerous imported emblem books like Ripa's, enjoying the high quality of engravings proceeding from European presses. But English book production, too, reworked the circulating standard emblems. Henry Peacham's *Minerva Britanna* (1612) trades on this emblem from Ripa, visually multiplying the complement of powers within the friendship emblem (fig. 3). Peacham's

    51. Robert Burton, *The Anatomy of Melancholy,* ed. Floyd Dell and Paul Jordan-Smith (New York: Tudor Publishing Co., 1927), p. 471.

Concordia infuperabilis. 40

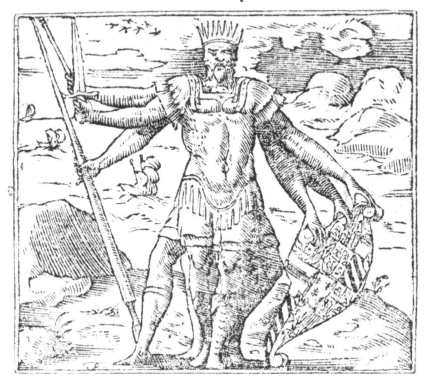

FIGURE 4. Andreas Alciati, *Concordia insuperabilis,* from *Emblemata* (Antwerp: Christopher Plantijn, 1577), p. 47. Photo courtesy of The Newberry Library, Chicago.

image, entitled *Amicitiae effigies* (The figure of friendship), offers a male figure. Notably, the poem glossing the image describes it as recording a "goodlie statue" that stood "in Rome." Friendship's arms are lifted, extending from the body, as is his billowing cloak. Now three ribbons list his powers and jurisdictions: "mors-vita" remains at the hem, "procul-prope" flows from a chest literally opened to expose the heart within it, and "hiems-aestas" streams from his brow.

In both graphic form and argument, this pair of friendship emblems bears direct comparison with another circulating motif in the emblem book vocabulary: those on concord or union. Andreas Alciati's *Concordia Insuperabilis* displays the conjoining of many into one as a multimembered body possessed of a panoply of weapons; comparable to the concord be-

Where many-Forces *joyned are,*
Vnconquerable-pow'r, *is there*

FIGURE 5. George Wither, *Where many forces joyned are,* from *A Collection of Emblemes, Ancient and Modern* (London: A. Mathewes, 1635), p. 179. Photo courtesy of The Newberry Library, Chicago.

tween twin brothers, the members share "unus amor." This, the motto explains, converts what would be weak singly into an undefeatable strength—a crowned strength that reigns (*regna*) (fig. 4). The same motto, "concordia insuperabilis," reappears in an English book in the early seventeenth century, George Wither's *A Collection of Emblemes, Ancient and Modern* (1635) (fig. 5). The crowned, bearded, six-armed, and multi-weaponed monarch represented here signifies the individual man who "hath many *Faculties,* or *Friends,*" and manages to conglomerate them "as if so many *Hands* they had been made; / And, in *One-Body,* useful being had"—to the end that such an individual can "attaine" and "crowne his honest *Hopes*" in whatever he endeavors to undertake. Holding all his possessions, masterful, superlative effectiveness is his. Such power proceeds from avowing it. Omnicompetent and crowned, this singular agentive personage requires a monarch to represent him.

"A Parfecte Consent": Being and Agreeing to Be Double

This sovereign singularity, gathered, perfected, master of accidents, and superior to need, proceeds to a nonobvious step: he finds another similarly situated and merges with him. This is the act of "sealing" to which Hamlet refers. The resulting sovereign amity, too, wears a crown. Wither's emblem of friendship conjoins these single and doubling iconographies (fig. 6) in an image still evident in contemporary popular culture. The crowned heart presides over a pair of clasped hands. Beneath the literal token of actual political sovereignty, friendship shows emblematically: "their *Affection* merits to be *crown'd,* / Whose *hearts* are fastned where they joyne their *hands.*" "True-love" here embodies both "perfect" friendship (as opposed to weak or even feigned instances) and the constancy or loyalty of the "true" heart, expressing itself in "fastening." This second sense, centered on performance more than on definitional categories, is at stake in the "good faith" (*bona fide*) handshake. The image indicates an agreement made by two sovereign selves who are, by that virtue, competent to agree; they are capable of consent. What they consent to is a "fastening," in Churchyard's rather astonishing words, "a willing bondage that brings freedom for ever."[52]

In Tiptoft's words, it is "co[n]venient to chese a frende such as is not double and . . . co[n]sente with hym in liuyng."[53] Renaissance writers hone in on the broad possibilities in *consensio*—they press the concept to govern an even wider range of matters, always keeping alive its double sense as an

52. Churchyard, *A Sparke of Frendship,* sig. 6a. For a persuasive consideration of this exact paradox, see François Rigolot, "Reviving Harmodious and Aristogiton in the Renaissance: Friendship and Tyranny as Voluntary Servitude," in *Montaigne Studies* 11 (1999): 107–19. Rigolot argues that Montaigne's essay takes up the contractualism of his friend Etienne de la Boétie's antityranny tract to suggest that friendship makes "the only imaginable case in which a human being would consent, by nobility of heart, to limit his or her liberty and accept that of another, without being disadvantaged by the resulting sacrifice" (p. 109).

53. Cicero, *De amicitia,* trans. Tiptoft, fol. 18v.

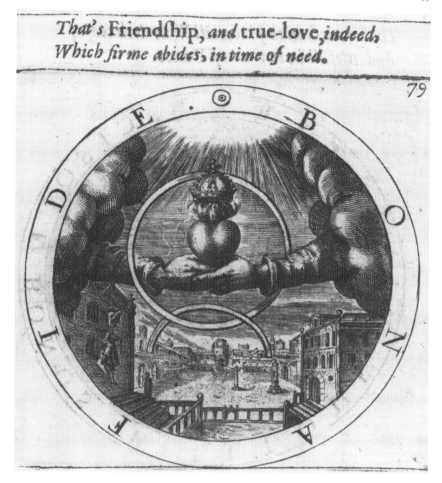

That's Friendſhip, *and* true-love, *indeed,*
Which firme abides, in time of need.

FIGURE 6. George Wither, *Bona fide,* from *A Collection of Emblemes, Ancient and Modern* (London: A. Mathewes, 1635), p. 237. Photo courtesy of The Newberry Library, Chicago.

act of contract and a condition of likeness. Indeed, likeness, as parity, fundamentally enables contractual consent insofar as some form of similitude is requisite for what contract law will later call a "meeting of the minds." [54] Equality between agreeing parties suggests a balance of wills, and only that parity can ensure that a contract has been freely entered. It is this utopian parity that the other-self logics of friendship fundamentally concern them-

54. Shakespeare's "marriage of true minds" and its possible "impediments" in Sonnet 116 and contract doctrine's "meeting of the minds" thus share a single logic.

selves to address, rather than an avoidance of diversity or a hierarchizing of difference. Consent and hierarchy here exclude one another mutually.

Examination of Cicero's persistent language shows the intensity and broad scope this prerequisite similitude accrues, but it also attests to similitude's virtual and metaphorical status. Cicero's proposition that "he who looks upon a true friend, looks, as it were, upon a sort of image of himself [tamquam exemplar aliquod intuetur sui]" rhetoricizes the meaning of likeness; it pertains in the realm of an "as it were" (pp. 132-33). *Exemplar* suggests a likeness or model (of "a sort") rather than an example *(exemplum)* or instance. Perhaps a translation like "contemplates some other *[aliquod]* likeness of himself" better shows the difference between this likeness and identity in the strongest philosophical sense. Tiptoft's idiom works likewise: "who so evir seeth his frende, seeth a maner lykenesse of hym self."[55] "A maner lykenesse" represents a kind of doubling, but it too eschews an absolute identity to render likeness metaphorical or true after a "manner."

In one of the most quoted passages of *De amicitia,* Cicero takes up an Aristotelian analogy between self-love and friendship. Self-love is routinized by specification as a "natural" principle ("this feeling is born alike in every living creature") and distinguished from selfishness or "a view of acquiring profit . . . from his self-love." The famous other-self phrasings follow: "everyone loves himself . . . because he is dear to himself on his own account; and unless this same feeling were transferred to friendship, the real friend would never be found; for he is, as it were, another self."[56] For reasons of translation, English versions of the gnomic sentiment concluding the passage must alter Cicero's phrasing of sameness. Elyot describes the friend as "properly named of Philosophers the other I" (p. 130); Francis Bacon recasts the locution as "A Frend is another Himself."[57] Newton's translation phrases this passage "for he is a freend, which is (as it were) an other himselfe" and highlights it with the marginal aid "Who a frend is."[58] But Cicero's language is neither *alter ego* nor *alter ipse,* but rather an even more intensely paradoxical *alter idem*—"another the same."

55. Cicero, *De amicitia,* trans. Tiptoft, fol. 7v.

56. Ibid., trans. Falconer, pp. 188–89 (referring to Aristotle, *Nicomachean Ethics,* bk. 8, pt. 3, sec. 6) [ipse enim se quisque diligit . . . quod per se quisque sibi carus est; quod nisi idem in amicitiam transferetur, verus amicus numquam reperietur: est enim is qui est tamquam alter idem].

57. Francis Bacon, "Of Frendship," in *The Essayes or Counsels, Civill and Moralll,* ed. Michael Kiernan (Cambridge, Mass.: Harvard University Press, 1985), p. 86.

58. Cicero, *Fowre Seuerall Treatises of M. Tullius Cicero,* trans. Newton, fol. 34r.

The phrase *alter idem,* in turn, is showily rhetorical, obtaining, again, with the suppositional caveat "as it were." The feeling of self-love itself is not friendship, but must actively be transferred, reconfigured toward another. By so traversing the gap within this sameness, one can "seek out another whose soul he may so mingle with his own as *almost* to make one out of two! [cuius animum ita cum suo misceat, ut efficiat paene unum ex duobus!]" (pp. 188–89) For Tiptoft, the phrasing emerges as the recommendation to "gete hym another / whos will he shold medle with his / that of tho tweyne he shold make wel nygh one"; and Newton translates with similar attention to the act of supposing: "as thoughe of two, hee oulde make (in a maner) but one."[59] The qualifiers—"almost," "wel nygh," "in a maner"—remain.

Laelius's opening gambit in *De amicitia* urges its most bracing definitional claim and accords a further perspective on this virtual and fashioned sameness as a species of consensus. He declares "the most complete agreement in wills, in pursuits, and in opinions [voluntatem studiorum sententiarum, summa consensio]" to be "the whole essence of friendship [id in quo omnis vis est amicitiae]" (pp. 124–25). The scope of this *summa consensio* is wide, as Laelius's other key formulation proposes: "friendship is nothing else than an accord in all things, human and divine, conjoined with a mutual goodwill and affection [Est . . . amicitia . . . omnium divinarum humanarumque rerum cum benevolentia et caritate consensio]" (pp. 130–31). Tiptoft's rendering of this constantly quoted passage varies the two instances of the Latin *consensio.* He references both a state of likeness and an act of conjoining: "the grettest force of frendship" is that two friends' "willes, studyes, and felynges *were all one*"; and "ffrendship fforsothe is nothyng ellis but *the knyttyng to gydre* of that thing that is goodly and of that thyng that is humayne with soueraigne benyuolence and charyte."[60] This same passage surfaces as Elyot's most obvious direct translation of Cicero in *The Governour,* and its phrases will echo throughout the Titus and Gyssipus story. "Frendship," he writes, "is none other thinge, but a parfecte consent of all thinges appertaynyng as well to god as to man, with beneuolence and charitie" (p. 130).[61] This "parfecte consent" (*summa*

59. Cicero, *De amicitia,* trans. Tiptoft, fol. 22v; Cicero, *Fowre Seuerall Treatises of M. Tullius Cicero,* trans. Newton, fol. 35r.

60. Cicero, *De amicitia,* trans. Tiptoft, fols. 5r–5v, 6v (emphasis mine).

61. Dorke tracks the line, too: "Friendship is a perfect consent and agreement with beneuolence & charitie in all things, appertaining as well towards God as men" (*A Tipe or Figure of Friendship,* sig. A4v).

consensio) doubles as a state of likeness or correspondence and the process of contracting or agreeing.

Renaissance texts—and Elyot's in particular—will expand the scope of *summa consensio,* which already seems broad, rather enormously. Aristotle had provided a compact classical perspective on that in which friends must be "like": "the perfect friendship is that between the good, and those who resemble each other in virtue . . . everyone is pleased by his own actions, and therefore by actions that resemble his own, and the actions of all good men are the same or similar."[62] Virtue has no signature; it is not idiosyncratic. Its expressions in different men's actions look the same ("or similar"). While Elyot's text certainly echoes the reference of friendship to virtue ("very amitie is vertue") (p. 184), he supplements virtue's role by suggesting a more colorful and variable reading of personal diversity. This has the effect of vastly expanding the domains within which friends must be "like."

Friendship remains "betwene good men onely," but, Elyot continues, "betwene all men that be good can nat all way be amitie" (p. 162). This is an avenue neither Cicero nor Aristotle concern themselves to explore, sharing the view that virtue is close enough to the same from one to another (within a certain civic status, at least). But Elyot freelances further rules: "it also requireth that they be of semblable or moche like maners." Listing "grauitie and affabilitie," "seueritie and placabilitie," "magnificence and liberalitie" and "frugalitie" as clear virtues, Elyot advances the likeness principle into a proliferating universe of virtuous varieties. Consent begins to take on a stronger sense of likeness beyond "agreeing": "wherfore it semeth that wherein the one deliteth, it is to the other repugnaunt unto his nature; and where is any repugnaunce, may be none amitie, sens frendshippe is *an entier consent* of willes and desires" (pp. 162–63, emphasis mine).[63] Likeness no longer inheres only in matters and opinions or even in abstract virtuousness, but now, also, in qualitatively variable natures, demeanor, and even personage.

When Cicero recounts the story of Orestes and Pylades (two exemplary friends who contended which of them would pay a death sentence imposed on Orestes), he describes a baffled king who was simply "ignorant which

---

62. Aristotle, *Nicomachean Ethics,* bk. 9, pt. 3, sec. 6.

63. Lewicke's versification of the story refracts the Ciceronian line, too: "Their willes and wits both, like did frame" (*The most wonderful and pleasaunt History of Titus and Gisippus,* p. 1).

of the two was Orestes" (p. 135). Compare Elyot's version of this classic tale of substitution: "Horestes and Pilades, beinge wonderfull like in all features, were taken to gider and presented unto a tyrant who [then] coulde nat discerne the one from the other" (p. 164). Friendship likeness has been literalized as a wonder-generating physical fact. Elyot frames the Titus and Gysippus story in the same terms. Gysippus "nat onely was equall to . . . Titus in yeres, but also in stature, proporcion of body, fauour, and colour of visage, countenaunce and speche"; their parents could not even tell them apart, since "they semed to be one in fourme and personage" (p. 166). As Edward Lewicke's versification of the tale rehearses, "on all the earth lo there were none: / So like of beautye blood and bone."[64] The extension of likeness to the body verges here on another likeness discourse: twinship.

As modes of resemblance, friendship and twinship take up different senses of shared "nature." The revealed twins in *Twelfth Night,* for example, display "one face, one voice, one habit, and two persons, / A natural perspective, that is and is not" (5.1.208–9). Bio-genealogically speaking, Viola and Sebastian are "one" in the sense that Antonio asks, "How have you made division of yourself? / An apple cleft in two is not more twin / Than these two creatures" (5.1.215–17). While friendship and twinship discourses alike depend on "natural" resemblances, what differs most between them is that while twinship seems to split or divide a preexisting single "nature," friendship is understood actively to conjoin preexisiting, separate, "unnaturally" like natures. John Donne will later suggest what is at stake in this difference in a 1607 letter to Henry Goodyere. After an extended conceit paralleling friendship and sexual reproduction, he asserts just "how well friendship performs that office," with exchange of letters affecting a retroactive constitution of friends as "twins at a latter conception."[65] The emphasis here positions choosing and consenting to membership in a (double) body as the locus of agency (even though the exercise of that choice selects a kind of self-loss in merger, as we shall see). While the likeness of twins (and siblings, too, from Cicero or Montaigne's point of view) seems accidental, the union effected by friends both recognizes nature in its acknowledgement of like natures and also exceeds it insofar as it creates a new body, an *institutio polis* of the tiniest, most speculative kind.

The sense of pact or contract in *consensio,* its focus on the action of fastening, sealing, or "conjoyning," represents the founding of a quasi-civic

64. Ibid.
65. John Donne, *Letters to Severall Persons of Honour* (London: n.p., 1651), p. 85.

body that has implications for both polity in its ordinary sense ("a singular and principall friendship dissolveth all other duties and freeth all other obligations") and for the sovereign selves incorporating themselves inside it. Elyot uses a very unusual term for the dissolving fate of the selves in friendship's separate polity. Of Titus and Gysippus, he writes, "their willes and appetites daily more and more . . . *confederated* them selfes" (p. 167, emphasis mine). The processual confederation of selves founds a new body in the corporate and political sense of an assemblage composed of multiple members. The action of the will as "genuine libertie" embarks on a friendship that will radically engage and bind that will:

> It is I wot not what kinde of quintessence, of all this commixture, which having seized all my will, induced the same to plunge and lose it selfe in his, which having likewise seized all his will, brought it to lose and plunge it selfe in mine . . . I may truly say, lose, reserving nothing . . . that was either his, or mine. (p. 149)

The "confusion so full of our wils" for Montaigne entails the expulsion of "words of division and difference" (p. 150). His sublime account of this process by which a new body is formed insistently deploys the *co-* or *con-* prefix: "in the amitie I speake of, they entermixe and confound themselves one in the other, with so universall a commixture, that they . . . can no more finde the seame that hath conjoyned them together" (p. 149). A "universall commixture" offers the same conundrum of singularity and diversity as the "e pluribus unum" on U.S. coins. The word *confound* suggests not only a baffling of distinguishability between the selves, but also a con-fusion, a co-founding of a new, double-bodied self fused in a seamless unit of alternative polity. The generation of this second body thus condenses the dilemmas of what Derrida calls "autonomy and heteronomy," what François Rigolot describes as a nondisadvantaging limitation of liberty, and what Churchyard in 1588 calls "a willing bondage that brings freedome."[66]

As for the oxymoronic interest of an amity that is sovereign, a contract or indenture within which sovereignty is paradoxically preserved, John Donne condenses its effects succinctly in the verse letter to Henry Wotton, "Sir, more than kisses." The sense of friendship as a social form set in opposition to everyday life and real politics emerges sharply. Friendship will provide a complex alternative to the poem's famous lines excoriating

66. Derrida, "The Politics of Friendship," pp. 632–44, 634; Rigolot, "Reviving Harmodious and Aristogiton in the Renaissance," p.109; Churchyard, *A Sparke of Frendship,* sig. Cv.

the depravities of ordinary sociability and its tainting effects: "Life is a voyage, and in our life's ways / Countries, Courts, Towns are Rockes, or Remoraes; / They break or stop all ships, yet our state's such, / That though then pitch they staine worse, wee must touch."[67] As the antidote to this morally self-eroding picture of social life, Donne proposes to Wotton that he "Be . . . thine owne home, and in thy self dwell; / . . . / Bee thine own palace or the world's thy gaole." (lines 47, 52). This strong utopian elsewhere of radical self-possession, of course, echoes the extreme formula of individual autonomy in which we have seen Cicero ground friendship itself. This Ciceronian call for a palatial self-residence translates the sovereign individual into the terms of the most visible sign of social and political establishment, the palace. Only in the very closing gesture of the poem does Donne offer an image of the non-depraved form of sociability announced in line 2 as friendship. He draws back from offering advice to his friend and instead suggests a preexisting *pedagogical* and intersubjective relation between them: "But, Sir, I advise not you, I rather doe / Say o'er those lessons which I learned of you" (lines 63–64). Such lessons, "said o'er" as a schoolboy might say them, concern Stoic self-sufficiency and offer a complex mutual voicing of the lessons of antiquity—just as we have seen in Ascham's episode with Whitney and *De amicitia*.

The poem's final lines vastly intensify the terms of a didactic sociability pertaining to the disciplines of self-construction: "but if myself, I've wonne / To know my rules, I have, and you have DONNE." The poem has brought Stoic individualism within the compass of another's "rule"; to the extent Donne has subjected his "self" (a virtual object here) to the terms of a "Bee thine owne Palace" doctrine now specified as Wotton's, *both* friends "have done" (having completed the joint project of his autonomy), and both friends "have Donne" (as a joint but absolute possession). "You have me" far exceeds the sensibility of the more ordinary signature line, "yours"; "you have me . . . exactly to the extent and on account of the fact that I have myself." This paradox is fundamental to the dense concept of "soveraigne amitie," posited here as absolutely separate from the ordinary terms of political and courtly life. This friendship, then, entails an act of self-erasure that can only magnify the self and improve its strengths; it disposes of a self but to that self's advantage. Unbordered, without seams: this kind of subject is empowered under such conditions. Friendship accomplishes this by gesturing to an elsewhere away from "politics," but the

---

67. John Donne, "Sir, more than kisses," in *The Complete English Poems*, ed. C. A. Patrides (London: Dent, 1985), lines 7–10.

gesture deploys a vocabulary that will subsequently play a part (at some historical distance) in the explicitly political discourses of social contract theory and modern liberal democracy. Friendship proceeds from a person's "genuine libertie," a "liberty of . . . hearte"; it transpires as an "election" effected by means of "plenare power"; by means of "parfecte consent," it "confederates" two into one, where it then "swaies in it all soveraigntie" as a "willing bondage that brings freedom forever."

This universe of affects and powers is endlessly marked as the polar opposite of practices "nowadays," excoriating the routines of dependency and subordination that govern patronage and practical governmental administration in Tudor and Jacobean contexts and the tainting spheres Donne's poem censures. "If," on the contrary, "friendship were thus imbraced in the Court," then

> there should be no Gnatho so often with filed tongue flattering, nor Thraso so commonly with brazen face bragging: nor Davus so continually with double heart dissembling. Currifauourers and clawbackes, should be contemned as irksome and perillous: Sicophants and Shifters, should be pronounced as execrable and odious: Parasites and platterfriends, should be proclaimed as pestilent and pernicious.[68]

Instead of alternative polity, here we are given real politics at its most intimate level; with these colorful, crusty, and very English words, we take friendship to Court.

Terms of Difference: Faithful Admonition and "Free" Speech

Erasmus's colloquy "Amicitia or Friendship" argues for something we might call chemistry; it describes natural sympathies and antipathies, or what "the Greeks call a natural Affection of Friendship [or] Enmity."[69] At the colloquy's end, the pedagogue in the dialogue (so thinly disguised that the headnote to one edition refers to him as Erasmus himself) makes a personal confession along these lines. "Erasmus at eight Years of Age," the headnote reads, "had a mortal Aversion to a Lyar"; the speaker explains, "I abhor'd him more than a Viper, and knew no Reason for it, but only a certain hidden Instinct in Nature."[70] And we do hear an Erasmian irony in the conclusion of the friendship colloquy: "but tho' I was born with this

---

68. Dorke, *A Tipe or Figure of Friendship,* sig. Bv.

69. Erasmus, *The Colloquies of Erasmus,* trans. N. Bailey (London: Reeves & Turner, 1878), p. 311.

70. Ibid., pp. 301, 314.

natural Disposition; yet, contrary to it, I seem to have been born to have to do with Liars and Imposters thro' the whole Course of my Life." False friends and flatterers may be ubiquitous (and, to judge from its protestations, the sixteenth century would seem to have had a special share of them), but they are not obvious, and entire treatises engage in supplying some method, short of the more convenient "mortal aversion," for detecting them.

Directly disjoining truth and language, flattery presents an epistemological dilemma for friendship practice; mere simulation can look a lot like the similitude friendship celebrates. For Cicero, the prospect of the dissembling flatterer triggered invective: "nothing is to be considered a greater bane of friendship than fawning, cajolery, or flattery . . . hypocrisy is not only wicked under all circumstances, because it pollutes truth and takes away the power to discern it, but also because it is especially inimical to friendship." Flattery also signals a self who will disable the production of friendship's unity: "since the effect of friendship is to make, as it were, one soul out of many, how will that be possible if not even in one man taken by himself shall there be a soul always one and the same, but fickle, changeable, and manifold?" (pp. 198–99) Treatments of flattery, as the flip side of friendship's other-self repertoire, concern the problems of discernment suggested here, a problem of epidemic interest to Renaissance commentators on the court, whether they stood "outside" it or passionately strove to enter it. Plutarch's "How to Tell a Flatterer from a Friend," from the *Moralia,* serves as the very heavily disseminated locus classicus for these ruminative worries.

Erasmus translated Plutarch's treatise into Latin in an edition published in Basel in 1514; it was included in the 1516 publication of *The Education of a Christian Prince,* which was first dedicated to the young Charles V. The Plutarch translation was characterized on the title page of this volume as "addressed to his Serene Highness, Henry the Eighth, King of England"; as Lisa Jardine points out, this edition of collected "advice to princes" material draws attention to the genre's pragmatic link "to the practical project of finding a generous and committed patron."[71] As part of an effort to procure a position in Henry VIII's government in 1517, Erasmus prepared a special copy of *The Education of a Christian Prince* (he also reinscribed it to Ferdinand of Spain in 1518). He did not secure this place, but Henry later requested Thomas Elyot to translate the Plutarch material from Latin into

---

71. Erasmus, *The Education of a Christian Prince,* ed. Lisa Jardine (Cambridge: Cambridge University Press, 1997), Introduction, pp. xvi, xviii–xix.

English.[72] In addition to these translations and redactions, Philemon Holland translated the text in 1603. The texts of friendship and flattery produced during the Renaissance substantially overlap with this complicated genre involving both advice to princes and, often enough, the solicitation of a post. Erasmus's *The Education of a Christian Prince* (1516), Baldessare Castiglione's *Il Cortegiano* (1528), Elyot's "The election of frendes and the diuersitie of flaterars" in *The Governour* (1531), and Bacon's *The Essayes or Counsels, Morall and Civill* (1597–1625) all take up Plutarch's logic.

Invariably, these iterations develop the scandal of the flatterer through metaphors of counterfeiting. Plutarch's version describes the linguistic trickster: "as false and counterfeit imitations of gold imitate only its brilliancy and luster, so . . . the flatterer, imitating the pleasant . . . characteristics of the friend, always presents himself in a cheerful and blithe mood, with never a whit of crossing or opposition."[73] For Plutarch, the flatterer is "false, spurious, and debased," and he understands "that he is committing a crime against friendship, which in his hands becomes a counterfeit coin."[74] In Holland's 1603 translation, "the supposed, false, and counterfeit friend [does] great injury to true amitie and friendship, which he doth corrupt in manner of a base piece of money."[75] For Erasmus, "the most deadly of all flatterers" are those who work "under a guise of candor" and by a "wonderful artifice."[76] Secretive and artificial, flattery endangers because "in many respects it coincides with friendship" and "blends itself with every emotion, every movement, need and habit" of friendship.[77] Elyot continues these themes of imitation, "resemblaunce," "studie," and "counterfaite" practices and concludes, translating Plutarch, that "harde it is all way to exchewe these flatterers," since "flatery from frendship is hardely seuered, for as moche as in euery motion and affecte of the minde they be mutually mengled to gether" (pp. 177, 181, 176).

The method of detection and discernment invoked by the classical discourses and their Renaissance voicers refers finally to the friend's speech.

72. Ibid., p. xxiii.

73. Plutarch, *Moralia,* trans. Frank Cole Babbitt (Cambridge, Mass.: Harvard University Press, 1927), p. 271.

74. Ibid., p.345.

75. Plutarch, *The philosophie commonlie called, the morals, written by the learned philosopher Plutarch of Charonea. Translated out of Greeke into English, and conferred with the latine translations and the French, by Philemon Holland* (London: Arnold Hatfield, 1603), p. 86.

76. Erasmus, *The Education of a Christian Prince,* p. 196.

77. Plutarch, *Moralia,* p. 275.

Speech can ultimately be discerned as that of a true friend, intriguingly, by its acidity in a conflict situation. For Cicero, the true friend deploys his influence, in Newton's translation, "not onely plainlye, but (if occasion so serve) sharplye: and let suche aucthoritie so geeven be throughly obeyed."[78] Plutarch's chapter on the discernment of true from false friends substantially entails a very practical protocol for the proper uses of candor and rebuke. For Elyot, "the company or communication of a persone familiar, whiche is always pleasaunt and without sharpnes . . . is alway to be suspected" (pp. 178–79). We do not need, in Holland's words, "a false friend to flatter us in our follies, . . . but rather of one that would frankely finde fault with our doings, and reprove us."[79] When circumstances require that an errant friend's course be "checked," the friend may be "sharp" and "vehement," because

> The admonition and reprehension of a friend, being sincere and cleansed pure from all private affection [i.e., personal investment], ought to be reverenced: . . . then, spare him not, but pierce and bite to the quick: vehemency of such free speech is invincible . . . for the mildness and good will of the chastiser doth fortifie the austerity and bitterness of the chastisement.[80]

Friendship speech practices thus involve the harsh words of a corrective or critical truth that the unctuous flatterer would not employ. For Francis Bacon, this practice is developed (in connection with Plutarch's notion that a man is his own worst flatterer) in a framework of "counsell": "so there is as much difference betweene the Counsell, that a Frend giveth, and that a Man giveth himselfe, as there is between the Counsell of a Frend, and of a Flatterer . . . the best Preservative . . . is the faithful Admonition of a Frend."[81] Sharp corrective speech arises here as the evidentiary test by which true and false friends and flattery and good counsel may be distinguished.

Categorically, we have seen likeness to be required for friendship to occur; a merger of selves and interests marks true friendship's separation from discredited forms of engagement. As Montaigne argues, "all things being by effect common between them; wils, thoughts, judgements, goods, wives, children, honour, and life; and their mutual agreement, [is] no other than one soule in two bodies" (pp. 149–50). And yet here, at the critical

78. Cicero, *Fowre Seuerall Treatises of M. Tullius Cicero*, trans. Newton, fol. 20v.
79. Plutarch, *The philosophie commonlie called, the morals*, p. 87.
80. Ibid., pp. 88, 91, 88.
81. Bacon, *Essayes*, p. 85.

moment of discernment, these standards must be suspended. You can identify the true friend because you have proof that he is not merged in your desire ("wils, thoughts, judgements"), but is acting now as a limit to it. The friend's differentiation proves the friend to be a friend. Instead of an evocative, poetic confusion of boundaries, suddenly we discover a disciplinarian, an admonisher, *a counselor.*

The affective figure of the intimate friend as a correcting advisor or fiduciary in a very real sense makes way for the emerging figure of the Renaissance humanist or professional political counselor. The mode of harsh-but-true speech desirable for a counselor to be able to employ trades on its proximity to the unquestionable virtue of true speech in friendship. "Private" friendship thus offers a rhetoric legitimating the truth-speaking counselor in other contexts. A striking fraction of the disseminators of Ciceronian and Plutarchan friendship theory, as we have seen, occupied or sought this counselor role (Erasmus, Castiglione, Elyot, and most obviously Bacon), and they address friendship in works that comprise the key instances of the advice to princes genre. If friendship's other-self logics serve widely to maximize the private subject's affective and personal powers, friendship's link to counselorship here begins to traverse the divide between this elsewhere of affective sovereignty and real political culture. It crafts a mode of speech to power.

Through this back door, so to speak, friendship discourses make their way into the overtly political question of right rule. Erasmus addresses Charles V and Henry VIII, among others; Elyot's *The Governour* aims to encompass the class that will function as the highest tier of "civil servants"; and Bacon's essays were variously dedicated to James I's son, Prince Henry, to George Villiers, Duke of Buckingham (the "royal favorite"), and to Prince Charles in Bacon's continuous effort to garner patronage as a counselor. Following Plutarch, Erasmus points out that flattery really is a prince's sort of problem: "to this malicious tribe [flatterers] the good fortune of great princes is especially exposed."[82] Elyot, too, proposes that discerning flatterers from friends concerns noble men most, "whome all men couayte to please, and to displease them is accounted no wysedom, perchaunce leste there shulde ensue thereby more parayle than profit" (p. 181). In "Of Counsell," Bacon makes this further preemptive argument in favor of kings attending to counsel: "the wisest Princes, need not think it any diminution to their Greatness, or derogation to their Suffi-

82. Erasmus, *The Education of a Christian Prince,* p. 193.

ciencie, to rely upon Counsell."[83] Elizabeth herself appears to have taken this humanist prescription to heart in her understanding of the protocols of giving and receiving advice. In her accession speech in 1558, she urges Cecil "without respect of my private will, you will give me that counsel that you think best."[84]

Thus, one of the most vital logics undergirding the flattery/friendship divide pertains not to friendly equals but to the more prickly relation between the prince and his counselor (or would-be counselor). By means of classical friendship discourses, Renaissance writers attempting to strike a balance between Elyot's "parayle and profit" accorded moral legitimacy to a certain kind of communicative mode, "a company or communication" not "without sharpnes," in Elyot's paraphrase. The invocation of these languages in contexts of royal patronage has two diverse effects. First, it authenticates the speech of the author by declaiming against false, self-interested, flattering speech in favor of an ethical friendship figure who gives loving and frank advice in the name of the hearer's good. This codes the advice as independent and upright, but also loyal and affective at the same time, drawing it from a personal or intimate register. Second, it legitimizes a difference of opinion between the counselor and his advisee-prince. The cool shade of an utterly valorized and uncontroversial discourse of friendship harbors the counselor's duty and desire to speak his differences.

It is in these lights that Renaissance translations of Plutarch's παρρησια ("candor," or "frankness," in contemporary translations) takes on special resonance. Elyot intermittently uses the phrase "liberty of speech"; Holland uses it countless times. When Elyot considers how the advancement of one friend "promoted in honour" ends similitude and severs friendship, the social distance between the friends begins to have effects, "suppressynge libertie of speech or familiar resorte" (p. 189). Holland's translation makes inordinate use of "liberty of speech" and its variants "speaking freely" or "free speaking," while the rules regarding its use stress balance, temperance, and moderation in the name of efficacy:

It behoveth that this liberty in fault finding, be tempered with a certain amiable affection, and accompanied with the judgement of reason . . . which mat take away the excessive vehemency and force of sharp words, like the over-bright beams of some glittering light, and for fear lest their

83. Bacon, *Essayes*, p. 63.
84. Elizabeth I, "Queen Elizabeth's First Speech," in *Elizabeth I: Collected Works*, ed. Leah Marcus, Janel Mueller, and Mary Beth Rose (Chicago: University of Chicago Press, 2000).

friends being dazeled as it were and frighted with the flashing beams of
their rebukes, seeing themselves so reproved for each thing . . . may take
such a grief . . . that for sorrow the be ready to flie unto the shadow of
some flatterer.[85]

At other times, however, the friend's "liberty of language and reprehension" may be "earnest and vehement," and he must "use his liberty of
speech and extend it to the full."[86] The liberty articulated here is being distinguished from mere licentiousness. Plutarch's sense of finding the desirable "mean" in all things applies to protocols of expression and free speaking, too. It is not "as if a freed slave newly franchised, should in a Comedie
think that he could not use and enjoy his liberty of speech unless he might
be allowed licenciously to accuse another without controlment."[87] A carefully balanced, responsible liberty attentive to protocols of expression and
concerned with its effects, the speech of the friend here begins to voice
a modern sense of "liberty of speech"—including its provisional and
counterbalanced condition as later spelled out in constitutional democracies. As Elyot exhorts, "O what domage have ensued to princes and their
realmes where liberte of speche hath ben restrayned?" (p. 132) The friend's
"faithful Admonition" sounds out the syllables of what would become the
"loyal opposition" in Parliamentary contexts.

If the harsh corrective speech of the counselor gains power from its
proximity to friendship, the prince's role within this structure remains to
be considered. It is here that the logics of friendship bring out their most
powerful weapon. In Cicero's formulation, "we live in one way with a
tyrant and in another with a friend" (p. 197). Only a tyrant fears or pro-
hibits "friendly" communications of a difference in views; only a tyrant
fails to see the virtue of a counselor speaking the sharp language of a
healthy truth in an exercise of liberty of speech. A ruler further signals his
tyranny by association with flatterers. According to Cicero, "such indeed
is the life of tyrants—a life, I mean . . . where friendship has no place"
(pp. 163–64). (Humanists can be seen as working to get friendship "a
place" in this sense.) Erasmus, too, pairs tyranny and flattery as inseparable
companions. "Nowhere do we read of a state which has been oppressed
under a great tyranny in which flatterers did not play leading roles in the
tragedy," he writes, and he recalls the famous saying of Diogenes: "when
asked what animal was the most dangerous one of all, he said, 'If you mean

85. Plutarch, *The philosophie commonlie called, the morals*, p. 87.
86. Ibid., pp. 88, 91.
87. Ibid., p. 87.

among wild beasts, I will say the tyrant; if you mean among the tame ones, the flatterer.'"[88] Princes hostile to advice from the learned risk the appellation of tyranny; under the logic of friendship, a conversation about the relations between kings and their counselors proceeds.

This conversation focuses on the intimate partnership of the pair (a king and his counselor), but it also shapes itself around the structures of reading we have seen applied to reader-subjects. Like those readers, the monarch too, it is to be hoped, is responsive to exempla. The spectacular power of virtuous friendship for the general reader is central to Elyot's friendship chapters in *The Governour*, as we have seen. But Elyot goes further. He recounts the effects of two exemplary friendship pairs on two tyrants. Orestes and Pilades' display of friendship "so relented the fierse and cruell harte of the tyrant, that wondringe at their marvelous frendship he suffred them frely to departe"; Damon and Pithias's show of friendship loyalty left a tyrant "all abasshed . . . and whan he had ynough wondred at their . . . constance in very frendship, he . . . desired them to receyve hym into their company" (pp. 165–66). In Dorke's *A Figure of Friendship*, this story reappears: "Dionisius the Tirant was so amazed at the friendship of Damon and Pythias that it translated his minde from being tirannous towards them, to become almost amorous with them, as it may appeare by his owne petition . . . I beseeche you (saith he) receave me also into your sacred societie."[89] Relenting tyrants, tyrants abashed and amazed, tyrants with their minds "translated" by friendship's irresistible example: this image qualifies as a humanist fantasy of the highest order, one in which the pedagogy of schoolroom exempla reaches the highest reader in the land.

Drawn from the perspective of a (royal) subject maximizing his agency in a stance of private sovereignty, friendship's stories and the figures populating them thus configure an intimate politics. The most diverse sixteenth- and early seventeenth-century readerships become familiar with sovereign, private selves who exercise virtually utopian powers of autonomy; with counselors whose liberty of speech is enshrined; and with kings who listen to that speech and also heed the examples that the "figures of perfet amitie" provide.

88. Erasmus, *The Education of a Christian Prince*, p. 193.
89. Dorke, *A Tipe or Figure of Friendship*, sig. A3–A3v.

Chaste Associations in Cary's *Tragedy of Mariam*: Sexual Mixtures, Same-Sex Friendship, and the Genders of Integrity

❧

> Myself and what is mine to you and yours
> Is now converted. But now I was the lord
> Of this fair mansion, master of my servants,
> *Queen o'er myself,* and even now, but now,
> This house, these servants, and this same myself
> Are yours, my lord's. I give them with this ring.
> —Portia's betrothal, *The Merchant
> of Venice* (3.2.166–71)

"Concerning marriage," writes Montaigne, as he excludes it from the "genuine and voluntarie acquaintance" that is friendship, "it is a covenant which hath nothing free but the entrance."[1] For Portia in *The Merchant of Venice,* of course, the irony of her self-bestowal to Bassanio in the lines quoted above is that while they sound like a speech-act by which she gives herself away, her words merely trace the compulsory effect of the lottery by which her deceased father has disposed of her, as property, to a "lord." The sovereignty she seems to give away (being "queen o'er [her]self") was only hers in brackets. In the light of Churchyard's "willing bondage that brings freedom forever" or Donne's subtly intersubjective "be thine owne palace" doctrine of friendship, Portia's handing over the keys to her mansion seems an even more telling "conversion" of both assets and identity. Even the entry to marriage need not be "free," as her case instances: "the lott'ry of my destiny / Bars me the right of voluntary choosing" (2.1.15–16). While gender has an expectedly asymmetrical impact here, Renaissance marriage offers little or no "utopian" freedom even to the men who would be "sov-

---

1. Michel de Montaigne, "Of Friendship," in *The Essayes of Montaigne: John Florio's Translation,* ed. J. I. M. Stewart (New York: Modern Library, 1933) [1603], p. 147. All subsequent references to Montaigne are to this edition and will appear in the text.

ereigns" within it. The utopian structures we have seen friendship compose through likeness or homogeneity in chapter 1 deeply engage the matter of gender differentiation. They also profoundly contextualize the historical meanings of the pairing of male and female (whether in love or marriage), since heterogeneous pairs, obviously, conjoin unlikes. In Renaissance social relations, this unlikeness reads either as hierarchy or as an endangering mixture in which the self is permeated by an intruding external force whose transforming effects are less than desired. As Parolles puns in *All's Well that Ends Well,* "A young man married is a man that's marred" (2.3.292).

The masculinity of Renaissance ideas of friendship is *almost* as prover-bial as the description of the friendship pair as "one soul in bodies twain." Extending Cicero's more oblique disqualification of women from ideal friendship in *De amicitia,* Montaigne argues that women's minds are "not strong enough to endure the pulling of a knot so hard, so fast, so durable" as that composing a friendship based on (male) virtue (p. 147).[2] In linking ideal friendship and masculinity and in relying on an ontological descrip-tion of woman as constitutionally of a weaker, more susceptible fabric, friendship writers themselves made gender a structuring presence in friend-ship theory. But the discourse itself, in valorizing virtuous self-possession, also sets off a critique of the social structures enshrining gender difference as a law of subordination. Gender constructions fundamentally concern the production and hierarchization of difference; heterosexual marital forms served as the institutional reflection of this differentiation as a law of unequals. Running athwart of the heterosexual organization of love and marriage, however, the powerfully homonormative bias in Renaissance thought favors both self-likeness (constancy) and same-sex affects. Insofar as diverse logics rendering disparate phenomena "normal" can coincide, given cultural moments contain competing "normativities." Disparate but equally "licit" discourses establishing incompatible "norms" coexist.

2. For Cicero's treatment of women and friendship, see *De amicitia* in *De senectute, De amicitia, De divinatione,* trans. W. A. Falconer (Cambridge, Mass.: Harvard University Press, 1923), bk. 13, sec. 46, pp. 156–57.

As a practical matter, of course, women's friendships are commonly portrayed in the Renaissance, but normally as coexistent with marriage. William Gouge's *Of Domesticall Duties* (1622), for example, reveals a kind of symmetry regarding friendship as it sets out the duties of husband and wife in marriage in the settings of quotidian life. Both parties have affective bonds outside of marriage, but a man's are to "boon companions," while a woman's friends are termed "gossips." William Gouge, *Of Domesticall Duties* (London: John Haviland and William Bladen, 1622), p. 251. See also *The Merry Wives of Wind-sor,* which casts female characters as "wives," but also emphasizes their relations with one another.

Though heterosexual coupling—it goes without saying—is a sine qua non of biological reproduction and so draws support from a range of other cultural imperatives, its merger of disparate, incommensurate "kinds," especially in marital or celebratory erotic forms, poses something of an intellectual *problem.* However normative it may be as hierarchy, it proves contradictory to the likeness topos at the center of positive ideas about union. This is not to say that certain normative affective paradigms act specifically in the name of (homo)eroticism, but that they act *against* the sense of "mixture" entailed by heterosexual forms of sex, love, and marriage. On account of notions about gender as a categorical difference in "kind," idealized friendship invariably takes a same-sex shape. Against the sense of a heterogeneity that dilutes or subdues, such friendship holds out a form of self-determination that can be mobilized—by either gender.

The rhetoricized virtues of ideal friendship (self-command, constancy, "liberty of heart," truthful and communicative speech) essentially repeat the criteria of manliness, so that the efforts by Elyot, Montaigne, Bacon, and others to define friendship describe the virtuous exchanges available to (certain) men. Cultural stress on the familiar "passive" virtues of chastity, silence, and obedience, on the other hand, attempts to structure female subjectivity by a limitation of social contacts but for one sort: the explicitly contingent relation of submission to an authority (i.e., paternal or marital hierarchy). This chapter, however, will address the specifically "feminine" virtue of chastity (a period ideal even more rhetoricized and heavily invested than friendship), and it will propose a substantive analogy between female chastity and the honest speech and restraint from passion, the self-possessed integrity, and the complex relation to authority encompassed within representations of male friendship. This analogy, in turn, sheds light on the signifying function proposed for friendship in chapter 1: namely, that its rhetoric tendentiously aims at the highest degree of integrity and unsubordinated being as a kind of private sovereignty of the self, a rhetoric formulated against the gendered contingencies of life within authoritative hierarchies whether political, social, or marital.

Writers commonly employed the trope of a virtuous friendship between equals as a contrast to the conditions of engagement with a political tyrant. The unsubordinating relation of friendly equals represents an alternative to the subordination without limits attempted by the tyrannical ruler and always potential in an ideology of more or less absolute monarchy. In gender terms, the manly autonomy of friendship virtue and its purported rule by reason contrast with the obedient deference deemed appropriate for both women/wives and political subjects. Friendship establishes a perspective from which marriage and monarchy are mirroring political forms, each tending toward a unilateral distribution of power. At the same time, friendship's autonomy also contrasts with the implication of "womanishness" or effeminacy on the part of the tyrant, whose personal subjection to private will, passion, and appetitiveness emasculates him in the gendered register of Renaissance moral values.[3] Womanishness, then, is another name for (bad) obedience, a contingent subordination—to passions or to power.

The mobility of gendered attributes in literary representation (womanish men and masculine women) usually preserves a gendered hierarchy of values.[4] But this flexibility also suggests a contiguity between sexes with respect to the concerns for autonomy and subordination that structure friendship's argument. Female chastity and idealized male friendship converge in opposing both heterosexual and tyrannical contingent states with a (gendered) model of an "integral" self. Historical variety in the notion of "chastity" reveals a sense of chastity as strength, an identity neither mixed nor marred by reference to a "lord," in Portia's terms. At the same time, its textual contexts indicate a chastity that is *associative*, not solitary. Though often denied by friendship writers, virtuous female friendship shows a relation equally marked by self-sufficiency, refusals to flatter or beguile, and homonormative social relations, and it harbors in chastity's social form.

The overlap of male friendship and this plural chastity suggests not only that they trope the same thing (a private sovereignty resistant to subordination), but also that male friendship itself configures what may well be called masculine political chastity. So, indeed, does no less a figure than Thomas More call it when he adapts a story from Tacitus to analogize resistance to Henry VIII. When the king tries to induce his council to countenance Anne Boleyn's coronation, More warns: "though your lordships have in the matter of the matrimony hitherto kept yourselves pure virgins, yet take good heed . . . that you keep your virginity still. . . . It lieth not in

3. Rebecca Bushnell argues that "the tyrant's love of pleasure, his impulse to shift shapes, and his improper sovereignty often generate the accusation that he is, in effect, 'feminized'" (*Tragedies of Tyrants: Political Thought and Theater in the English Renaissance* [Ithaca, N.Y.: Cornell University Press, 1990], p. 9). Bushnell also discusses the classical sources of these gender associations and their implications for the Renaissance stage (pp. 20–25).

4. In Spenser's *The Faerie Queene*, for example, masculinity in a female character tends to solidify her moral fabric (Britomart), while the feminine male tends to signify moral laxity (the unfortunate lover in the Bower of Bliss); Spenserian androgyny is not coded symmetrically. See also Patricia Parker, "Gender Ideology, Gender Change: The Case of Marie Germain," *Critical Inquiry* 19 (1993): 337–64.

my power but that they may devour me. But . . . I will provide that they shall never deflower me!"[5] Cross-gender identifications of this kind will suggest that male writers, too, have something at stake in female friendship's possibility. And for female writers? The network of logics interconnecting discourses of chastity, friendship, marriage, and tyranny will be further specified in a reading of Elizabeth Cary's *The Tragedy of Mariam, the Fair Queen of Jewry* (written 1602–5, published 1613). *Mariam* is the first published, original play in English known to have been written by a woman.[6] Cary's closet drama conscripts tropes of male friendship to craft a nuanced political critique of social organization (whether marital or political) at the turn of the seventeenth century.

Womanishness, Sovereign Friendship, and Marital Rule

As Ian Maclean has outlined, ancient ideas of women as "failed men" circulated widely in the Renaissance; such notions shape explicit treatments of female friendship by its theorists.[7] Considering wavering men, Cicero asks "syth the force of frendship resteth in that one wylle sholde be made of many willes / how maye it be so made, yf one wille be not in one man, ne yet the same alwey, but variaunt, manyfolde, and mevable?"[8] In both Cicero and Montaigne, the avowed nature of woman serves as proof that women, just like such "bad" or unconstant men, cannot fulfill friendship's demanding offices. As an afterthought to classifying marriage as a subordinate form of friendship (i.e., of utility and pleasure, but not of virtue), Aristotle's *Nicomachean Ethics* proposes that marriage can approximate friendship insofar as its sexually disparate partners may each be virtuous in his or her kind.[9] But Cicero and Montaigne decline to explore a separate

5. William Roper, *The Life of Sir Thomas More* [1557], in *Two Early Tudor Lives,* eds. Richard Sylvester and Davis Harding (New Haven, Conn.: Yale University Press, 1962), pp. 229–30. I am grateful to Jonathan Goldberg for bringing this passage to my attention.

6. *The Tragedie of Mariam, Faire Queene of Jewry* was printed by Thomas Creede, for Richard Hawkins, London, 1613. The time of the play's actual composition has been difficult to pinpoint, but a date sometime between 1602 and 1605 appears to be most likely. *See* Elaine Beilin, "Elizabeth Cary and *The Tragedie of Mariam,*" *Papers on Language and Literature* 16 (1980): n. 6.

7. See Ian Maclean, The Renaissance Notion of Woman: A Study in the Fortunes of Scholasticism and European Intellectual Life (Cambridge: Cambridge University Press, 1980), pp. 8–27.

8. Cicero, *De amicitia,* trans. John Tiptoft (London: William Caxton, 1481), fol. 25r.

9. Aristotle, *The Nicomachean Ethics,* trans. Horace Rackham (Cambridge: Harvard University Press, 1999), bk. 8, pt. 7, sec. 1–2, pp. 476–79.

excellence for women. They content themselves instead with the perennial allegation of a disabling womanly weakness. In describing "friendships" sought for defense and protection (i.e., friendships of utility), Cicero points out "that those least endowed with firmness of character and strength of body have the greatest longing for [that sort of] friendship," arguing that "helpless women, more than men, seek its shelter." [10] John Tiptoft's translation refers to the special neediness of "sely wymmen," comparing them to "they that were nedy rather than they that were riche & they that were wretchid than they that were weleful." [11] The prima facie impulse motivating a woman's relationship is weakness or need rather than self-sufficiency, liberality, or volition. In stark contrast to the tendentious, Stoic supposition of individual "plenare power" we have seen *De amicitia* to offer, the weakness argument suggests a person vulnerable to whatever "fortune, happe or chaunge" befalls her. [12] A weak constitution leaves woman vulnerable to random external forces; this permeability in turn grounds a further charge of mutability or fickleness—women are accorded a contingent condition, and political subordination only regularizes that contingency. To the extent that such weakness implies not simply a circumstantial failure, but in fact a woman's constitution or nature, a woman will not have the capacity to perform the friendship role.

While Montaigne begins by disqualifying "the affection *toward* women" (an emotion in a man) from the friendship he is trying to describe, he quickly makes an unmarked transition from this male disability to a discussion of women's nature; the instability of male sexual desire entails the insufficiency of women. The shifting reference of Montaigne's excluded affection begins to make gender look very much like an auxiliary metaphor for moral qualities, rather than any essential bedrock for them. He proceeds to disqualify woman as such, for

> (to speake truly) . . . the ordinary sufficiency of women cannot answer this conference and communication, the nurse of this sacred bond: nor seem their mindes strong enough to endure the pulling of a knot so hard, so fast, so durable . . . this sex could never yet by any example attain unto it, and is by ancient schools rejected thence. (p. 146)

10. Cicero, *De amicitia,* trans. Falconer, bk. 13, sec. 46, pp. 156–57 [minimum firmitatis haberet minimumque virium, ita amicitias appetere maxime: ex eo fieri ut mulierculae magis amicitiarum praesidia quaerant quam viri].

11. Cicero, *De amicitia,* trans. Tiptoft, fol. 14r.

12. Ibid., fol. 3r.

While this is not an accurate account of "the ancients,"[13] Montaigne casts friendship as a demanding discipline of which women are incapable, on account of their constitutive weakness; they lack the "stuff" or fiber required for its knotting practices. Masculine gender signifies some fundamental internal substantiality or indomitability—firmness of character or strength of mind (qualities not inherent in all males). Friendship, for Montaigne, must be "guided by vertue and conduct of reason" because "without them it is altogether impossible to combine and proportion" one another's "inclination" (p. 146). Woman's uneven, irregular "nature" precludes the kind of *mutual* self-regulation he envisions.

Unsurprisingly, the charge of weakness unsuiting women for true friendship also grounds their specific suitability for marriage in emerging sixteenth-century discourses on the subject. The ubiquitous sixteenth-century analogy between the husband's rule in the family and the monarch's rule in the state specifically presumes upon the need of the weak to be ruled and the requirement of the weak to obey. As Constance Jordan has demonstrated, in treatises on marital duties, "marriage remains largely politicized and regarded as a form of government, [and] a wife, like a subject, is instructed in the virtues of obedience."[14] For example, *The Second Tome of Homilees* (1570) proposes that the wife has "relinquished the libertie of [her] own rule," in exactly the equation of personal liberty and sovereignty (as self-rule) Portia's speech verbalizes.[15] Incapable of forming a friendship relation of equality and stable self-presence, monstrous in a position of superiority or rule, weak and wavering woman—logically—can only be offered a role of subordinate obedience.

The preceding chapter argued that the currency of friendship dis-

---

13. Plato's *Symposium* and Plutarch's *Moralia,* for example, propose otherwise. Plutarch defends women on this score: "to holde, that being by nature not indisposed unto other vertues, they are untoward for amitie onely and friendship, (which is an imputation laid upon them) is altogether beside all reason" (*The philosophie commonlie called, the morals, written by the learned philosopher Plutarch of Chaeronea. Translated out of Greeke into English, and conferred with the Latine translations and the French, by Philemon Holland* [London: Arnold Hatfield, 1603], p. 1155). (This defense is one in which marriage is being considered as a form of friendship, however, rather than addressing women as practitioners of exalted friendship).

14. Constance Jordan, *Renaissance Feminism: Literary Texts and Political Models* (Ithaca, N.Y.: Cornell University Press, 1990), p. 215. For a discussion of Elizabethan marriage treatises, their new attention to the affective lives of spouses, and the ongoing political metaphor, see pp. 214–20.

15. *The Second Tome of Homilees* (London: n.p., 1570), sig. H2v, quoted in ibid., p. 215.

courses in the English Renaissance must be read in relation to the unilateralism implicit in the ideology of monarchy. Operating less within a political discourse of Parliamentary powers and more within a model of the face-to-face relations of embodied power, friendship suggests a mode of communication or counsel for addressing a potentially tyrannical power, a strategy operating by association with friendship's moral discourse of candor. In the intense opprobrium accorded to the figure of the flatterer, who is promiscuous with respect to truth and bends in whatever direction power requires, and in the anxiety registered as defiance to the tyrant's demands, the rhetoric of male friendship represents a powerful vision of an unsubordinated selfhood. By means of likeness, friendship discourses imagine a self capable of "entier consent" freely entering a speculative polity without subordination.

If friendship discourses establish a counterpoint to absolutism (monarchical or tyrannical), marriage, in contrast, operates by analogies to it in the mirroring logics of Renaissance thought. Montaigne's sense of marriage as a contract having "nothing free but the entrance, the continuance being forced and constrained" stresses the complex question of *ongoing* consent (p. 147). The bond of friendship presents no such dilemma. In Cicero's much repeated articulation, "if you remove goodwill from friendship, the very name of friendship is gone"; Tiptoft translates, "But from frendship nevir for to take awey benyvolence, ffor the'ne take awey the name of frendship."[16] Interestingly, Milton later actually proposes for marriage the ongoing volitional status that friendship held for Cicero. For him, the fact that the "name" of marriage persisted after the death of the affection it should embody, leaving "a drooping and disconsolate household captivity," constituted just cause for revising marriage rules.[17] Thus, even from a male point of view, marriage seemed something far from an opportunity for power or self-expression; to a high degree, its regime looked "compulsory."[18]

16. Cicero, *De amicitia,* trans. Falconer, bk. 5, sec. 19, pp. 128–29 [sublata enim benevolentia amicitiae nomen tollitur]; trans. Tiptoft, fol. 6r.

17. John Milton, *The Doctrine and Discipline of Divorce Restored to the Good of Both Sexes,* in *John Milton,* ed. Stephen Orgel and Jonathan Goldberg (Oxford: Oxford University Press, 1990), pp. 182–226, 183. Milton laments the continuance of forced union as "unspeakable wearisomeness, and despair of all sociable delight" (p. 183).

18. I take this term from another context: Adrienne Rich, "Compulsory Heterosexuality and Lesbian Existence," *Signs: A Journal of Women and Culture and Society* 5, no. 4 (summer 1980): 631–60. The taint of economic considerations in marriage further displaces it from the realm of ideal friendship. See Laurence Stone, *The Family, Sex, and*

The level of male resistance to or noninterest in marriage registers in
the surge of religiously based tracts and domestic propaganda apparently
deemed necessary to address it, suggesting a strong counterweight to what
Philippa Berry calls an "emergent ideology of married love" in the late sixteenth and early seventeenth centuries.[19] Voluminous pro-marriage publications advocated the direction of affect into heterosexual, marital love, no
doubt contending with both a focus on same-sex bonding and an understanding of romance as extramarital. Ironically, it is the bachelor Erasmus
who offers an early version of this argument: through the experience of
married love, the individual learns to exercise charity, and this practice
contributes to Christian spiritual development and even salvation.[20] The
increasing prestige ascribed to marriage in the English church and the
plethora of marriage tracts during the Stuart period show the cumulative
effect of these ideas, their gathering force.[21] These marriage texts variously
take the form of treatises, instructional manifestos, and juridical documents. Beyond Spenser's *Amoretti,* it is a rare sixteenth-century text in
which the marriage form harbors a fantasy of individual happiness or
in which marriage offers a utopian or celebratory discourse like that of
amity. Even dramatic comedy such as John Lyly's or Shakespeare's, as

---

Marriage in England, 1500–1800 (New York: Harper, 1979), in which Stone claims that
marriage and love were detached systems, with marriage "usually arranged rather than consensual" and "emotional ties [if they developed] . . . left . . . to a later date" (p. 81).

19. Philippa Berry, *Of Chastity and Power: Elizabethan Literature and the Unmarried
Queen* (London: Routledge, 1989), p. 146. The idea of marriage as "emergent" focuses in
on very specific historical moments. Peter Brown observes, "it appears that the nuclear family, and with it a tendency to lay stress on the affective bonds between husband and wife . . .
was already a well-established feature of Roman society at least in the west" (*Body and
Society: Men, Women, and Sexual Renunciation in Early Christianity* [New York: Columbia
University Press, 1988], p. 16). Also, Caroline Walker Bynum suggests that recent work on
the Middle Ages disputes the findings of Lawrence Stone, Philippe Ariès, and Peter Laslett,
affirming instead that a notion of a close, affective nuclear family did exist in the Middle
Ages. See her *Holy Feast, Holy Fast: The Religious Significance of Food to Medieval Women*
(Berkeley and Los Angeles: University of California Press, 1987), p. 225. See also Alan
Macfarlane, *Marriage and Love in England: Modes of Reproduction, 1300–1840* (New York:
Blackwell, 1986).

20. See Jordan's discussion of Erasmus on marital love as an essential Christian virtue
and experience (*Renaissance Feminism,* pp. 56–64).

21. For example, Robert Pricke, *Doctrine of Superioritie and of Subjection, Contained
in the Fifthe Commandement* (London: T. Creed, 1609); William Gouge, *Of Domesticall
Duties* (London: John Haviland, 1622); and William Whateley, *A Bride Bush or a Direction
for Married Persons* (London: Bernard Alsop, 1623). For a discussion of these Stuart materials, see Jordan, *Renaissance Feminism,* pp. 286–307.

Stephen Orgel has wryly noted, effect stunningly less in the way of marital encomium than they are normally said to do.[22] What celebration comedy affords, in the ritual sense, marks its social function rather than its work as a crucible of selfhood. Marriage, to judge from literary evidence at least, was not captivating imaginative attention. In the sharpest contrast, in Florio's transliteration of Montaigne's *jouissance,* friendship offered a highly individuated "jovissance" (p. 147).

If male writers record objections to marriage as a forced relation under law, for women, as many scholars have detailed, the situation could routinely be much more onerous. Much work has considered the legal implications of marriage for Renaissance women and the corresponding impact on women's sense of self. Unmarried women and widows had greater legal rights than a married woman, who, as a *feme covert,* lost autonomy and legal existence upon entrance into marriage.[23] In the Earl of Leicester's entertainment of Queen Elizabeth at Kenilworth in 1575, Diana (a key figure for chastity and female friendship, as we shall see) figured resistance to its captivity and subordination when she condemned the "wedded state, which is to thraldome bent."[24] Edmund Tilney's formulation exemplifies this commonplace of Renaissance marriage theory: "the man both by reason, and law, hath soveraigntie over his wyfe."[25] The duty of obedience, loyalty, and love to someone who held absolute legal sway (as the terms *thraldome* and *soveraigntie* here suggest) placed wives in the same position with respect to husbands that citizens occupied with respect to tyrants or

22. "We are always told that comedies end in marriages, and that this is normative. A few of Shakespeare's do, but the much more characteristic Shakespearean conclusion comes just before the marriage, and . . . sometimes with an entirely unexpected delay or postponement" (Stephen Orgel, *Impersonations: The Performance of Gender in Shakespeare's England* [Cambridge: Cambridge University Press, 1996], p.17).

23. For a general discussion of the legal status of married women and its application to *The Tragedie of Mariam,* see Betty Travitsky, "The *Feme Covert* in Elizabeth Cary's *Mariam,*" in *Ambiguous Realities: Women in the Middle Ages and the Renaissance,* ed. Carol Levin and Jeanie Watson (Detroit: Wayne State University Press, 1987), pp. 184–96. For all the putative progress in infusing the marital bond with affection and in the recognition thus accorded to women's spiritual existence, the problem of virtually absolute power remained; Jordan discusses the ambiguities for women as the political subordinates, natural inferiors, but "spiritual equals" of men (*Renaissance Feminism,* p. 61).

24. Quoted in Louis Montrose, "*A Midsummer Night's Dream* and the Shaping Fantasies of Elizabethan Culture," in *Rewriting the Renaissance: The Discourses of Sexual Difference in Early Modern Europe,* ed. Margaret Ferguson, Maureen Quilligan, and Nancy Vickers (Chicago: University of Chicago Press, 1986), pp. 65–87, 81.

25. Edmund Tilney, *The Flower of Friendship: A Renaissance Dialogue Contesting Marriage,* ed. Valerie Wayne (Ithaca, N.Y.: Cornell University Press, 1992), p. 134.

absolutists. Jordan remarks, "It is tempting to speculate that the whole concept of legitimate resistance to political authority was developed by analogy to the wife's traditional right to disobey the unrighteous orders of her husband, although as far as I know there is not the slightest evidence for such a conclusion." [26] Causal evidence, indeed, would be hard to find. But, as chapter 1 has argued, friendship discourses gather an array of powers that partially suggest a later theory of political rights. The micropolity of marriage similarly gives occasion for reflections on governance, and the synergies Jordan suggests do arise in the critiques and resistances shaping the cultural conversation on marriage.

Homonormative Selves: A Caveat about "Love"

Heterosexual romantic love and marriage are not the same in the period—even more than they are not the same now. But they do have one key thing in common that suggests much about how Renaissance notions of gender work. To the extent that love and marriage are both sexually heterogeneous, they present an intellectual problem: the mixing of disparate kinds. As Foucault describes the sixteenth-century episteme I am calling homonormativity in its affective instance, "resemblance" plays a constitutive role in the organization of knowledge. Proposing that "the semantic web of resemblance in the sixteenth-century is extremely rich," he lists *Amicitia, Aequalitas, Paritas, Similitudo, Conjunctio* as some of its forms and references analogy and sympathy as two of its processes.[27] Friendship, in its invariably same-sex form, fits smoothly into this norm. Concurrently, Renaissance texts frequently reckon gender as a substance that is diluted and altered by cross-gender exchanges. "Effeminacy," as criticism has recently pointed out, marks men who indulge their interest in women too much and, by overly close association with them, become "womanly"; as other scholars have shown in the female case, the dedication to chastity can be seen to enhance power.[28] Renaissance anxieties about sexual mixing offer heavy weather to an emergent ideology urging a form of marriage that (as long as it is presumably heterosexual) can only preside over just such a mix-

26. Jordan, *Renaissance Feminism,* p. 121, n. 54.
27. Michel Foucault, *The Order of Things: An Archaeology of the Human Sciences* (New York: Vintage, 1970), pp. 17–23.
28. See Bushnell, *Tragedies of Tyrants,* pp. 9, 20–25, 34–36; Jonathan Goldberg, *Sodometries: Renaissance Texts, Modern Sexualities* (Stanford, Calif.: Stanford University Press, 1993), p.111; and Berry, *Of Chastity and Power.*

ing; this is the trouble with love, from a Renaissance perspective.[29] In John Lyly's *Gallathea* (1592), for example, one of Diana's nymphs (the object of Cupid's games) complains that her heart is "I know not how affected or infected."[30] The line between affection and infection wavers. The sense of love as something one might greet with lamentation seems historically very distant to twenty-first-century readers trained to consider it the most real thing.

Here is Montaigne's account of a man in love, which conflates sexual desire in men with a woman's nature, both of which run counter to the firmer fabric of amity. A man's "affection toward women" is "more active, more fervent, and more sharpe" than the affection of friendship. The passage is marked by the usual Renaissance adjectives describing suspect passion as an illness threatening identity and self-possession. A man's heterosexual desire "is a rash and wavering fire, waving and diverse: the fire of an ague subject to fits and stints, . . . a ranging and mad desire in following that which flies us," whereas "true friendship . . . is a generall and universall heat, and equally tempered, a constant and settled heat, all pleasure and smoothnes" (p. 146). And so "womanliness," as a lack of resistance to external effects or influence, though alleged to be a woman's nature, characterizes men, too. It arises through the very permeability attributed to women. As Montaigne writes, such "passions [have] entered into me," and "these fading affections have sometimes found place in me" (p. 147). In a sense, these locutions frame an eroticism not expressive of or central to identity construction, but representing its temporary collapse.

Views of heterosexual love can also consider it a monstrous form of male subordination, not only to a passion (as in Montaigne) but to a person, an inferior, a woman. John Lyly's court drama, deeply informed by the humanist teachings of the earlier century and composed for Elizabeth I's milieu, contains much of this perspective. His *Campaspe* (1584) provides an example. Alexander, having fallen in love, is addressed by his martial male companion, Hephestion, who laments that it seems "monstrous . . . that the heart of the greatest conqueror of the world should be found in the hands of the weakest creature of nature." Hephestion alleges that to fall in

---

29. On the role of sexual likeness in specifically comic contexts, see my "Nature's Bias: Renaissance Homonormativity and Elizabethan Comic Likeness," *Modern Philology*, 98, no. 2 (November 2000): 183–210.

30. John Lyly, *Gallathea*, in *The Complete Works of John Lyly*, ed. R. Warwick Bond (Oxford: Clarendon Press, 1902), 3.1.47.

love is to be "worse than a man."[31] Here Hephestion invokes the assertive
and sharp corrective speech appropriate to the friend as counselor, and he
uses it to address a political superior.

Urging resistance to heterosexual enchantment, Hephestion's speech
argues that love, associated with peace, the court, and womanish activities,
induces weakness and softness in the man committed to soldierly enterprise.[32] The related antitheses of war and peace, masculinity and womanishness, and plain versus deceptive speech are commonplaces in Renaissance drama, but they are relevant here for the doubts they raise about the
security of any notion of heterosexual normativity (let alone married love)
when male association with women could be considered weak, immoral,
base, and risky.[33] As Bertram vows in *All's Well*, "Great Mars, I put myself
into thy file, / Make me but like my thoughts and I shall prove / A lover
of thy drum, hater of love" (3.3.9–11). Heterosexual passion, rather than
serving as an identity, instead threatens the gendered self by this logic.
Male heterosexual desire could entail a loss of masculinity, a contamination
of a precarious *virtu* sustainable only in the martial company of men.[34]

Same-sex association and the homonormative self it produced thus
were part of an inertia against which the marriage tracts set themselves. But
this homosociality differs in part from that encompassed in Eve Sedgwick's
original conception of homosocial desire as a masculine economy in which
the circulation of women functions to signify and impart value to relations

31. John Lyly, *Campaspe and Sappho and Phao,* ed. G. K. Hunter and David Bevington (Manchester: Manchester University Press, 1991), p. 79. This legendary friendship is
mentioned by Mortimer Senior in his friendship speech in Marlowe's *Edward II* (1.4.391).

32. Lyly offers extended metaphors contrasting the music of the drum and the lyre,
the handling of the spear or the spindle. See, especially, Hephestion's "counselor's" speech,
ibid., pp. 79–81. The metaphors are ubiquitous in Shakespeare's *Much Ado About Nothing* (Benedick's soldierly resistance) and *All's Well That Ends Well* (Bertram's boyish martial
ambition).

33. See Janet Adelman, *Suffocating Mothers: Fantasies of Maternal Origin in Shakespeare's Plays, Hamlet to The Tempest* (New York: Routledge, 1992), which makes a related
argument about Renaissance masculinity's panicky effort to relieve itself from the taint of
female, i.e., maternal, origin.

34. For the precariousness and preservation of masculine gender through activity, see
Thomas Laqueur, "Orgasm, Generation," in *Representations* 14 (1986): 1–14. See also
Stephen Greenblatt, "Fiction and Friction," in *Reconstructing Individualism: Autonomy,
Individuality, and the Self in Western Thought,* ed. Thomas Heller (Stanford, Calif.: Stan-
ford University Press, 1986), pp. 30–52. Lorna Hutson provides a critique, however, of
the evidentiary groundings of these claims in "On Not Being Deceived: Rhetoric and the
Body in *Twelfth Night*," *Texas Studies in Literature and Language* 38, no. 2 (summer 1996):
140–74.

between men.[35] Instead of a triangle within which a female beloved appears primary but serves as an object mediating a more fundamental affective bond between men, the same-sex economy explicitly eschews or down-grades cross-sex association. When Mercutio welcomes Romeo back into the company of the Montague boys, he exclaims, "Is this not better than groaning for love? Now art thou sociable, now art thou Romeo; now art thou what thou art" (*Romeo and Juliet,* 2.4.83–84). The sexual other functions as a definitional opposite to be avoided; heterosexual *aversion* arises here. In Tiptoft's Cicero, we see friendship's relation to that aversion: each natural thing "desireth his lyke & fleeth his contrarye."[36] In Lyly's *Gallathea,* one of Diana's followers taunts Cupid in language suggestive not only of friendship as oppositional to love, but also of the ways heterosexual mixings can undo the integrity of a gendered "kind": "This difference is betweene my Mistris Diana, and your Mother . . . Venus, that all [Diana's] nimphes are *amiable . . . in theyr kinde,* the other amorous and too kinde for their sexe."[37] The passage also indicates a homosociality among women.

These possibilities complicate Mary Beth Rose's thesis that two dominant discourses of affect and love compete during the Renaissance (both incorporating an exclusively heterosexual pattern): first, a "dualistic sensibility in which women and eros are perceived either as idealized . . . or as degraded and sinful" and then a "Protestant idealization of 'holy matrimony' which constitutes a coherent, elaborate, and self-conscious effort to construct a new ideology of private life." She thus understands her question as a history "of the relations *between* the sexes."[38] But a martial male version of same-sex association offers a semiotics of masculinity based on concentratedness or saturation: masculinity, whether a substance, a practice, an attitude, or a humor, is preserved, even exponentialized, in asso-

35. Eve Kosofsky Sedgwick, *Between Men: English Literature and Male Homosocial Desire* (New York: Columbia University Press, 1985). The structure of triangulation, however, is not at all absent from the twinning friendship I am describing; as I argue in the introduction, the third term in this form of friendship is in fact the sovereign. Unlike the female beloved in Sedgwick's triangle, the sovereign is not sought, but perhaps pursues or intrudes upon friendship's private world. For a more direct application of a homosociality like Sedgwick's to the economics of Renaissance humanist *amicitia, see* Lorna Hutson, *The Usurer's Daughter: Male Friendship and Fictions of Women in Sixteenth-Century England* (New York: Routledge, 1994).

36. Cicero, *De amicitia,* trans. Tiptoft, fol. 8r.

37. Lyly, *Gallathea,* 1.2.26–29.

38. Mary Beth Rose, *The Expense of Spirit: Love and Sexuality in English Renaissance Drama* (Ithaca, N.Y.: Cornell University Press, 1988), pp. 14, 4.

ciation with other men. An "effeminate" man is a man too heterosexually captivated. Within such a logic, then, even from a male point of view, heterosexual bonds contended with both a fear of diminution and a desire for (the identity produced by) male companions. It also resonated with the anxiety-producing specter of tyranny—whether domestic or political.

Female Chastity; Female Choice

Attention to the antitheses and analogues at play in friendship's counter-point with both marriage and tyranny will show that the conventional masculinity of the friendship discourses did not place female friendship so far outside the sweep of representation as to escape both female articulation and the speculations of male writers. In the notion of chastity, a figure or space for friendship gendered female can be found. If heterosexual mixing could diminish male power and if male association intensifies masculinity, chastity presents a concomitant form or meaning for female association. Female chastity in literary representation corresponds to the symbolics of male friendship in key respects. With respect to the self "itself," the freestanding individual envisioned in friendship discourses finds its precise analogue there. As Jordan describes, chastity "was important chiefly insofar as it could lead to a woman's escape from patriarchal proprietorship . . . feminists [as she broadly defines the term for the period] generally portrayed [the woman choosing chastity] as possessing a kind of liberty," a liberty Jordan glosses as "psychic freedom." [39] In the stirring words of *A Midsummer Night's Dream,* Hermia resists both her father and the Duke's marriage choice for her and prefers an unmarried state: "So will I grow, so live, so die, my lord, / Ere I will yield my virgin patent up / Unto his lordship whose unwishèd yoke / My soul consents not to give sovereignty" (1.1.79–82). Consent and sovereignty, along with the sense of a quasi-legal title to oneself inhering in the term *patent,* echo the terms central to friendship discourses. Masculine friendship and female chastity both proffer self-sufficiency, autonomy, and constancy, as well as a freedom from servility, mutability, or contingency.

A number of competing models of chastity can be seen in Elizabethan and Jacobean contexts. Our modern conflation of chastity with celibacy only approximates one of a variety of Renaissance senses. The sense of

---

39. Jordan, *Renaissance Feminism,* p. 30, referring to Margaret L. King, "Book-Lined Cells: Women and Humanism in the Early Italian Renaissance," in *Beyond Their Sex: Learned Women of the European Past,* ed. Patricia H. Labalme (New York: New York University Press, 1980), p. 37.

chastity as celibacy coexists in some tension with the familiar Renaissance innovation of "marital chastity," understood as a wife's sexual fidelity to her husband.[40] Another sense could exceed both of these more regulatory modes: a morally ambitious chastity, a pursuit of integrity and autonomy, familiar as virtue in the masculine case and similarly embodying power. This symbolic function doubtless benefited from Elizabeth's spectacular example, and Hermia's vow in *A Midsummer Night's Dream* and Rose's "I mean to live a maid" in *The Shoemaker's Holiday* (1599) evidence a kind of rhetorical currency for the choice not to marry.[41] Philippa Berry likewise argues that the terms of chastity articulate a powerful condition. Berry considers the use of Petrarchan models in poet-courtiers' representations of Elizabeth I, whose own grand improvisation on her choice "to live out of the state of marriage" provides the most (in)famous historical reference for chastity as a "determination."[42] Berry examines the role of Elizabeth as chaste beloved in the development of masculinity through Petrarchan forms, suggesting that

> the most vital aspect of the beloved's role as mediator of a new masculinity, her chastity, had a disturbing habit of eluding or contradicting the significance accorded to it by the male lover as poet or philosopher. It often seemed to connote, not the negation of a woman's bodily difference, of her own sexual desires, but rather the survival of a quality of feminine autonomy and self-sufficiency.[43]

Echoing the Ciceronian self-sufficiency required of friends, by this interpretation, female chastity takes on a volitional character; the chaste virgin expressed an active "femall pride."[44]

Independence from males is often signified by a reliance on and alliance with the goddess Diana. This formation harbors a heroic femininity similar to the "gender concentrate" of male friendship. While the association of

40. For example, "Thy lady's noble, fruitfull, chast withall, /His children thy great lord may call his own." Ben Jonson, "To Penshurst," lines 90–91, in *Ben Jonson*, ed. Ian Donaldson (Oxford: Oxford University Press, 1995), p. 68.

41. *A Midsummer Night's Dream*, 1.1.79–82); Thomas Dekker, *The Shoemaker's Holiday*, ed. Anthony Parr (London: A & C Black, 1990), scene 9, line 30.

42. Elizabeth I, "Queen Elizabeth's First Speech before Parliament," in *Elizabeth I: Collected Works*, ed. Leah Marcus, Janel Mueller, and Mary Beth Rose (Chicago: University of Chicago Press, 2000), pp. 58, 57. Subsequent references are to this edition and appear in the text.

43. Berry, *Of Chastity and Power*, p. 18.

44. George Chapman, *Hero and Leander* (1598), in *Elizabethan Narrative Verse*, ed. Nigel Alexander (Cambridge, Mass.: Harvard University Press, 1968), p. 105, line 244.

chastity with Diana's tribe will be further investigated at this chapter's
close, the form of chastity evidenced here strongly parallels male friendship
in its avoidance of marriage and in its uneasy relation with tyrannical control. In the discussion that follows, I will consider Cary's closet drama *The
Tragedy of Mariam,* its view of the contest over who will define chastity,
and the linkage of these "chastities" with the symbolics of friendship. The
play critically engages both Cicero and Montaigne to consider the dilemma
in which the legally disabled female subject finds herself. Cary's protago-
nist finds herself among both inadequate and impossible discursive regimes
of female chastity (as sexual fidelity) and marriage, and unavailable forms
of male friendship. A revision of female chastity (as a constancy of mind)
reflects back on male friendship, highlighting how it seeks a kind of citizen's chastity in a polity without subordination. Thus Cary's closet drama
comes close to Jordan's speculative relation between critiques of marital and
political subordination. In Cary's hands, the linkage empowers both critiques. The play is nothing short of a critical intervention in both debates,
pairing monarchy and marriage, and juxtaposing them with contrary—
but still licit—discourses of friendship and chastity.

Chastity and Friendship in *The Tragedy of Mariam*

Increasing critical attention has focused on Cary's closet drama. Much
discussion has approached *The Tragedy of Mariam* in a spirit of feminist,
biographical interpretation, considering the play in the context of docu-
menting the emergence of women writers, exploring the difficulties attendant on the formation of a woman's authorial voice, and understanding the
play's treatment of marriage and political power as the voicing of Cary's
biographical experiences (which are astonishing in themselves and should
not be overlooked).[45] This research has yielded crucial insights into the

45. Earlier critical treatments, generally disparaging, have addressed *Mariam* in the
context of genre and of the Mariam-Herod story in general. More recent criticism, which
has explored feminist issues, includes: Nancy Cotton Pearse, "Elizabeth Cary, Renaissance
Playwright," *Texas Studies in Literature and Language* 18 (1977): 601–8; Elaine Beilin, *Re-
deeming Eve: Women Writers of the English Renaissance* (Princeton, N.J.: Princeton University Press, 1987), pp. 157–76; Sandra Fischer, "Elizabeth Cary and Tyranny, Domestic
and Religious," in *Silent but for the Word,* ed. Margaret P. Hannay (Kent, Ohio: Kent State
University Press, 1985), pp. 225–37; Betty Travitsky, "The *Feme Covert* in Elizabeth Cary's
Mariam," in *Ambiguous Realities: Women in the Middle Ages and Renaissance,* ed. Carole
Levin and Jeanie Watson (Detroit: Wayne State University Press, 1987), pp. 184–96; Betty
Travitsky, *A Paradise of Women* (Westport, Conn.: Greenwood Press, 1981); Nancy Gu-
tierrez, "Valuing *Mariam*: Genre Study and Feminist Analysis," *Tulsa Studies in Women's
Literature* (autumn 1991): 233–51; Margaret Ferguson, "Running On with Almost Pub-

historical context of female authorship and essential information on the history and struggle of women's subjectivity, but it has been less concerned to read *Mariam* as a profoundly analytical contribution to political debates at the turn of the century.

More recently, criticism has reacted to the gap created by a biographical focus, particularly attempting to account for Cary's handling of the closet drama or Senecan tragedy as a generic type and as an engagement with the discourse of Stoicism and with debates over the subject's powers of resistance within the ideology of absolute monarchy.[46] Cary's engagement with contemporary debates represents a marbled mix of analytical critique and the reaffirmation of prevailing values. She places the two paradigmatic forms of gendered virtue beside each other as parallel forms of resistance to political and marital tyranny, and, in doing so, traces the disastrous dilemma they create, specifically, for female subjectivity. In effect, she outlines the negative impact of gender differentiation in the legal rules governing marriage (which placed the woman in a position of contingency and obedience) and in the classically derived notion of ideal friendship. Thus, Cary's drama not only actively participates in contemporary interest in a self preserved against the inroads of tyrannical power, she also comments on the effectiveness of the gendered rhetorics used to conduct that conversation.

After a dedicatory sonnet (to be discussed below), the play begins with a summary of events leading up to the concentrated twenty-four hours in the kingdom of Herod and his queen, Mariam, that are dramatized in the verse text. The very first sentence of this "Argument" reveals that "Herod, the son of Antipater . . . repudiated Doris, his former wife, by whome he had children."[47] It is this action of divorce, in significant part, that sets off the chain of mishaps leading to Mariam's death. Herod had divorced Doris in favor of Mariam and the dual attractions of her beauty and royal blood. Having earlier usurped the throne, Herod sought to approximate legiti-

---

lic Voice: The Case of 'E.C.,'" in *Tradition and the Talents of Women,* ed. Florence Henderson (Urbana: University of Illinois Press, 1991); and Barbara Kiefer Lewalski, *Writing Women in Jacobean England* (Cambridge, Mass.: Harvard University Press, 1993).

46. For example, Gutierrez, "Valuing *Mariam*"; and Marta Straznicky, "'Profane Stoical Paradoxes': *The Tragedie of Mariam* and Sidnean Closet Drama," and Laurie Shannon, "*The Tragedie of Mariam:* Cary's Critique of the Terms of Founding Social Discourses," both in *English Literary Renaissance* (winter 1994): 104–34 and 135–53.

47. Elizabeth Cary, *The Tragedy of Mariam, the Fair Queen of Jewry,* ed. Margaret Ferguson and Barry Weller (Berkeley and Los Angeles: University of California Press, 1994), p. 67. Subsequent references are to this edition and are in the text.

mate succession by marriage to the granddaughter of Hircanus, the rightful king. Then Herod embarked on the course of violence necessary to consolidate his original criminal move. Herod charged Hircanus with treason, eliminating him and his claim; he also killed Mariam's brother to eliminate all claims superior to his own. Meanwhile in Rome, Caesar had overthrown Anthony, on whose good graces Herod had relied, so Herod undertook a journey to Rome, since the change "was likely to make an alteration of his fortune" (p. 67). Leaving Mariam—who is referred to throughout the play as chaste and guiltless—in the custody of Sohemus, his own counselor, Herod ordered Sohemus to put Mariam to death if he himself should die at Caesar's command, since he could not bear the prospect of her outliving him and marrying another. In Herod's absence, rumors of his death reach Jerusalem, and "their willingness it should be so, together with the likelihood" (p. 67) cause the citizens to believe it.

It is this mistaken belief that prompts the characters to take actions they would never have considered had Herod been present. Significantly, Sohemus divulges the truth about his secret orders to Mariam; Mariam, troubled by her ambivalent response to the news of her consort's death, nevertheless asserts her moral independence from Herod in dialogue with Sohemus. Pheroras, Herod's brother, proceeds with a marriage that Herod had forbidden, and Constabarus, present husband of Herod's conniving sister, Salome, brings the sons of Baba out of hiding where he had loyally preserved them from Herod at risk to himself. This, of course, is the paradigmatic classical friendship plot.

Naturally, as is hinted early on by the chorus, Herod was never put to death. He returns, to the horror and surprise of all but Salome, whose fortunes alone would improve if Herod lived. Salome, in her desire for a new marriage, had attempted to divorce Constabarus in contravention of Hebrew law. With Herod's return, she can make a deal with Pheroras: she will protect him if he will accuse Constabarus of treason and cause Herod to execute him. Long an enemy of Mariam's, Salome also utilizes the evident communication between Mariam and Sohemus to suggest to Herod that Mariam is adulterous, unchaste; his jealousy and suggestibility dispose him to believe it. Although fatally endangered, Mariam decides against trying to manipulate Herod and save herself by amorous dissemblances. Finally, the passionate and impulsive Herod orders the execution of Constabarus and Baba's sons as well as the murder of Mariam, "which rashness was afterward punished in him, with an intolerable almost frantic passion" (p. 68).

Cary's narrative juxtaposes all of the following elements: tyranny, in politics and marriage; conjugal chastity; chastity as personal integrity; and classically derived, expressly male friendship, which shapes the relationship of political virtue between Constabarus and the sons of Baba. The representation of masculine friendship in the play is itself uncomplicated.[48] Cary, as a skilled Latinist, no doubt knew Cicero's *De amicitia;* she certainly was familiar with Florio's translation of Montaigne.[49] Their echoes recur throughout the play. The friendship between Constabarus (whose name itself reflects the constancy at issue here) and the sons of Baba is specifically played out as a form of resistance to tyranny. After Constabarus hides Baba's sons, preserving their lives while risking his own, they hope to give him "recompence" and "requittal" for their debt. But Constabarus responds, "Oh, how you wrong our friendship, valiant youth! / With friends there is not such a word as 'debt'" (2.2.99–100). Such a relationship is above the "base mechanic traffic that doth lend" (4.6.289). A grounding in truth anchors a union of such friends: "Where amity is tied with bond of truth, / All benefits are there in common set. / Then is the golden age with them renew'd, / All names of properties are banish'd quite: / Division, and distinction are eschew'd: / Each hath to what belongs to others right" (2.2.101–6).[50] Constabarus refers to the biblical paradigm of David and Jonathan, and the pattern of friendship becomes an ultimate form of personal loyalty, one explicitly prioritized over political and familial forms of authority: "For neither sovereign's nor father's hate / A friendship fix'd on *virtue* sever can" (2.2.114–15). Abiding by this transcendent code of truth and virtue affirms values beyond self-interest and self-preservation, for the cost of wronging such a friend would entail a "dearer price than life" (2.2.138). Thus, the form of friendship here involves all the notions of merged selves, unaccountable economies, and alternative polity so important in friendship writing generally.

The personification of tyranny is straightforwardly presented in Herod, an archetypical despot. Not only is he passionate and cruel, he is also a usurper, reflecting ancient and early modern understandings of *tyranny* as

48. Compare the complex role of the male friendship frame in *The Two Noble Kinsmen,* developed in chapter 3, in which the two friends are drawn in a manner parodying the exorbitant rhetoric of which friendship is capable and so illustrate friendship failure.

49. See Straznicky, "'Profane Stoical Paradoxes,'" p. 125, n. 60.

50. Here we see an echo of Montaigne's language on friendship and the united ownership of property: friends "expell from one another these words of division and difference" (p. 150).

unlawfulness in either obtaining or administering power. These details enhance the onus of tyrannical cruelty in the period's moral commentary.[51]
The play conventionally characterizes tyrannical rule as a negation of reason, restraint, virtue, and law in favor of the lawless regime of abandonment to passion.[52] Under Herod's improperly personal governance,
willfulness prevails across his kingdom, because it has prevailed in him.
Herod's brother Pheroras, contrasting himself with the king, says that
"[h]e, for his passion, Doris did remove; / I needed not a lawful wife displace" (2.1.31–32). Salome states the hegemony of will and passion as
blatantly as can be imagined: "I mean not to be led by precedent, / My will
shall be to me instead of Law" (1.6.453–54).[53] Both references to passion's sovereignty over reason and law speak in terms of marital instability.
Othello, too, uses this language, announcing ominously that "My blood
begins my safer guides to rule" (2.3.195).

Cary's pointed contribution to the profile of tyrannical personality thus
unites in Herod the roles of tyrant and husband. The tyrant in Thomas
Middleton's *The Second Maiden's Tragedy* (1611) compares himself to
Herod and justifies his own succumbing to the rule of passion in similar
terms: "In vain my spirit wrestles with my blood; Affection [passion] will
be mistress here on earth. The house is hers; the soul is but a tenant." But
Middleton's tyrant pursues (and martyrs) a virgin, not a wife, and that virgin's moral constancy is specifically contrasted with the susceptibility and
sensuality of a character titled, simply, "the Wife." The convergence of
roles of tyrant with husband and martyr with wife facilitates *Mariam*'s
demonstration that a "domestic" fault on the ruler's part spirals out to create chaos in the realm. But it also suggests the indistinguishability of the
roles, in terms of power, from the point of view of women (or at least of
wives). Here Cary innovatively gathers the force of anti-tyranny rhetoric to
address marriage as an instance of tyranny.

The unilateral, tyrannical power of the husband to divorce a wife (cen-

51. On the original scope of the Greek term, see Antony Andrewes, *The Greek Tyrants*
(London: Hutchinson, 1956). Renaissance conceptions of tyranny include the same range
of "improper sovereignties," both as a question of character in the conduct of office and in
terms of the method of obtaining it. See, for example, Sir Thomas Smith, *De Republica
Anglorum,* ed. Mary Dewar (Cambridge: Cambridge University Press, 1982), chaps. 7–9.

52. In effect, the tyrant becomes a woman and is as monstrous as the prospect of a
woman ruler to those like John Knox, who referred to female rule as a "monstrous regiment."

53. Thomas Middleton, *The Second Maiden's Tragedy* (London: n.p., 1611), 5.2.1–3.
See also R. V. Holdsworth, "Middleton and *The Tragedie of Mariam,*" *Notes and Queries*
231 (1986): 379–80, on connections between the two plays.

tral to Herod's prior bad acts) and his power here to have her executed are blunt examples of Herod's power over Mariam. But Cary is also interested in another aspect of this power: the tyrant-husband's power to define chastity. The drama puts the idea of female chastity under a kind of pressure quite different from the trials of chastity dramatized in *The Second Maiden's Tragedy,* where a foolish husband asserts, "O what lazy virtue is chastity in a woman if no sin should lay temptation to it."[54] Instead, Cary develops a pair of contesting definitions, one from the point of view of the tyrant-husband, and one defined by the woman whose chastity is being scrutinized.

The first operative definition in the drama—it is Herod's—casts chastity as sexual fidelity to one person, a familiar idea. By way of comparison, masculine friendship discourses had invoked a fidelity always mediated through an abstract and unchanging measure: a standard of virtue that could not fluctuate. As Constabarus claims, nothing can sever "a friendship fix'd on virtue" (2.2.114). Such virtue could function as a constant for simply assessing loyalty between friends. Either the friends remained virtuous (and were thus constant), or they swerved from loyalty and friendship at the same time. This swerving or instability had been Cicero's basis for excluding "bad men" from friendship. In his call for sameness and sympathy, he argues, "the support and stay of that unswerving constancy, which we look for in friendship, is loyalty . . . it is impossible for a man to be loyal whose nature is full of twists and twinings."[55] The emphasis here is on the good man's being one with himself, his self-possession rendering him a master over the accidents and circumstances that befall him, as we have seen in chapter 1.

Twists and twinings in Herod, however, radiate to an entire "wavering" kingdom. As the first chorus indicates, once passion is in charge, it sets an unstable cycle in motion. Passion is viewed as changeable and, hence, insatiable and tormenting; one moves from desire to desire, "For no content attends a wavering mind" (1.6.498). Since "To wish variety is a sign of grief, / . . . / That man is only happy in his fate, / That is delighted in a settled state" (1.6.515–16). Under passion's reign, instability and inconstancy mark Herod's kingdom. The first chorus describes the condition of the "wavering mind" (1.6.498); Constabarus condemns Salome's "wavering

54. Middleton, *The Second Maiden's Tragedy,* 1.2.37–39.
55. Cicero, *De amicitia,* trans. Falconer, bk. 18, sec. 65, pp. 174–75 [Firmamentum . . . stabilitatis constantiaeque est eius quam in amicitia quaerimus fides est. . . . Neque enim fidum potest esse multiplex ingenium et tortuosum].

thoughts" (1.6.474); Salome herself describes her own "wand'ring heart" (1.4.321); and Constabarus, facing execution, curses the whole "wavering crew" (4.6.311).

Herod's capriciousness generates a community sense of contingency and provisionality. The characters are thrown into a rough game of musical chairs, for as Doris was displaced, so Mariam, as a wife, is dependent on Herod's whims; and Constabarus recognizes that as a husband to Salome, he is exposed to the same risks from new lovers as the husband before him: "I was Silleus and not long ago / Josephus then was Constabarus now" (1.6.461–62). Speeches frequently take on a conditional cast when a character considers his or her future in the kingdom as contingent on whether Herod lives or dies: Salome (1.4), Constabarus (1.4), Pheroras and Graphina (2.1), Doris and her son (2.3), and Mariam (i.e., 3.3).

In assessing woman's chastity in terms of loyalty, if it is impossible for a man to be loyal whose soul is full of perturbations, it can only be more difficult, as well as morally risky, to be "constant" to such a person. Indeed, the provisionality of all the characters' circumstances emphasizes the impracticability of requiring constancy toward an object that is always in motion on account of its own subjection to appetitiveness. Female (wifely) chastity thus understood confronts just this sort of dilemma—Cary illustrates the double bind of a male-defined chastity when it turns out to require the kind of inconstancy of spirit that the friendship discourses mercilessly attack. As Mariam argues in her opening speech, regarding her ambivalent feelings and vacillating response, "And blame me not, for Herod's jealousy / Had power even constancy itself to change" (1.1.23–24). Because society measures a wife's constancy in relation to something outside herself, and not by inquiring into her state of mind, Mariam finds herself in a terrible dilemma: "Now do I find by self-experience taught, / One object yields both grief and joy" (1.1.9–10). Consequently, the measure of constancy for this chastity lies in another person, placing the woman in the same position as the citizen, courtier, or counselor at risk with a capricious monarch. This is a sort of political risk. But further, if constancy is acknowledged as one of the most serious individual virtues for both genders (and Cary's play advocates this virtue at all turns), the obeisance, the wife's submissive deference in marriage, also poses a moral risk to her integrity. To adhere to that duty entails a contingency, dependency, and subordination that, even worse, is always under revision.

But the option offered by Salome as a route out of this dilemma also ranks as morally wrong in the drama. Salome's extended criticism of the gender differential in divorce, on the one hand, is developed with flawless logic. She argues, "Why should such privilege to man be given? / Or given to them, why barr'd from women then? / Are men than we in greater grace with Heaven? / Or cannot women hate as well as men? / I'll be the custom-breaker: and begin / To show my sex the way to freedom's door" (1.4.305–10). Nevertheless, from the perspective of the drama, her claim to an equal right to divorce exposes her as a part of the disease from which the kingdom suffers. From the point of view of constancy, she wants the right to be "as bad" as the men.

It is in response to these moral prospects that Mariam opts to pursue her own, diverging conception of chastity, adopting a moral code arguably proper to males, understood especially as constancy, honesty, and truth-speaking. In this mode she will measure her integrity by reference to an internal standard, a constancy within, echoing Elizabeth I's motto, *semper eadem,* or "always the same." Two critical moments express this decision on Mariam's part. First she communicates her true convictions to Sohemus: "I will not to [Herod's] love be reconcil'd, / With solemn vows I have forsworn his bed" (3.3.133–34). This level of communicative freedom is a benefit associated with ideal friendship. Cicero had asked, "What is sweeter than to have someone with whom you may dare discuss anything as if you were communing with yourself?"[56] Indeed, some treatments of friendship consider such communication an essential duty. In Beaumont and Fletcher's *The Maid's Tragedy* (1611), for example, Amintor attempts to hide an injury from his friend Melantius, who responds, "You may shape, Amintor, / Causes to cozen the whole world withall, / And your-selfe, too, but 'tis not like a friend, / To hide your soul from me . . . Fare-well, / From this time have acquaintance but no friend."[57] Cary's depiction of Mariam here poses the question of what will happen, in the climate of tyranny and gender differentiation, if a woman "dares" to adopt the mode of frank disclosure so valorized within the male friendship model. She portrays this audacity as a collision of two disparate sets of assumptions. The values on which Cary shows this profound affection to be based are truth and virtue, and virtue for men is, of course, not defined simply as chastity. Within the format prescribed for women by custom and the law, women are barred from entering such friendship not because of a constitutional

56. Ibid., bk. 6, sec. 22, pp. 130–31 [Quid dulcius quam habere quicum omnia audeas sic loqui ut tecum?]. (There is no unchaste mixing there!)

57. Francis Beaumont and John Fletcher, *The Maid's Tragedy* [1611], in *The Dramatic Works in the Beaumont and Fletcher Canon,* ed. Fredson Bowers (Cambridge: Cambridge University Press, 1970), 3.2.89–93, 104–05, p. 56.

weakness but because the attributes on which those friendships rest have different social meanings for women.

Since truth is involved in friendship, so are communication and knowledge. "Friendship," Montaigne declares, "is nourished by communication" (p. 145). But the constraints attaching to women's chastity render communication and exchange impossible: to be chaste, a woman must be silent; to appear chaste (which is at least equally important), she must give special, additional care to performance and appearances, even using misinformation or dissembling to protect her reputation. Speech by women is seen, in the world the drama portrays, as publicity, and the publicity of a wife is unchastity. In the first line of the drama, Mariam asks, "How oft have I with public voice run on?" (1.1.1) Herod's remark that Mariam's "mouth will ope to ev'ry stranger's ear" (4.7.434) clearly indicates the (convoluted) assimilation of promiscuity and conversation. The third chorus stresses the infamy of a wife's speaking publicly: "That wife her hand against her fame doth rear, / That more than to her Lord alone will give / A private word to any second ear" (3.3.227–29). Later, the chorus articulates a further conflation of body and mind: "Her mind if not peculiar is not chaste" (3.3.242). Even Salome is reprimanded for violating this rule against private exchanges with nonhusbands: "A stranger's private conference is shame, / I blush for you that have your blushing lost" (1.6.377–78). Such open communication as that between Mariam and Sohemus is a fatal attempt by a woman to utilize the truth-and-virtue model of friendship. He reveals his secret instructions to kill her, and she reveals her decision not to reconcile with Herod. Herod's eye sees in that conversation between them, in which they express to each other the profound, moral positions that lead to their respective deaths, one thing: adultery. Here, Cary links a revised notion of female chastity to the ideals of masculine friendship.

The second critical moment expressing Mariam's decision to choose an idea of chastity as fidelity to oneself (a chastity not only of the body, but also of the mind) is her resolution not to save herself by means of dissimulation. While the open communication between Mariam and Sohemus creates an appearance of unchastity, dissembling and beguiling conduct are seen as useful props in properly maintaining a chaste reputation. The third chorus brings out another dimension of the semiotics of women's chastity that poses a further obstacle to the direct honesty of the male friendship celebrated by Constabarus: "'Tis not enough for one that is a wife / To keep her spotless from an act of ill: / But from suspicion she should free her life, / And bare herself of power as well as will" (3.3.215–18). Actually being innocent is not enough.

Although Mariam could have overcome Herod's rage and saved her life by pretending love and ingratiating herself, she chooses not to: "I know I could enchain him with a smile: / And lead him captive with a gentle word, / I scorn my look should ever man beguile, / Or other speech than meaning to afford" (3.3.163–66). She here refuses to say anything she does not mean, repudiating the modes of communication to which women are consigned and, instead, fatally operating in the mode central to transcendent male friendship. Women, bound by customary thinking about chastity, are limited to silence or forms of false communication that are antithetical to Constabarus's friendships of communication and knowledge. Further, Mariam's speech refusing to seduce Herod with a smile discloses another connection between her version of female chastity and the discourses of ideal friendship. Not only does Mariam refuse to employ the "feminine" model of beguiling speech; she also refuses to practice that technique already shown to be preferred by tyrants and abhorred in friendship: *flattery.*

Shortly before her execution, Mariam describes the effectual exclusion of women from the practices and principles of male friendship: "I did think because I knew me chaste, / One virtue for a woman, might suffice." She now realizes the "glory of our sex" can only stand where actual chastity is supplemented (or undercut) by a willingness to dissemble and comply (4.8.561–66). *The Tragedy of Mariam* thus records under protest the fatal effects of a woman's attempt to enact a chaste or constant integrity specifically created for males. The exclusion of women from male friendship practices coheres as an effect of tyrannical power. Herod's victims are linked by the two virtues tyranny cannot tolerate: Herod the husband-tyrant executes his wife Mariam, who is heralded throughout the play as a paragon of chastity by others, and he executes Constabarus and Baba's sons, archetypical practitioners of classically derived male friendship. Thus Cary's argument conjoins these characters as exemplars of resistance to political and marital subordination, which in turn are linked as threats to virtuous constancy.

Much current discussion of Cary's play considers its political posture, analyzing it, for example, as an attempt to subvert a patriarchal construct (i.e., Senecan tragedy); examining it as a form of resistance to patriarchal models; or describing it as ambivalent.[58] As an active attempt to articulate a dilemma, the play itself partly resists such conclusions. As I have argued

---

58. Gutierrez, "Valuing *Mariam*"; Lewalski, *Writing Women in Jacobean England,* pp. 179–211; and Ferguson, "Running on with Almost Public Voice."

earlier, Cary can only be seen as deeply committed, for example, to a traditional and arguably patriarchal idea of constancy—she sounds a sharp interrogative note only as to its differential application to the two sexes. Further, her faith in the value of Montaigne's Ciceronian friendship seems quite strong; she scrutinizes not the doctrine itself but its inaccessibility for women. With this critical focus, she neither debunks Montaigne nor simply copies him as so many contemporaries did. Instead, she engages in a dialogue with him, scrutinizing the gender assumptions and developing the implications of his model.

"We live in one way with a tyrant and in another with a friend." [59] Indeed. Cary's play forcefully details the differences between these "ways" of living and what is at stake for the self of either gender situated between them. She also relates this configuration to a parallel opposition: (female) chastity and (tyrannical) marriage. Cary thus applies the developed rhetoric of friendship's resistance to tyranny to strengthen an idea of a morally ambitious female chastity as against the "absolute monarchy" of the husband in marriage—whether in Herod's Old Testament setting or in Jacobean England. Further, she mobilizes chastity—a "female" virtue—to say something about the terms of political obedience.

Framing *Mariam:* Women among Themselves

Berry's analysis in *Of Chastity and Power* occasionally notes that imaginings of female chastity in Elizabethan literary representation can suggest a female community and that the "quality of feminine autonomy and self-sufficiency" could be troped in the plural. She proposes, for example, that male fear of an active female sexuality presented "the disturbing possibility of woman taking narcissistic, and possibly even homosexual, pleasure in the female body," and that this latter "possible possibility" is suggested by "the recurrence of the figure of the goddess Diana . . . whose association with close-knit communities of women . . . is stressed." [60] Despite this indication, the question of the associative aspects of a chastity figured by Diana's circle is never explored. Berry reads such plural moments in terms of female narcissism,[61] or in terms of Elizabeth's female "community" with

59. Cicero, *De amicitia,* trans. Falconer, bk. 24, sec. 89, pp. 196–97 [aliter enim cum tyranno, aliter cum amico vivitur].

60. Berry, *Of Chastity and Power,* p. 8.

61. For example, the concept of female marriage presents "the unsettling phenomenon of the feminine in relation to itself" (ibid., p. 41); "Elizabeth's rule figured the feminine in a mystical or symbolic relation with itself" (p. 67); and a reference to the "links between a specifically female eroticism and chastity which are always implied in Elizabethan iconog-

her mother, Anne Boleyn,[62] or in terms of a sphere with a unified feminine quality, by which the masculine is excluded or civilized.[63] Where these categories fail, Berry defaults to a language of "ambiguity" rather than directly argue the implications of a self-specified, same-sex association that her texts would seem to offer.[64] The possible elements of female association within chastity are not strictly relevant to Berry's primary interest in charting the role of chastity in male subjectivity. Neither are they necessary to her attempt to relate chastity to the deeply troubled issue of female religious and political authority in the period. However, her systematic rendering of these textual moments as "ambiguous," perhaps from an overly erotic interpretation of such moments, obscures an aspect of her "feminine sphere."[65]

A fuller understanding of Renaissance representations of female chastity, however, requires an account of its frequent configuration as female association, often by reference to Diana and her followers (Lyly's *Gallathea* may be the fullest exploration of this reference, expertly directed to Elizabeth I as its first audience). Not only a resistance to marriage, a commitment to chastity can signify a choice for the company of women. Berry suggests an "implied recognition" of Elizabeth's close ties with other women from the following song;[66] emphasizing the spirit of the second line, the close of this chapter attempts to render that recognition explicit:

---

raphy" is construed as "the female body in touch with itself" (p. 188, n. 76). These formulations derive from Irigarayan theory (ibid. and n. 1, p. 166). See also Valerie Traub, who notes the limitedness of narcissism as a model for early modern (female) homoerotics: *Desire and Anxiety: Circulations of Sexuality in Shakespearian Drama* (New York: Routledge, 1992), p. 104.

62. Berry, *Of Chastity and Power,* p. 82. This sense of female community as a biological and religious genealogy emphasizes a female tradition at a distance in time rather than as a companionate present, and perhaps the relationship of Elizabeth with Katharine Parr would be even more interesting to consider under this rubric. Barbara Lewalski's concept of "female community," as she uses that phrase to consider Aemilia Lanier's *Salve Deus Rex Judeorum* (1611), similarly focuses on female "community" understood as a tradition of "good women" throughout (religious) history, rather than as a social present: "Imagining Female Community: Aemilia Lanyer's Poems," in *Writing Women in Jacobean England,* pp. 213–41.

63. See, for example, Berry's discussion of Spenser's "April Eclogue": *Of Chastity and Power,* pp. 78–80.

64. Ibid., pp. xi, 123, 124, 132.

65. Berry's use of the adjective *deviant* to describe a relationship to a "heterosexual norm" is incongruous in light of the work her book does to complicate that "norm" (ibid., p. 125).

66. Ibid., p. 82.

Hey downe a downe did Dian sing,
Amongst her maidens sitting,
Than love there is no vainer thing,
For Maydens most unfitting

.   .   .   .

When women knew no woe,
But liu-ed them-selues to please:

.   .   .   .

From wanton toyes and fond affect,
The Virgins life was free.[67]

Diana's most resonant presence in sixteenth-century lore appears in
Ovid's *Metamorphoses*.[68] In his narration of Diana's explosive encounter
with Actaeon, she is discovered in a place sacred and proper to her; indeed, she is in its deepest, wooded recess, in a grotto ("Vallis erat . . . sacra
Dianae / cuius in extremo est antrum nemorale recessu").[69] The withdrawn
privacy of the spot enhances the sense of Actaeon's transgression when he
enters it. The locale is private, indeed, but not lonely: Ovid enumerates the
activities of Diana's companions, and he lists many of their names (lines
165–72). When Actaeon bursts upon them, they use their bodies to knit
a protective wall around Diana ("circumfusaeque Dianam / corporibus
texere suis") (lines 180–81), and she is surrounded by the throng of her
companions ("[Diana] comitum turba est stipata suarum") (line 186).[70]
Here, in its most frequent source version for the Renaissance, this mani-
festation of Diana locates powerful female chastity in a sacred, enclosed, or
withdrawn realm, while also populating that space with a plural female
company, a voluntary "band."[71]

67. "A Nimphs Disdaine of Loue," *England's Helicon, Reprinted from the Edition of
1600,* ed. Hugh Macdonald (London: The Haslewood Books, 1925) p. 123, lines 1–4, 6–
7, 12–13.

68. Leonard Barkan details the reception history of this mythical encounter in
"Diana and Actaeon: The Myth as Synthesis," *English Literary Renaissance* (autumn 1980):
317–59.

69. Ovid, *The Metamorphoses,* trans. Frank Justus Miller (Cambridge: Harvard University Press, Loeb Classical Library, 1916), bk. 3, lines 155–57, pp. 134–35.

70. Goldberg's observation regarding the circumstances of Elizabeth I parallels those
of Ovid's Diana: "It was literally true that access to the queen's body was in the hands of a
small number of women; no approach to her privy chamber without passing by the female
guard. These women are the only people we can be sure were intimate with the queen's
body" (*Sodometries,* p. 47).

71. Nancy Vickers, in her effective arraignment of Petrarchan technique, observes that
"in *The Metamorphoses,* [Diana] is surrounded by protective nymphs, but Petrarch makes

An adherent of Diana's takes a vow and joins a group; she becomes a "votaress." Diana's votaries are members of a "company," a "sweet troop";[72] they belong to a "band."[73] In this pluralized form, female chastity takes on the morally ambitious, volitional character of idealized male friendship: such a votaress espouses a "virgin's faith."[74] Renaissance writers generally situated images of Diana and her company in the kind of private locale depicted in Ovid, a zone of feminine autonomy physicalized as the grove, the locus amoenus, the garden (indeed, this spatialization gives female friendship an even more marked sense of place than idealized male friendship enjoyed). For example, in Spenser's "April Eclogue," Hobbinoll's voicing of Colin's song calls upon "Nymphs," "Virgins," "daintie Damsells," and a "bevie of Ladies bright" (who together comprise a "troupe") to help him celebrate a reigning presence variously called Phoebe, Cynthia, and Eliza.[75] Colin observes her, and them, at a distance; the sense of remove is enhanced by Colin's own absence. In book 3 of *The Faerie Queene*, Belphoebe, "shadowing forth" Elizabeth in Diana's guise, hunts in her woods with her "Damzels." They discover the wounded Timias and, to heal him, "into that forest farre they thence him led, / Where was their dwelling, in a pleasant glade."[76]

In practical, social terms, of course, the seclusion of women within the garden and within domestic space has primarily a regulatory purpose.[77] As Georgiana Zeigler describes, there is a developing homology or identi-

no mention of either her company or of Actaeon's" ("Diana Described: Scattered Woman and Scattered Rhyme," *Critical Inquiry* (winter 1981): pp. 265–79, 268).

72. John Lyly, *Gallathea and Midas,* ed. Anne Begor Lancashire (Lincoln: University of Nebraska Press, 1969), 2.2.12, p. 11.

73. William Shakespeare and John Fletcher, *The Two Noble Kinsmen,* ed. Eugene Waith (Oxford: Clarendon Press, 1989), 5.1.162.

74. Ibid., 4.2.46.

75. Edmund Spenser, "April Eclogue," from *The Shepheardes Calender,* in *The Poetical Works of Edmund Spenser,* ed. J. C. Smith and E. de Selincourt (Oxford: Oxford University Press, 1912), lines 37, 41, 147, 118, and 149.

76. Edmund Spenser, *The Faerie Queene,* ed. A. C. Hamilton (London: Longman, 1977), bk. 3, sec. 5, cantos 28–41; canto 39, lines 1–2.

77. Peter Stallybrass considers the regulatory function of the "enclosure" of the female body in Bakhtinian terms, arguing that the ideal woman is "rigidly 'finished': her signs are the enclosed body, the closed mouth, the locked house" ("Patriarchal Territories: The Body Enclosed," in *Rewriting the Renaissance: The Discourses of Sexual Difference in Early Modern Europe,* ed. Margaret Ferguson, Maureen Quilligan, and Nancy Vickers [Chicago: University of Chicago Press, 1986], p. 127). See also Hutson's discussion of the sixteenth-century use of Xenophon's *Oeconomicus* in constructing masculinity through the confinement of women in *The Usurer's Daughter,* pp. 17–51.

fication between women and household, chamber, garden, or closet that plays a role in the rise of the idea of the private; she notes the degree to which "the woman's room signifies her 'self'" in Shakespearean drama.[78] As her materials indicate, the will to keep women within the domestic sphere also generates an anxiety about their conduct within the women's quarters. How to ensure proper conduct in this separate world? The act of seclusion is slightly at odds with the desire to control women's "private" conduct, as the continuous recommendation of activities such as sewing and prayer attests.[79] What these literary feminine places begin to suggest is the prospect that the "proper" zone of female persons accorded by the conduct books and gender ideology of the period could take on a "proprietary" sense.

As Cary shapes a constellation of female chastity and male friendship, of marriage and tyranny, what is the place of a specifically female friendship or association? Within the narrative of the drama, the relations between women are unqualifiedly hostile. Their interests under a tyrannous regime are directly opposed. Salome is delighted by the return of Herod because it jeopardizes Mariam, and Salome vows to take an ultimately successful, extreme revenge on Mariam: "Now tongue of mine with scandal load her name, / Turn hers to fountains, Herod's eyes to flame" (3.2.97–98). Similarly, Doris, whose fortunes waned when Herod preferred Mariam to her, is in a state of open hostility toward Mariam: "Had I ten thousand tongues, and ev'ry tongue / Inflam'd with poison's power and steep'd in gall: / My curses would not answer for my wrong, / Though I in cursing [Mariam] employ'd them all" (4.8.609–12). Even Mariam's own mother scorns her on the way to her execution: "as [Mariam] came she Alexandra met, / Who did her death (sweet Queen) no whit bewaile, / But as if nature she did quite forget, / She did upon her daughter loudly rail" (5.1.33–36). Not only is women's friendship conspicuously absent in the universe that the drama depicts; even a basic neutrality between women is precluded by a patriarchal social organization that directs women's anger toward each other.

It is in light of the impossibility of women's friendships in *The Tragedy of Mariam* that the dedicatory sonnet prefixed to the play becomes retrospectively suggestive:

78. Georgiana Zeigler, "My Lady's Chamber: Female Space, Female Chastity in Shakespeare," in *Textual Practice* (spring 1980): 73–90, 73.

79. Ibid., pp. 75, 77, 86.

To Diana's Earthly Deputess, and My Worthy Sister,
Mistress Elizabeth Carye

When cheerful Phoebus his full course has run,
His sister's fainter beams our hearts doth cheer:
So your fair brother is to me the sun,
And you his sister as my moon appear.

You are my next belov'd, my second friend,
For when my Phoebus absence makes it night,
Whilst to th' Antipodes his beams do bend,
From you my Phoebe, shines my second light.

He like to Sol, clear-sighted, constant, free,
You Luna-like, unspotted, chaste, divine:
He shone on Sicily, you destin'd be,
T'illumine the now obscurèd Palestine.
My first was consecrated to Apollo,
My second to Diana now shall follow.
                                   —E.C. (p. 66)

Cary's sonnet dedicates the play to her sister-in-law, her "Worthy Sister, Mistress Elizabeth Carye." Thus while the final chorus consigns the play to the benefit of posterity, the opening dedication sends it to (another) Elizabeth Cary, another woman, described as "my next belov'd, my second friend." This testimony to a female friendship of a type both absent from and impossible within the text of the play provides the outermost frame for the drama. The extended complementarity of the two roles of husband and woman friend suggests a female association that, while "fainter," "second," and dependent on the absence of "Phoebus," is nevertheless an equally present reality, as are Night and Day in Cary's metaphor. The woman to whom the dramatic text is dedicated plays an inspirational role in its composition: "you destin'd be, / T'illumine the now obscurèd Palestine." This dedicatory sonnet also suggests a female version of Montaigne's unspotted friendship. Not only does Cary denominate the recipient as "my next belov'd, my second friend"; the fact that the drama is offered from one Elizabeth Cary ("E.C.") to another Elizabeth Carye suggests the mirroring or merger that is so complicated and striking in Montaigne: "Because it was he, because it was myself" (p. 149).[80]

Finally, the female friendship acknowledged in Cary's dedication is

80. The French reads: "Par ce que c'estoit luy; par ce que c'estoit moy" (p. 188).

articulated precisely in terms of Diana imagery, completely disregarding any difficulty possibly arising from the fact that both Elizabeth Carys are married women. The reference to the goddess of chastity, of virginity, as the matrix enabling female association is thoroughgoing in the sonnet: not only is one E.C. "Diana's Earthly Deputess," but the other E.C. is "consecrating" her work to Diana. The former E.C. is "unspotted, chaste, divine" and, "Luna-like," is linked to the feminine moon. A network of female relations is imagined through Diana's governance, the functioning of her deputy, and Cary's offering as a votary of Diana's. If the dedication offers as reality what the tragedy describes as impossible, it too comments on the constraints of the drama's world. While idealized male friendship is present-in-exile within the walls of the play, female friendship is envisioned and thematized outside it, by an invocation of a range of images associated with the pluralized chastity of "Diana's tribe." By dramatizing female chastity as victimized by an illegitimate tyrant and immoral husband and framing female association in terms of the mythical figure of Diana, Elizabeth Cary links a reconfigured female chastity with a homosocial paradigm of women's bonds. These bonds compose the play's outermost frame, denoting what seems impossible within it, raising the stakes of personal integrity, heightening the moral force of a friendship doubly exiled because of gender, and suggesting a community of female readers.

"Double Shee": Cross-Gender Exemplarity and Tyrannicide

The enabling female friendship Elizabeth Cary thus envisions warrants one further consideration as a figure for agency of a very powerful kind. Using a religious idiom flatly to contradict Montaigne's claim that "the ordinary sufficiency of women . . . cannot endure the pulling of a knot so hard, so fast, so durable," (p. 147), in the "Elegie on the Lady *Marckham*" John Donne describes Lady Markham as "meet, / To have reform'd this forward heresie, / That women can no parts of friendship bee."[81] In Donne's "Elegie to the Lady Bedford," we can trace some of the extraordinary effects of this challenge. By involving a degree of cross-gender identification through friendship, the poem goes outside the paradigmatic friendship terms of Donne's literary-philosophical context, representing one of the few idealized friendships gendered female in Renaissance literature up to the midseventeenth century. Donne addresses the Countess

81. John Donne, "Elegie on the Lady Marckham," in *The Complete English Poems*, ed. C. A. Patrides (London: Dent, 1985), p. 380, lines 56–58. Subsequent references to Donne's poetry are to this edition.

on the death of a close female friend, combining elegy with verse letter. But the "Elegie" goes beyond simply revising the gender inscriptions within friendship doctrine by imagining female friendship. Like Cary's play, Donne's poem raises the possibility of cross-gender identification within friendship's terrain, but it does so by suggesting that female friendship can set an example for males, particularly with respect to its didactic force in a practice of self-government. At the very same time, the poem connects the feminine virtue that friendship enshrines to an act of political murder.

The poem opens with a doctrinally perfect rehearsal of friendship arguments, except for its unremarked-upon feminine gendering. The Countess has lost a friend; the elegaic moment following such a loss is a signature aspect of friendship's philosophical tradition: Cicero voices Laelius's speech after the death of Scipio, Montaigne raises a discourse on friendship to the memory of la Boetie, and Maurice Blanchot makes the question of death definitive of friendship.[82] The privileging of a relation between only two, "that but themselves no third can fit" (line 5) accords with the limited size of friendly polities.

Donne traces the logic of friendship's "one soul in two bodies" formulation: "so they doe / Which build them friendships, become one of two" (lines 3–4), and he explores the strange post-mortem economies familiar from Montaigne: Who, exactly, is dead? How does the remaining "halfe" constitute both the nothing and the all of a friendship? Though two friends "as divers stars one constellation make," when one dies, it is the survivor who becomes "a carcasse," "not a live friend: but th'other halfe of clay" (lines 11, 14). For Montaigne, "all things were with us at halfe; me thinkes I have stolne his part from him" (p. 153).

To this extent, Donne's tropes are very orthodox—indeed, the orthodoxy itself highlights the major departure. Despite Montaigne's claim about women's capacities, Donne envisions female friendship in terms that can only be described as fully commensurate with the masculine norm; *no difference is noted,* and friendship tries to be an omni-sufficient, totalizing bond exceeding all others even when it fails or is cut off by death. Lady Bedford, as survivor, must "act that part" of being "but one part," which must stand for "the whole" (lines 15, 16, 18). Here Donne initiates an almost incantatory repetition of the word *all,* invoking its double sense as an "all that is left" (a mere remainder) and an "all" that encompasses the totality of the universe (lines 20, 26). In lines 20 through 34, "all" recurs eight times. The verbal excess of this compensatory repetition situates the

82. Maurice Blanchot, *L'Amitié* (Paris: Gallimard, 1971), pp. 326–30.

friendship of the women within the terms of male friendship's normally exalted tones.

What Donne adds to the friendship scenario here, however, in addition to making a case of female friendship, is a position from which both female friendship and its memorialization in Lady Bedford may be observed, a position upon which friendship exerts a reforming and didactic power. The spectacular power of virtuous friendship is central to Thomas Elyot's friendship chapters in *The Boke of the Governour,* as we have seen, which recounts the effects of two friendship pairs on two tyrants. Orestes and Pilades' display of friendship "so relented the fierse and cruell harte of the tyrant, that wondringe at their marvelous frendship he suffred them frely to departe"; Damon and Pithias's show of friendship loyalty left a tyrant "all abasshed . . . and whan he had ynough wondred at their . . . constance in very frendship, he . . . desired them to receyve hym into their company."[83] Visions of friendship virtue are high-impact experiences. Donne voices a "wee" that, here, similarly observes female friendship as a model of exemplary virtues—virtues jointly applicable to *both* sexes.

In key respects, this observer resembles the lover of Petrarchan poetry: he speaks from a quasi-religious adoration, and it is the gaze that prominently orders the exchange. Constituting an observing "wee" instead of a Petrarchan "I," Donne elaborates: "Had you dy'd first . . . / Wee your rich Tombe in her face had seen" (lines 11–12). Since Lady Bedford now embodies the whole of the friendship, "so wee all reverence you" (line 18). Finally, inventorying the colonial wealth Kim Hall has shown to underwrite the sonnet's semiotic,[84] "She was all spices, you all metalls; so / In you two wee did both rich Indies know" (lines 33–34). But instead of a vision of the Petrarchan beloved, Donne places a female pair as the object of the gaze of a "wee" voice united in reverence for what Donne has described as his "second religion, friendship."[85] Along with the Petrarchan mistress, Donne has displaced the eroticism structuring traditional sonnet logics, supplanting it with a cross-gendered triangle of a rather unusual type. The exceptional gender relations of this triangle offer a non-erotic mode of cross-gender identification, one with intense didactic and moral seriousness. The spectacularly effective vision of friendship, gendered female, ap-

---

83. Thomas Elyot, *The Boke Named the Governour,* ed. Foster Watson (New York: Everyman, 1907), pp. 165–66.

84. Kim F. Hall, *Things of Darkness: Economies of Race and Gender in Early Modern England* (Ithaca, N.Y.: Cornell University Press, 1995), pp. 62–122.

85. John Donne, *Letters to Severall Persons of Honour* (London: n.p., 1651), p.87. This letter is to Henry Goodyere and probably dates from 1607.

pears as exemplary to the male gaze instead of serving as an object of its desire in an erotic sense.

The final lines of the poem discover John Donne imagining Lady Bedford compensating for her friendship loss by contemplating the exemplary Old Testament Jewish heroine, Judith. Her story has key parallels with Mariam's: a male political figure (the Assyrian general Holofernes, who besieged the Jews) offers a bargain to Judith that would exchange her chastity for the safety of her people. Judith struck her own blow against tyranny by slaying Holofernes with her maidservant's help—in yet another refraction of a "doubled shee" alliance. Caravaggio painted a *Judith* about 1598–99, but the painting career of another contemporary artist shows a radical, feminist refiguration of this Judith story. Artemisia Gentileschi painted a number of Judith paintings in the early seventeenth century; Judith's maidservant is no longer the very aged observer Caravaggio portrays. Instead, she is of similar age to Judith and a copartner in the decapitation of Holofernes.[86]

To Donne, nothing less than an image of a tyrannical force undone by a pair of women seems to be the proper compensatory contemplation for a Lady mourning her friend. Moreover, he offers the friendship itself and the parties to it as exemplary models for a mixed-gender readership. With such a local gesture of cross-gender identification in "Elegie on the Lady *Marckham*," Donne uses friendship to convey a vision of gender difference as neither negligible nor beyond navigation, but rather just large enough and just small enough for analogies to be worth drawing. By this joint invocation and infraction of friendship doctrine, Donne *virtually* subverts gender difference—while reverencing an act of tyrannicide.

86. For a comparison of the various images, see Mary D. Garrard, *Artemisia Gentileschi* (New York: Rizzoli, 1993).

THREE

Professing Friendship:
Erotic Prerogatives and "Human Title"
in *The Two Noble Kinsmen*

☙

The first published English translation of Cicero's *De amicitia* (by John Tiptoft in 1481) shows just how strangely friendship collides with hetero-sexual logics, appropriating the image of animal coupling to a tellingly different end. Following the passage in which Cicero terms the friend an *alter idem* ("the/an other the same"), Tiptoft's English proceeds:

> And yf that appereth in beestys and fowles bredyng in the woodes or in the waters tame or wilde that fyrste they love theym self / ffor that is a thyng that is innate unto everiche that hath lyf Secundly that they seke and desire suche beestys as they wolde couple them self with and be of the same kynde / . . . how moche more it is caused by nature in a man that he sholde love hym self and gete hym another / whos will he shold medle with his / that of tho tweyne he shold make wel nygh one.[1]

Here, the natural world offers likeness as the basis for affect and equality, not difference as the ground of superiority, as, for example, Luciana does in *The Comedy of Errors*: "The beasts, the fishes, and the winged fowls / Are their males subjects and at their controls. / Men, more divine, the masters of all these, / . . . / Are masters to their females, and their lords" (2.1.18–19, 23–24). Even more striking, Cicero's Latin says nothing about animals "bredyng"; it only lists the various habitats where they typically flock together. Tiptoft's inserted verb, to "couple," suggests quite different valences than the Latin *se applicare,* "to attach" or "to devote oneself or one's attention to" an object.[2] While Tiptoft's word does not yet signify only the

---

1. Cicero, *De amicitia,* trans. John Tiptoft (London: William Caxton, 1481), fols. 22r–22v.

2. Cicero, *De senectute, De amicitia, De divinatione,* trans. W. A. Falconer (Cambridge: Harvard University Press, 1923), pp. 188–89 (21.81).

sexual coupling of male and female, it does move the translation toward individuated pairs and away from the collective species implied by animals seeking other "beestys" (plural) "of the same *kynde*." In this passage, animal "keeping-to-kind" (i.e., species) grounds a homonormative logic of affectionate kinds (i.e., sex); it is as if a powerful investment in gender differentiation raises male and female sex to the level of species difference.[3] And while *De amicitia*'s same-sex "meddled wills" in 1481 may bear an ancient Roman provenance, a century or so later they will appear at the heart of the Shakespearean sonnets as "the marriage of true minds" (or "like kinds")—a phrase which, in turn, would be unmoored from its same-sex origins to preside over scores upon scores of Anglophone ceremonies of gender-mixed legal or ecclesiastical marriage.

What stands out about Tiptoft's translation, of course, is its obliviousness to the possibly analogy-defeating difference we might sense between his introduced animal "bredyng" or coupling and a male friendship that grounds itself neither on procreation[4] nor eroticism as such. A very rich criticism has emerged that traces the phenomenon of same-sex and especially male same-sex eroticism in Renaissance culture. In an impulse to specify practices, however, its procedures sometimes invoke eroticism as an organizing principle in tension with Foucault's dating of the hermeneutic impulse regarding erotic acts as a later nineteenth-century *scientia sexualis*. How, then, to hear the classificatory significance of the Renaissance's own nomenclatures? Jonathan Goldberg considers this problem and argues that in Renaissance England, "there was . . . no recognition of homosexuality *per se*, no terms to identify a homosexual except within a seditious behavior that knew no limits," and that sodomy was not visible unless linked "with the much more visible signs of social disruption represented by unorthodox religious or social posi-

---

3. For a more detailed treatment of the ways early modern natural laws construed gender as a matter of virtual species and therefore do not (and cannot) ratify a fully heteronormative concept of sex or gender, see my "Nature's Bias: Renaissance Homonormativity and Elizabethan Comic Likeness," *Modern Philology* 98, no. 2 (November 2000), pp. 183–210, which considers John Lyly's *Gallathea* and Shakespeare's *Twelfth Night*.

4. The procreative logics of male friendship, however, are explored in Jeffrey Masten, *Textual Intercourse: Collaboration, Authorship, and Sexualities in Renaissance Drama* (Cambridge: Cambridge University Press, 1997), chap. 2; see also George Klawitter, "Verse Letters to T.W. from John Donne: 'By you my love is sent,'" in *Homosexuality in Renaissance and Enlightenment England,* ed. Claude Summers (New York: Haworth, 1992), pp. 85–102, who discusses the ways Donne and Thomas Woodward link a shared poetic productivity to lesbian forms in their exchange of verse letters.

tions."[5] Rather than generate identifying terms to fill this silence by using a hermeneutics that supposes something is hidden from language, examining the patterns of what Renaissance writers do say can help us grasp a serious difference in affective organization before the regime of contemporary sexuality Foucault has described.

Male same-sex eroticism does garner a specified designation when it appears, for example, hierarchized above the love of women, in an extraordinarily direct formulation in Spenser's *Shepheard's Calendar*. E.K.'s gloss reports there that "paederistice [is] much to be praeferred before gynerastice, that is the love whiche enflameth men with lust toward woman kind."[6] This construction emphasizes the greater degree of category-crossing involved in heterosexuality (an approach to woman as a "kind"). But the naming of pederasty also highlights a question of unequals, or unlikes. This inequality seems to be what actually triggers articulation. In "Of Friendship," Montaigne shows just the same technology of thought. When he dismisses "Greeke licence" from true friendship, the problem is not eroticism, but difference: "it had so necessary a disparity of ages, and difference of offices between lovers, [and so] did no more sufficiently answer the perfect union and agreement, which here we require."[7] In a series of exclusions from friendship (heterosexuality, pederasty, utilitarianism, and blood relations), Montaigne leaves the prospect of eroticism between male equals utterly, and probably pointedly, unaddressed.

And female homoeroticism? Even within "chaste" female association, the presence or absence of sexual acts would be even less dispositive than it would have been for males. Considering sodomy, Goldberg writes that "if sodomy named sexual acts only in particularly stigmatizing contexts, there is no reason not to believe that such acts went on . . . called, among other things, friendship or patronage, and facilitated by beds shared, for instance, by servants or students, by teachers and pupils, by kings and their minions

5. Jonathan Goldberg, "Sodomy and Society: the Case of Christopher Marlowe," in *Staging the Renaissance: Reinterpretations of Elizabethan and Jacobean Drama,* ed. David Scott Kastan and Peter Stallybrass (New York: Routledge, 1991), pp. 75–82, 75–76.

6. Edmund Spenser, *Shepheardes Calender* ("Januarye"), in *The Poetical Works of Edmund Spenser,* ed. J. C. Smith and E. de Selincourt (Oxford: Oxford University Press, 1912). This reference is discussed in Jonathan Goldberg, *Sodometries: Renaissance Texts, Modern Sexualities* (Stanford, Calif.: Stanford University Press, 1992), p.66; and Stephen Orgel, *Impersonations: The Performance of Gender in Shakespeare's England* (Cambridge: Cambridge University Press, 1996), p. 43.

7. Michel de Montaigne, "Of Friendship," in *The Essayes of Montaigne: John Florio's Translation,* ed. J. I. M. Stewart (New York: Modern Library, 1933)[1603], p. 147. Subsequent references to Montaigne are to this edition and will appear in the text.

or queens and their ladies."[8] From a social viewpoint, Valerie Traub compares the asymmetry of the voluble regulation of female heterosexuality and relative silence on female homoerotics to suggest that "the nature of [women's] erotic contacts did not invite sexual interpretation . . . [since] such behavior did not threaten the basis of the social contract—the open lineage family" and that "women's relative confinement in the household" privatized their sexual contact and precluded the formation of "homoerotic subcultures," which might have been the basis for a more marked presence in discourse.[9]

In a separate essay entitled "The (In)Significance of 'Lesbian' Desire," Traub offers a typology of lesbian representations in the Renaissance ("the French female sodomite, the English tribade, and the theatrical 'femme'"), and she proposes that the first two discursive figures achieve representation because they transgress the patriarchal specification of proper female roles (by usurping male sexual agency), while the latter made her way into dramatic representation because she does not. In other words, "whereas the 'tribade' and 'sodomite' functioned as magnets for cultural fantasies and fears . . . the 'femme' woman, who challenged neither gender roles nor reproductive imperatives, seems to have been so unworthy of notice that little note was taken of her at all."[10] Traub concludes that "theatrical representations suggest that 'feminine' homoerotic desires were dramatized precisely because they did not signify."[11] The strategy of reading employed here with respect to "lesbian (in)significance" associates signification with transgression, and so declines to take up the ways in which the textual or discursive phenomena of female homoeroticism may participate in "established" structures of thought. As I have argued in chapter 2, heterosexual imperatives jostled with homonormative trends in Renaissance thinking about affect, showing that the "licit" itself is fractured and contradictory, less monumental than our generalizations about it. The principle of likeness that friendship celebrates privileges certain relations more than others, depending on the circumstances.

Eroticism, especially homoeroticism, then, seems not to operate as a device governing meanings in the Renaissance; its presence or absence is

8. Goldberg, *Sodometries,* p. 19.
9. Valerie Traub, *Desire and Anxiety: Circulations of Sexuality in Shakespearean Drama* (London and New York: Routledge, 1992), p. 108.
10. Valerie Traub, "The (In)Significance of 'Lesbian' Desire in Early Modern England," in *Queering the Renaissance,* ed. Jonathan Goldberg (Durham, N.C.: Duke University Press, 1994), pp. 62–83, 79.
11. Traub, *Desire and Anxiety,* p.80.

not determining in nomenclatures, knowledges, or social practices. Alan Bray's work on the relation between friendship and homosexual practices may be taken as definitive: what we can know about Renaissance orderings of these matters is that unequal friendship—in terms of class or status— could, but need not invariably, trigger an allegation of sodomy.[12] *Sodomy* itself, in turn, describes an "utterly confused category," as Foucault termed it and as Goldberg has shown in detail for Renaissance England.[13] Categories of relation and their transgression derive less from erotic designations and more from the status of the parties as like or unlike. In the naming of Renaissance desires and affects, then, principles of likeness control more than either an inventorying eye to sexual practices or even eroticism itself can control.

Because the presence or absence of same-sex eroticism sets no necessary interpretive limits, the texts of the period have proven enormously fruitful for historians and critics concerned to explore the social and signifying functions of homoeroticism. Although Lorna Hutson has argued that much of this work has to do with seeing our own obsessions in the cornucopian Shakespearean text,[14] it gets much of its power from what I am calling Renaissance homonormativity: an almost philosophical preference for likeness or a structure of thinking based on resemblance. Indeed, as Janel Mueller has shown in the contexts of John Donne's remarkable poem, "Sapho to Philenis," such likeness in and of itself serves a legitimating role in the astonishingly direct case she terms Donne's "brief for lesbianism."[15] Homoeroticism instances this likeness norm, so while the "-eroticism" may, sometimes, be transgressive, the "homo-" prefix itself describes something commonplace, "normal," and even proverbial in its affirmation that "like seeks like."

Another aspect of Donne's poem warrants further consideration here.

12. Alan Bray, *Homosexuality in Renaissance England* (London: Gay Men's Press, 1982) and "Homosexuality and the Signs of Male Friendship in Elizabethan England," in *Queering the Renaissance,* ed. Jonathan Goldberg (Durham, N.C.: Duke University Press, 1994), pp. 40–61.

13. Jonathan Goldberg, "Sodomy and Society: The Case of Christopher Marlowe," in *Staging the Renaissance: Reinterpretations of Elizabethan and Jacobean Drama,* ed. David Scott Kastan and Peter Stallybrass (New York: Routledge, 1991).

14. Lorna Hutson, "On Not Being Deceived: Rhetoric and the Body in *Twelfth Night," Texas Studies in Literature and Language* 38, no. 2 (Summer, 1996): 140–74. This essay also entails a strong critique of the Thomas Laquer's "single sex theory."

15. Janel Mueller, "Troping Utopia: Donne's Brief for Lesbianism in 'Sappho to Philenis'," in *Sexuality and Gender in Early Modern Europe,* ed. James Grantham Turner (Cambridge: Cambridge University Press, 1993), pp. 182–207.

In the verse epistle, Donne's Sappho voices a range of persuasions to Philaenis as to the preferability of lesbian eroticism. One of those arguments is, in fact, its relation to chastity. This rationale translates Traub's sense that lesbianism and chastity are related (through negligibility) by advocating that link as a positive inducement. In contrast with the "side effects" of heterosexuality (pregnancy), Philaenis is urged to choose lesbian erotic practice, because it neither marks nor mars the body: "Men leave behinde them that which their sin shows, / And are as theeves trac'd, which rob when it snows. / But of our dallyance no more signes there are, / Than fishes leave in streames, or Birds in aire."[16] An uncanny reverberation occurs here, as the "fishes in streams" image recalls key language from Donne's friendship poem to Henry Wotton, "Sir, more than kisses, letters mingle souls," discussed in chapter 1. There, Donne urges Wotton carefully to traverse the soul-endangering world of courts and ambition in just the same manner: as "Fishes glide, leaving no print where they passe."[17] The untraceable submarine paths of fish can emblematize both the masculine integrity enabled through friendship and female same-sex erotic choice, because each turns from the norms of subordination to which they are mutually averse. Elusive female homoeroticism and exalted male friendship are, in this sense and for these purposes, the same.

While Elizabeth Cary linked female chastity and male friendship as counterparts in a struggle with tyrannical power, Shakespeare and John Fletcher's *The Two Noble Kinsmen* (1613) goes in a different direction, pressing the issues of gender and eroticism within friendship. Shakespeare and Fletcher collaborate to construct a female voice as the preeminent advocate of a tyranny-resisting, same-sex principle of friendship, a principle of female association that, doubly revising Montaigne, admits sexuality into the friendship script. Although generally read in accord with conventions privileging marriage in dramatic comedy, *The Two Noble Kinsmen* associates marriage with unreasonable rule, juxtaposing both with principles of friendship and choice. The play thus construes "human title"[18]— authority over the disposition of the self—as a bedraggled prize in the struggle between personal affective autonomy and a monarchical preroga-

16. John Donne, "Sapho to Philaenis," in *Poetical Works,* ed. Herbert Grierson (Oxford: Oxford University Press, 1990), pp. 110–12, lines 39–42.

17. John Donne, "Sir, more than kisses," in *The Complete English Poems,* ed. C. A. Patrides (London: Dent, 1985), pp.159–62, line 56.

18. William Shakespeare and John Fletcher, *The Two Noble Kinsmen,* ed. Eugene M. Waith (Oxford: Clarendon Press, 1989), 1.1.233. All references are to this edition and appear in the text.

tive understood less as state power than as a personal excess by a "tyran-nical" ruler.[19] Derrida describes this opposition between autonomy and heteronomy as a philosophical trademark of "the tradition of a certain concept of friendship."[20] But here, against that tradition, a female voice dramatizes friendship and reason, and it is the voice of an Amazon, a figure much more likely to serve as an absolute other beyond reason's pale.[21]

In the following discussion of *The Two Noble Kinsmen,* I extend chap-ter 2's argument locating idealized female friendship in a specifically social kind of female chastity, despite both the characteristic masculinity of friendship rhetoric in the period and a sense of chastity that envisions females in isolation or in a male's jurisdiction. In *The Two Noble Kinsmen,* Emilia, a votaress of Diana's and a lady knight, articulates a commitment to such a chastity of women among themselves. Chastity thus envisioned (rather than as a "single blessedness") carries political charges analogous to the autonomy valorized in male friendship. But Emilia's case also extends the range of this principle of self-rule, and so it complicates the already vibrant scholarship considering early modern sexuality.[22] Shakespeare and

19. For a concise expression of this Renaissance understanding, see Sir Thomas Smith, *De Republica Anglorum,* ed. Mary Dewar (Cambridge: Cambridge University Press, 1982), bk. 1, chaps. 7–9. Smith views tyranny in terms of the ruler's subjugation of government institutions to his own personal desires, motivated by "pleasure" and self-interest. Chap-ter 8 suggests the conceptual difficulties in separating this sense of tyranny from absolutism in general, calling the latter (at best) a "lawful tyrannie for a time" (p. 54).

20. Jacques Derrida, "The Politics of Friendship," *The Journal of Philosophy* 85 (1988): 634.

21. Louis Montrose argues that "invariably, the Amazons are relocated just within the receding boundary of *terra incognita,*" and are commonly configured in "an anti-culture that precisely inverts European norms of political authority, sexual license, marriage prac-tices, and inheritance rules." "*A Midsummer Night's Dream* and the Shaping Fantasies of Elizabethan Culture: Gender, Power, Form", in *Rewriting the Renaissance: The Discourses of Sexual Difference in Early Modern Europe,* ed. Margaret Ferguson, Maureen Quilligan, and Nancy Vickers (Chicago: University of Chicago Press, 1986), p. 71. Recently, Kathryn Schwarz's *Tough Love: Amazon Encounters in the English Renaissance* (Durham, N.C.: Duke University Press, 2000) has challenged this sense of Amazon exoticism, urging that the domestication of Amazons is a recurrent theme in the texts of the period and that the Ama-zon figure stimulates both homoerotic and heteroerotic response. *Tough Love* appeared dur-ing the final stages of this book's production, but its insistence on the ways Amazons chal-lenge *and* establish social orders clearly offers a home for *The Two Noble Kinsmen*'s Emilia.

22. For a summary of the basic debate, see Claude J. Summers's well-annotated dis-cussion in "Homosexuality and Renaissance Literature, or the Anxieties of Anachronism," *South Central Review* 9, no. 1 (spring 1992): 2–23. Compare, for example, Bruce Smith, *Homosexual Desire in Shakespeare's England: A Cultural Poetics* (Chicago: University of Chicago Press, 1991); and Bray, *Homosexuality in Renaissance England.*

Fletcher's drama conceives same-sex associations, including those that are erotic, as a matter of "persuasion" and even "faith." In this the play exceeds the usual poles of the historical debate.[23] It reflects neither the antiidentitarian view that same-sex eroticism transpired without any means to directly articulate it, nor the more essentialist view that such eroticism pertained to those whose "nature" prescribed it. Instead, same-sex associational primacy appears as something one might "profess" or choose, as an espousal of a "faith," or as a "way of life,"[24] echoing distantly the vital idea of conscience so resonant in the period.[25]

Reading a female character's primary commitment to other women as an argument or position gives an obverse perspective on the word *sodometries* as Goldberg has explicated it: citing its "nonce-word suggestiveness," he expands on its sense of logics or metrics, citing the term's use "to impugn . . . customs . . . and arguments."[26] Goldberg's elucidation of sodometry as a period allegation of false logic and "preposterousness"[27] is neatly reversed in this case of female homoerotics. For rather than representing an

23. The spectrum of views on historical approaches to sexuality extends between these two poles. John Boswell's *Christianity, Social Tolerance, and Homosexuality,* on the one hand, is often characterized as "essentialist" in its effort to trace a history of homosexuality; volume 1 of Michel Foucault's influential *History of Sexuality* has inspired much scholarship in a "constructivist" mode. See Summers, "Homosexuality and Renaissance Literature, or the Anxieties of Anachronism," p. 20, n. 7; and Traub, *Desire and Anxiety,* p. 103. Both Boswell and Foucault, however, attempted to modulate these characterizations. Boswell concludes that "most of the current spectrum of belief [about what homosexuality is] appears to have been represented in previous societies. . . . Both realists and nominalists must lower their voices." John Boswell, "Revolutions, Universals, Categories," *Salmagundi* 58–59 (fall 1982–winter 1983): 89–113, 112–13. In an interview, Foucault commented specifically on Boswell's methodology, characterizing it as, in effect, nonessentialist and claiming that Boswell's emphasis on how people conceived the meanings of their own behaviors is essential to an archeology of sexuality. "Sexual Choice, Sexual Act" in Michel Foucault, *Foucault Live,* trans. J. Johnston, ed. Sylvère Lotringer (New York: Columbia University Press, Semiotext(e) Foreign Agents Series, 1989), pp. 211–31.

24. Foucault's interview in *Le Gai Pied* reveals an emphasis on this sense of choice and innovation, which is not often associated with his work. There, Foucault offers a notion of (modern) homosexuality/friendship as "a way of life" involving invention, improvisation, and communicative experimentation not far from the sense of choice and articulate persuasion to be found in *The Two Noble Kinsmen.* Michel Foucault, "Friendship as a Way of Life," reprinted in *Foucault Live,* pp. 203–9.

25. In contemporary, U.S. terms, this implies same-sex erotic choice as kind of a performative power pertaining to rights under the First Amendment of the Constitution (1791), as a blend of the related freedoms of expression and association.

26. Goldberg, *Sodometries,* pp. xiv–xv.

27. Ibid., p. 4 and passim.

unorthodox or negativized position or a sedition without limits as sodomy seems to have done,[28] female association here instead reprehends a tyranny without limits, reproving the abuse of absolute power from the established viewpoint of reason. In *The Two Noble Kinsmen,* same-sex association, inclusive of homoerotics, takes a position not only on the content of sexual meanings, but also in the contest over who shall determine them, thus emblematizing the threatened terrain of the subject's prerogative.

Consequently, female association is not only thinkable in this drama; friendship gendered female appears to extraordinary effect, linking marriage and tyranny and intensifying the otherwise familiar disapprobation the play registers toward absolute (or unreasoning, unbounded, "tyrannical") power. Gendering friendship female makes metaphors of chastity available to express an urgent rationale for opposing a tyrant's powers of incursion. As a final matter, I will consider the viability of this troping of the tension between autonomy and tyranny, extending the implications more broadly to critical approaches to gender and sexuality in Renaissance dramatic texts. For the possibility that both gender and sexuality can be mobilized in this unexpected manner suggests a kind of superior urgency for political "station" or hierarchical status as an organizing principle in Renaissance self-conception. While gender emerges as flexible, even reversible,[29] and while sexuality attaches only variably to gender[30] and "sodomy" only variably to transgression,[31] birth or station, especially the relation of "degree" between sovereign and subject, seems to have a special fixity as a vertical differentiation backed by divine will. The Renaissance sense of public personage or "great persons,"[32] those holding offices in public

28. Goldberg, "Sodomy and Society," pp. 75–76.

29. See Thomas Laqueur's "one sex model" in *Making Sex: The Body and Gender from the Greeks to Freud* (Cambridge, Mass.: Harvard University Press, 1990), especially chaps. 2–4.

30. Traub, *Desire and Anxiety,* chap. 4, pp. 91–116.

31. Commenting on the fact that James I, "notorious for his overtly homosexual behavior," nonetheless considered "sodomy" a felony in his *Basilikon Doron,* Goldberg argues that James's "treatise does not . . . dissimulate; rather it shows that sodomy was so fully politicized that *no king could possibly apply the term to himself,*" in "Sodomy and Society," p. 80.

32. On this special sense of the word *great,* Francis Bacon's essay "Of Great Place" conveys a view of "greatness" as a position structured by the complementary categories of personage colloquially familiar as the "greater" and the "meaner" sort. In that essay, Bacon's own way of rhetorically circumscribing the power of the great is to emphasize that "Men in Great Place, are thrice Servants: Servants of the Soveraigne or State; Servants of Fame; and Servants of Businesse. So as they have no Freedome. . . ." *The Essayes or Counsels, Civill and Morall,* ed. Michael Kiernan (Cambridge, Mass.: Harvard University Press, 1985), p. 33.

power, informs and constrains selves in ways that have no corresponding discourse in the modern era.

Emilia's Argument in *The Two Noble Kinsmen*

The drama begins as Theseus, Duke of Athens, returns from military victory over the Amazons and plans to marry Hippolyta, his captive Amazon queen. Pirithous, Theseus's friend, and Emilia, Hippolyta's sister and co-captive, attend the proceedings. Three widows arrive and interrupt the nuptials. They complain that their slain husbands lie rotting on the battlefield because Creon has forbidden removal of the bodies. The widows, with the help of Hippolyta and Emilia, persuade Theseus to suspend the ceremony and punish Creon. As Theseus and Pirithous depart, the Amazon sisters reflect on friendship and Emilia speaks on behalf of "true love 'tween maid and maid," averring that she never wants to marry. In the ensuing battle, Theseus witnesses the ardor and the wounding of Palamon and Arcite. Rather than allowing them to die, he orders that their lives be saved so that he may imprison them for life. Their imprisonment introduces a subplot of the Jailer, the Wooer, and the Jailer's Daughter, who observe the courtesy of Palamon and Arcite in prison.

There, the two kinsmen employ strong protestations of friendship to celebrate their confinement as a preservative against worldly corruptions. Within fewer than sixty lines, however, they disclaim this friendship. For both Palamon and Arcite fall in love with Emilia, whom they see from the prison window as she walks in a garden with her Woman. Freed from prison but banished from the kingdom, Arcite encounters countrymen on their way to Theseus's games and resolves to disguise himself in hopes of joining Emilia. Back in prison, the Jailer's Daughter goes mad with love for Palamon and helps him escape. Arcite distinguishes himself at the games and joins Emilia's service. Encounters between Arcite and Palamon result in a plan to duel over the right to love her. Their meetings alternate with mad soliloquies by the Jailer's Daughter, who joins the countrymen's morris dance. This dance is performed for Theseus, Pirithous, Hippolyta, and Emilia, who are in the woods hunting. When the sound of dueling draws the courtly hunters to discover the kinsmen, the enraged Theseus vows to execute them for their offense to his authority. The others beg him, on their knees, to show mercy; he responds by proposing that Emilia pick one as a husband and send the other to death. Shocked and unwilling, she refrains from choosing. Theseus then resolves that they shall duel and the winner shall take her, with the loser being immediately put to death.

Palamon, Arcite, and Emilia all visit the altars of their tutelary divinities, Venus, Mars, and Diana respectively. Emilia is ordered to attend the duel and refuses, exclaiming, "I am extinct" (5.3.20). In the duel, Palamon is wounded and Arcite declared the winner. Just as Palamon is about to be executed, news arrives that Arcite, an accomplished horseman, has been crushed by Emilia's horse. The dying Arcite bequeaths Emilia to Palamon, whose marriage is deferred, as Theseus's had been, by funeral business. Concluding the drama, Theseus exclaims by way of a moral, "O you heavenly charmers, / What things you make of us!" (5.4.131–32)

Much of the critical consideration of *The Two Noble Kinsmen* has concerned itself with allocating authorship between Shakespeare and Fletcher.[33] Treatments undertaking more thematic interpretation have often utilized an idea of the "naturalness" of marriage to interpret this drama, which, I will show, could hardly go further than it does to argue that marriage is a (brutally) political institution, both within itself and as an instrument of third-party power. As one editor of *The Two Noble Kinsmen* suggests, "perhaps the chief difficulty is that the play seems to compel us to attribute to Shakespeare . . . an apparently partial and distorted attitude to love."[34] Instead of reaching such an undesirable conclusion, some critics compensate: they read the play as a representation of the inevitable defeat of such a "distorted" attitude. One describes the play's concern with "resisting a stage of life on which nature insists, the life of sexual relations."[35] Mary Beth Rose argues that "the best studies of the play have relied on the psychoanalytic conception of individual development to argue . . . that *The Two Noble Kinsmen* concerns . . . the unavoidable process of growth."[36] Barry Weller, whose reading encompasses a brief reference to Adrienne Rich's formulation of "compulsory heterosexuality," neverthe-

33. Both G. R. Proudfoot, "*Henry VIII, The Two Noble Kinsmen,* and the Apocryphal Plays," in *Shakespeare: Select Bibliographical Guides,* ed. Stanley Wells (London: Oxford University Press, 1973) and Paul Bertram, *Shakespeare and "The Two Noble Kinsmen"* (New Brunswick, N.J.: Rutgers University Press, 1965) offer summaries of the authorship debates. In general, Fletcher is accorded the greater part of the play, with act 1, substantial parts of act 5, and scattered scenes attributed to Shakespeare. See also Mary Beth Rose, *The Expense of Spirit: Love and Sexuality in Renaissance Drama* (Ithaca, N.Y.: Cornell University Press, 1988), p. 213 and accompanying note.

34. *The Two Noble Kinsmen,* ed. N. W. Bawcutt (London: Penguin Books, 1977), introduction, p. 9.

35. Philip Edwards, quoted in Barry Weller, "*The Two Noble Kinsmen,* The Friendship Tradition, and the Flight from Eros," in *Shakespeare, Fletcher, and "The Two Noble Kinsmen,"* ed. Charles H. Frey (Columbia: University of Missouri Press, 1989), p. 100.

36. Rose, *The Expense of Spirit,* p. 222.

less characterizes marriage in terms of "the inevitability of this institution as both the building block of the social order and the seal of adult sexuality."[37] Rose, again, reflecting on the historical moment in which marriage was just becoming a normative locus of affectivity, sees *The Two Noble Kinsmen* as a "representation of neurotic suffering"; in her reading the play equates resistance to marriage as a celebratory zone for self-fulfillment with "perversity" and an "unnatural recoil from experience and, specifically, from sexual love."[38]

Given the historical change marriage was undergoing, these critical approaches underestimate the power of the theories of friendship in the play by conflating sexuality, nature, growth, and love with marriage. They fail to grapple with the stunningly negative conception of marriage the drama projects. In doing so, they also diminish the force of the character Emilia, who walks onstage to dramatize the most explicit case for same-sex association in the period except for Donne's "Sapho to Philenis." Mueller argues that the "brief for lesbianism" in Donne's astonishing thought experiment is unprecedented and extraordinary given the inherited imageries of Sappho in the sixteenth-century context.[39] In this poem, the same-sex relationship is not represented as inevitably temporary or short-lived. Mueller proposes that Donne envisions lesbianism, in both erotic and economic terms, as a utopian resolution of the sexual dilemma in Montaigne's friendship theory.[40] *The Two Noble Kinsmen*'s Emilia, in comparison, appears as an advocate of female homoerotics in a contest situation, as a representative of individual, volitional association against the sovereign's power to reorganize one's affective arrangements. In a sense, the play moves female homoerotics from utopia into the realm of political contest, where it remains positively coded as utopian; its apparent defeat by marriage is

37. Weller, "*The Two Noble Kinsmen,* The Friendship Tradition, and the Flight from Eros," p. 104.

38. Rose, *The Expense of Spirit,* pp. 224, 223.

39. Mueller, "Troping Utopia."

40. Ibid., pp. 184, 194—96. In a recent essay, Paula Blank disagrees with Mueller's claim that the erotics represented in Donne's poem constitutes a "fully utopian moment." Blank argues that the structure of comparison, of sameness, ultimately fails in Donne's poem, in a way consistent with the corpus of his poetry. Paula Blank, "Comparing Sappho to Philaenis: John Donne's Homopoetics," *PMLA* 110, no. 3 (May 1995): 358–68, 359. But while Blank's concern is to show the way the poem fits into Donne's poetic practice ("homopoetics," or "the cultural making of likenesses," p. 359), Mueller's contextualization takes on a different project—placing Donne's "imagining" against a backdrop of virtually complete silence on the subject of female homoeroticism.

marked by funerals rather than celebration. Since the power of the sovereign and the imposition of marriage are so morally tainted in *The Two Noble Kinsmen*, Emilia's advocacy is not simply another example of what James Holstun usefully terms "lesbian elegy."[41] Instead, the "inevitability" of a female homoerotics pressed into the past tense is just what Shakespeare and Fletcher qualify and recast as political injustice.

The literary rarity of Emilia's position, its specifically political role in the drama, and its connection to female proprietary spaces make *The Two Noble Kinsmen* an extraordinary text, one that distinguishes itself from the mere co-optation of female (homo)eroticism that is perhaps a more probable scenario.[42] For Emilia's combined dedication to women and to chastity develops the case for a chastity that specifically configures itself as female friendship or association. This chastity opposes not only tyrannical or coercive marriage, but also tyranny in its plain political sense. While Rose locates the play's conflict between "erotic love and friendship"[43] and Weller considers the play to "dramatize the conflict between friendship and marriage,"[44] friendship and marriage arguably trope another conflict. That conflict places nonsubordinating affective bonds in opposition to compulsory and hierarchical ones, an opposition in which relations achieved by a frankly articulable preference counter those enforced by tyrannical compulsion. In my view, the conflict of the play is best understood as pitting Emilia as a spokesperson for volitional association against Theseus as the agent of imposed marriage. Theirs is a contest over which of the two paradigms will capture "human title."

Which Friendship?

The prologue to *The Two Noble Kinsmen* signals its source in the tale of Palamon and Arcite, originally from *The Decameron*, by referring to Chaucer's "The Knight's Tale." The points of deviation are even more important, however, for they all tend to highlight friendship—for both sexes—and to darken marriage and diminish its prestige. In Chaucer's tale,

41. James Holstun, "'Will you rent our ancient love asunder?': Lesbian Elegy in Donne, Marvell, and Milton," *ELH* 54 (winter 1987): 835—67.
42. For a discussion of co-optation in the drama of the period, see Douglas Bruster, "Female-Female Eroticism and the Early Modern Stage," *Renaissance Drama* 24 (1995): 1–32.
43. Rose, *The Expense of Spirit*, p. 216.
44. Weller, "*The Two Noble Kinsmen*, The Friendship Tradition, and the Flight from Eros," p. 101.

Theseus's marriage to the captured queen of "Femenye" is already effected, not indefinitely deferred as in the drama. The playwrights have also de-emphasized the marriage of Emilia and Palamon, postponing it beyond the play's borders. The drama enhances Pirithous's presence, giving his friend-ship with Theseus sufficient weight to counterbalance that of Palamon and Arcite; the kinsmen's friendship attains a new degree of articulation. Most unusually, the play vastly expands the role of Emelye into a character who articulates an entirely new argument, connecting a female preference for chastity with the cultivation of a camaraderie of women. All these changes weaken the marriage element that Shakespeare and Fletcher adapt from Chaucer while substantiating the counterpresence of friendship.

The friendship topic is strengthened by the playwrights, but they also make it more complex; criticism has not registered this complicating di-vergence in "the" friendship theme of the play. Indeed, one critic has as-serted that Palamon and Arcite are just "younger versions of Theseus and Pirithous."[45] While the moral problems with Theseus's character will be explored shortly, the case of Palamon and Arcite so markedly deviates from model friendship that it can only be considered a parody of that highly rhetoricized period ideal. On the one hand, the secure friendship of The-seus and Pirithous is recorded by others' observation. In a rich conversa-tion between Hippolyta and Emilia, the two sisters analyze both the scope and basis of this famous friendship. Their dialogue proceeds as Pirithous leaves them to follow Theseus to war:

> EMILIA: How his longing
> Follows his friend! . . .
> Have you observed him
> Since our great lord departed?
>
> HIPPOLYTA: With much labor;
> And I did love him for it. They two have cabined
> In many a dangerous as poor a corner,
> Peril and want contending . . .
>
> .   .   .   .
>
> Their knot of love,
> Tied, weaved, entangled, with so true, so long,
> And with a finger of so deep a cunning,
> May be outworn, never undone. I think
> Theseus cannot be umpire to himself,

45. Jeanne Roberts, "Crises of Male Self-Definition in *The Two Noble Kinsmen*," in Frey, ed., *Shakespeare, Fletcher, and "The Two Noble Kinsmen,"* pp. 133–44, p. 138.

Cleaving his conscience into twain and doing
Each side like justice, which he loves best.
(1.3.26–47)[46]

The sisters, experienced in war themselves, assess this friendship with war-credentialed eyes and they find it to be rooted in mutual experience and tested over time. Emilia subsequently comments on the friendship's sense of "ground" and its "maturely seasoned" quality (1.3.56). This perspective sets the Theseus-Pirithous friendship apart from the rapturous immediacy of Montaigne's formulation.[47]

For their part, Palamon and Arcite articulate their twinning friendship with a youthful excess that effectively parodies the declamatory rhetoric of Florio's Montaigne. The Jailer's Daughter had observed that the imprisoned kinsmen (not unlike Donne's lovers in "The Good-Morrow") "have all the world in their chamber" (2.1.25). Arcite begins to imagine that they can thrive in confinement:

>   And here being thus together,
> We are an endless mine to one another;
> We are one another's wife, ever begetting
> New births of love; we are father, friends, acquaintance;
> We are, in one another, families.
> I am your heir, and you are mine; this place
> Is our inheritance; . . .
>   here . . .
> We shall live long and loving.
>   (2.1.132–40)[48]

---

46. This "knot of love" ("so true, so long, . . . so deep") directly incorporates the language and cadence of Florio's Montaigne describing the "knot" of friendship as "so hard, so fast, so durable" (p. 147) that women are too weak to sustain it. Here, the women have the power to appreciate it; Emilia, of course, will go on to describe her experience of it, despite Montaigne's theory. Florio's language exceeds Montaigne's ("un neud si pressé et si durable" [p. 186]) and would appear to have influenced this play.

47. "Wee sought one another before we had seene one another, and by the reports we heard of one another; . . . we embraced one another by our names" (Montaigne, "Of Friendship," p. 149).

48. *The Maid's Tragedy* similarly reflects a use of familial language to describe a friendship that exceeds it: lamenting his friend's death, Melantius proclaims "here was Sister, Father, Brother, Sonne, / All that I had" (p. 98). (Melantius here reflects the desire to "escape" from one's maternal origin that Janet Adelman describes in *Suffocating Mothers: Fantasies of Maternal Origin in Shakespeare's Plays, Hamlet to The Tempest* [New York: Routledge, 1992]).

A few lines before this extravagantly rhetoricized relationship abruptly ends, Palamon asks, "is there record of any two that loved / Better than we do Arcite?" (2.1.166–67) and concludes in the same self-congratulatory tone, "I do not think it possible our friendship / Should ever leave us" (2.1.168–69). However, the entire declamation of Palamon and Arcite's friendship notably transpires in the shadow of a captivity that serves as both its context and its caveat. Unlike Theseus and Pirithous, the kinsmen envision their friendship both as a haven from the worldly trial of their virtue and as a bond vulnerable in the circumstance of liberty. The prison is a "holy sanctuary" to keep them from corruption (2.1.125). "Were we at liberty, / A wife might part us lawfully, or business; / Quarrels consume us. . . . a thousand chances, / Were we from hence, would sever us" (2.1.142–49). On the contrary, within Renaissance friendship theory, "neither Soveraignes nor fathers hate / A friendship fixt on vertue seuer can." [49] The kinsmen's declamations are premature and untested.

Montaigne refers to Cicero on this issue: "Clearly friendships are to be judged by wits, and ages already strengthened and confirmed." [50] Compared to Theseus's "knot of love," as Hippolyta and Emilia had just described it, the kinsmen's friendship is precarious in the extreme. This precariousness is immediately dramatized as the onset of their love for Emilia engenders a quarrel over their respective rights to love her. [51] The collapse of Palamon and Arcite's friendship falls decisively short of the right result, according to friendship lore, when two virtuous friends fall in love with the same woman. The paradigm for this dilemma is Boccaccio's story of Tito and Gesippo in *The Decameron,* a tale circulated further in Elyot's *The Boke Named the Governour.* In Weller's words, "one friend surrenders his bride to the other, but this gift creates an asymmetry that, in the second move-

49. Elizabeth Cary, *The Tragedy of Mariam, the Fair Queen of Jewry,* eds. Margaret Ferguson and Barry Weller (Berkeley and Los Angeles: University of California Press, 1994), 2.2.113–14, p. 21.

50. Cicero, *De amicitia,* trans. Falconer, p. 148.

51. Whether in homoerotic or homosocial terms, a number of critics have noted the degree to which Palamon and Arcite's love for Emilia is a figuration of a primary love for each other. See, for example, Weller, "*The Two Noble Kinsmen,* The Friendship Tradition, and the Flight from Eros," p. 96; and Roberts, "Crises of Male Self-Definition in *The Two Noble Kinsmen,*" p. 141. While I emphasize here the measurement of failure in this friendship in terms of classically derived doctrine, their warm affectivity survives both their disclaimers of love and their murderous oaths. See, for example, act 3, scene 2, in which they promise "no mention of this woman, 'twill disturb us" (line 15), and the scene where they lovingly dress each other for combat (3.6).

ment of the tale, is presumably rectified when the recipient of the bride offers to die for the donor. The crises of death and sexual desire test the proposition that a friend is an 'other self' under extreme conditions."[52] False to form, the noble kinsmen Palamon and Arcite instantly pursue their separate interests, and vow to take each other's lives.[53] A "true" friendship would not have collapsed under this pressure.

Subjections to Love, to Madness, to Power

The two kinsmen's deviation from form follows the decidedly un-Ciceronian convention of (courtly) love at first sight. Love appears in its standard role as the antidote to same-sex friendship; it shows here, however, no trace of the "prestige" that Rose claims is accruing to love and marriage. Instead, the kinsmen's passion better resembles a medieval view of love as a medical illness or the familiar Renaissance view of love as subordination to dangerous passion, a weak succumbing to a form of madness. In Montaigne's words, again, love is "a mad desire in following that which flies us"(p. 146). In that mad pursuit, the kinsmen, who thought themselves "twins of honor" (2.1.72), become murderous. Erotic love thus engenders all the instability Montaigne had described and produces the erratic behavior that Cary and Cicero both link to subjection to a passionate appetite. Herod in *Mariam* followed his subjection to desire first into inconstancy and finally into a "franticke passion." Such a desire Lyly had called "the desease of love . . . whose assaults neyther the wise can resist by pollicie nor the valiaunt by strength."[54] And what about the simple and the weak? For it is in connection with the kinsmen's yielding to passion that the Jailer's Daughter must be considered; her madness literalizes the state in which the kinsmen place themselves.[55] Upon liberating Palamon, she soliloquizes, "I love him beyond love, and beyond reason, / Or wit, or

52. Weller, "*The Two Noble Kinsmen,* The Friendship Tradition, and the Flight from Eros," p. 93.

53. A similar, though unilateral, collapse of friendship happens in the earlier *Two Gentlemen of Verona,* and Valentine calls his friend Proteus "thou friend of an ill fashion!" (*The Two Gentlemen of Verona,* 5.4.61)

54. John Lyly, *Euphues and His England,* in *The Complete Works of John Lyly,* vol. 2, ed. R. Warwick Bond (Oxford: Clarendon, 1902), p. 158, cited in Rose, *The Expense of Spirit,* p. 23.

55. In considering the introduction of a threat of disorder into Theseus's realm, presenting crises for Theseus's authority, Michael D. Bristol argues that from Palamon and Arcite, disruption "spreads first to the Jailer's Daughter. This secondary plot completes the social and erotic pathology of the action." "Shakespeare and the Problem of Authority," in Frey, ed., *Shakespeare, Fletcher, and "The Two Noble Kinsmen,"* pp. 78–92, 90.

safety . . . / . . . I am desperate" (2.5.11–13). The Jailer's Daughter, like the kinsmen, embarks beyond reason's pale along the wavering, self-destructive path of subordination to desire.

In an effort to prove that "it would be wrong to say that love is invariably seen in an unfavorable light" in the play, Eugene Waith argues that the Jailer's Daughter's "simple unaffected desire" (never mind that "its hopelessness does indeed unsettle her mind") establishes her as a foil to the kinsmen's less direct, quarrelsome passion.[56] For Waith, the "destructive power of love" upon the Jailer's Daughter is likely to be overlooked by the spectator in favor of the "pathos of her situation."[57] Rose records a similar empathic response: "the Jailer's Daughter plot is the most appealing aspect of *The Two Noble Kinsmen*."[58] For Rose, this subplot is "distinctively modern" insofar as the Doctor appears "more successful at regulating sexuality" than Theseus the Duke. Rose also argues that futurity, otherwise absent from the play, is "suggested and affirmed" by this successful strategy of regulatory power. Given that the Jailer's Daughter's cure is effected by a professional intervention, however, it is unclear how she can represent a future that is "attached to creating a realm of private experience."[59] For rather than moving "happily, if obliviously" into the future, as she enters the bed-trick "cure" the Jailer's Daughter's last lines are spoken to her dissembling Wooer: "But you shall not hurt me" and "If you do, love, I'll cry" (5.2.109–10). She moves from a fitting role in a mad morris to a sane role in a mad illusion, another performance. Thus even in the most colorful and vigorously heterosexual part of the plot, erotic love remains in the terrain of illness (under a Doctor's jurisdiction), and the Jailer's Daughter exits with a haunting premonition that the world upon which she is entering may cause her "hurt."

Susan Green has considered the Jailer's Daughter a crux in an array of authorship questions and "crises of creativity," and, provocatively, suggests an analogy between the base-born young daughter of Theseus's jailer and Theseus himself. She describes them as "contrasting 'playwright' figures" in the drama.[60] The Jailer's Daughter's authorial power, of course, is drastically qualified by the Doctor's power to encompass her mad narrative into

56. Waith, *The Two Noble Kinsmen,* introduction, pp. 56, 57.
57. Ibid., p. 57.
58. Rose, *The Expense of Spirit,* p. 226.
59. Ibid., p. 228.
60. Susan Green, "'A mad woman? We are made, boys!' The Jailer's Daughter in *The Two Noble Kinsmen*," in Frey, ed., *Shakespeare, Fletcher, and "The Two Noble Kinsmen,"* pp. 121–32, 124.

a ruse designed to displace and correct her narrative. What qualifies the "authorial" control of Theseus? Theseus himself takes on the role of spokesman for a sense of fate, in which outcomes are controlled by some unpredictable external power. In the final speech of the play, he offers this commentary on the bizarre—and appallingly serious—turn of events: "Never fortune / Did play a subtler game . . . yet in the passage / The gods have been most equal. . . . The gods my justice / Take from my hand, and they themselves become the executioners / . . . O you heavenly charmers, / What things you make of us!" (5.4.112–32) Theseus's light tone here belies the spiritual bruises, long faces, and blood that surround him. Though "subtle," the occasion is a "game"; Theseus rightly perceives himself as a (friendly) competitor with the gods, gaming with other people's lives. His claim that the outcomes here have been effected by fortune or the gods, however, masks his agency in setting up the original "fateful" dilemmas in over-passionate exercises of his unilateral power. While much criticism seems to accept the role of fate in the drama,[61] the absolute power, the tyranny, of Theseus remains to be explored.

Authority: Theseus Unbounded

In act 1, we find the kinsmen discussing the nature of Creon's power in Thebes. They call him "a most *unbounded* tyrant" and prepare to exile themselves, when the approach of warring Theseus revives their political loyalty to Creon: "we must / With him stand to the mercy of our fates / Who hath *bounded* our last minute" (1.2.63, 101–3, emphasis mine). Such is the tyrant's character. He has a boundary problem, exceeding his own and contracting or violating the boundedness of others. Theseus displays exactly this problem, insisting upon a relationship of intimacy with persons over whom he has absolute power.

Both the kinsmen and both the Amazons are *less than subjects* in Theseus's dukedom. They are captives, prisoners of war, lives to be disposed of by decrees. They are lower than citizens; their position vis-à-vis Theseus is exactly the same as that of a "citizen" under a tyrant. Previous criticism has not factored this specifically political circumstance into readings concerned with individualistic or exclusively private meanings of love and sexuality. Hippolyta and Emilia are captive soldiers, Amazons to be domesticated by Theseus's phallic power; Palamon and Arcite were combatants near death when Theseus ordered, "All our surgeons / Convent in their be-

61. Bawcutt, introduction, *The Two Noble Kinsmen,* Penguin edition, p. 10; Waith, introduction to the Clarendon Press edition, pp. 58–59.

hoof . . . we had rather have 'em / Prisoners to us than death!" (1.4.30–37) All four are in effect Theseus's property; none arrived in his dukedom voluntarily. His comportment toward them combines domination with desire, aggression with affection and admiration as he blurs personal inclination with political office. Hippolyta, his enemy, will be his bride; Emilia, her sister, he will marry off in a gesture of paternal authority; and Palamon and Arcite, his prisoners, he will celebrate and call friends. All their fates will be determined by Theseus's imagination and will be effected by the mechanisms of his political power; none will be motivated by individual growth.

The Renaissance associations with Theseus's character were deeply mixed, despite what D'Orsay Pearson describes as a "critical myth": that Theseus represented the ideal Renaissance prince, a reasonable man and an equitable ruler.[62] Instead, Pearson argues, Theseus's "Renaissance image as an unnatural, perfidious, and unfaithful father and lover far outweighed . . . his accomplishment in organizing the *demes* of Athens . . . or his reputation as an icon of the virtues of friendship."[63] Reckoning up the various representations of Theseus in the sixteenth century, Pearson concludes that the saliency of his reputation for savage betrayals of women and wives and for the murder of his own son is critical to understanding *A Midsummer Night's Dream,* making it "an even more serious and ironic comedy," especially if it is to be regarded as a "marriage play."[64] *The Two Noble Kinsmen,* however, even more fully dramatizes a Theseus ruled by his own desires rather than reason.

In Theseus the roles of absolute ruler and husband ominously converge, as they did in Cary's Herod. The battle with the Amazons that preceded Hippolyta's captivity starkly literalizes the trope of love as a battle in which marriage is the fate of the defeated. In the first scene of the play, the Second Queen addresses Hipployta: "this thy *lord,* / . . . *shrunk thee* into the *bound* thou wast o'erflowing, at once subduing / Thy force and thy affection" (1.1.77–85, emphasis mine).[65] Before the scene is over, Hippolyta, queen of the Amazons, joins the other queens in a position com-

62. D'Orsay Pearson, "Unkinde Theseus: A Study in Renaissance Mythography," *English Literary Renaissance* (spring 1974): 276–98, 276.

63. Ibid.

64. Ibid., p. 280—81.

65. In *A Midsummer Night's Dream,* Theseus had proclaimed, "Hippolyta, I woo'd thee with my sword, / And won thy love doing thee injuries." (1.1.16–17). William Shakespeare, *The Complete Works of Shakespeare,* ed. David Bevington (New York: Longman, 1997).

monly used to address Theseus: she is on her knees (1.1.86). Theseus at
first protests the queens' insistence upon kneeling ("Pray you, kneel not"
and "O no knees, none, widow" [1.1.54, 74]). But after he has once re-
fused them, the widows ask Hippolyta to "Lend us a knee" and of Emilia,
"O help now! / Our cause cries for your knee" (1.1.96, 199200). When the
spectacle of the kneeling ladies finally affects Theseus, "All the Ladies rise"
(1.1.207, stage directions).

This is not the only time an extravagant display of deference bespeaks
Theseus's tyrannical capriciousness as a ruler. When Arcite and Palamon
are discovered dueling, Theseus becomes enraged and orders that both
must die. He is besieged by another wave of entreaties, this time not for
revenge, but for forbearance. Lacking princely probity, he appears not to
know which is appropriate to a given case. When he decides to let the kinsmen duel first and then kill the winner, the ladies resort to their knees,
again, in supplication, with Emilia proclaiming, "I will be woman and
have pity. / My knees shall grow to th' ground but I'll get mercy. / . . . the
powers of all women will be with us" (3.6.191–4). As the sisters beg to no
avail, Pirithous enters the fray: "Nay, then, I'll in too" (3.6.201). Their
combined and repeated pleas for mercy finally cause Theseus to relent,
only to produce a more arbitrary decree.

Theseus's disposition of the problem that Palamon and Arcite raise en-
meshes an innocent bystander: the single-by-choice Emilia. In the mode of
reasoned counsel that friendship discourses avow, Emilia urges him to take
back his oath to execute the kinsmen: "That oath was rashly made, and in
your anger; / Your reason will not hold it" (3.6.227–28). Further, she re-
minds him of a prior oath made to her "of more authority . . . / Not made
in passion neither, but good heed" (3.6.231–32). By this oath, Theseus
had promised to fulfill any reasonable request of Emilia's, and she proclaims, "I tie you to your word now" (3.6.236). Emilia on her knees has
presented Theseus with a morally serious challenge. In asking him to stand
firm to his word and to be ruled by reason in his own rule-making, Emilia
mobilizes all the humanist principles of good rule by reason against the
inconstant, wavering rule by passion or anger associated with the tyrant.
Here Emilia distinguishes herself from the madness and unreason variously
displayed by the kinsmen, Theseus, and the Jailer's mad daughter. She asks
Theseus to banish both the kinsmen and to make them "swear . . . never
more / To make me their contention, or to know me" (3.6.251–53). Thus,
framed within a demonstration of marked moral clarity in Renaissance
terms, Emilia's one request is that these kinsmen, without violence, leave
her alone.

Instead of heeding her request to be given neither of the knights, Theseus responds by offering her the "choice" to have one as a husband and to send the other to death. This entails exactly the degree of involvement and responsibility from which she has just sought to be relieved. When Emilia refuses to implicate herself in Theseus's process of "justice" ("for me, a hair shall never fall of these men" [3.6.287]), he improvises. He decides to permit the duel, execute the loser, and give her to the winner. Death is a fate the kinsmen had already undertaken to risk, yet there is now an additional prospect of reward. In violating his word, Theseus casually, as if his attention has already lapsed, transgresses the known, stated desire of Emilia, who seconds earlier was hunting with him as an equal. Only Emilia, who has lowered her body and raised her voice for mercy, has been punished by the end of the whole transaction.[66] She is arbitrarily thrust out of the role of a reasoning interlocutor and into that of a silent item of booty by the decree Theseus establishes unilaterally, in violation of reason. His autocratic conduct suggests a wavering, divided mind, but one nevertheless possessed of final authority.

While Theseus's treatment of Emilia illustrates the brutality of his thought, it also highlights the equivocal position in which all the characters subject to his power find themselves. Theseus's injection of marriage here is important, for, as Rose notes, "marrying Emilia is never an explicit concern [even] of the kinsmen, who quarrel only over the right to love her."[67] In this sense, Theseus imposes marriage on *everyone,* as an expression of his control over them. Situated only as an element of his fantasy and imagination, marriage is instituted through an act of Theseus's political capacity. Arcite upon his "victory" tells Emilia, "To buy you I have lost what's dearest to me / Save what is bought" (5.3.112–13). Palamon, swept by Arcite's demise into "victory," reflects on the paradox "that we should things desire which do cost us / The loss of our desire! That naught could buy dear love but loss of dear love!" (5.4.110–12) While Palamon and Arcite equate the passions of friendship and love, Theseus's regime sets the

66. Rose considers Theseus's command that one kinsman must die as a "pointed deviation from Chaucer" that "emphasizes the harsh, arbitrary, human irrationality of the monarch's decree." She does not address the matter of any cruelty here toward Emilia (*The Expense of Spirit,* p. 219). Compare Theseus's similarly harsh decree in *A Midsummer Night's Dream,* in which Hermia, insisting on her own choice of a husband, violates her father's authority; Theseus, escalating the threat there, too, offers a dilemma inversely related to Emilia's: Hermia must choose "either to die the death or to abjure / For ever the society of men." (1.1.65–66).

67. Rose, *The Expense of Spirit,* p. 220.

two forms in a life-or-death struggle. As a consequence, both kinsmen register mixed evaluations of the fate Theseus has wrought for them. Subjection to passionate desire, subjection to absolute power: both place Palamon and Arcite as well as Emilia under a tyranny of false choices, in the thrall of others' imperatives.

On the other hand, as the only politically unsubordinated character, Theseus can exercise choices he considers consistent with maintaining what he calls "our human title" (1.1.233). Despite his use of language suggesting a view that Rose terms "the heroics of marriage," where marriage figures as a threshold of human identity, it is precisely the prospective threat posed to his "human title" by marriage that moves Theseus to defer his own. He goes to war instead, claiming, "As we are man, / Thus should we do; being sensually subdued, / We lose our human title" (1.1.231–33). While he can compel or defer his own marriage, his compulsion of connections among other characters represents for them a constraint inconsistent with that "human title" as volitional freedom or self-disposition. When Emilia, facing the prospect of the duel and its results, announces "I am extinct" (5.3.20) and, given to the victor, laments "Is this winning?" (5.3.138) it is clear that the right to freely choose one's affective association expresses self-ownership and integrity. But all these characters find that Theseus's unlimited authority cancels their self-possession. Theseus holds "title" to their lives.

Emilia's Choice

Emilia is the dramatic counterweight to Theseus as well as his political victim. Although she is the only figure in the drama capable of what Weller describes as a "conscious articulation"[68] of desire (for chastity and the company of women), criticism has neglected and misread her to a frankly astonishing degree. Roberts argues that "the Amazonian Emilia comes closer to being a simple allegorical figure than any of the men. Like Hippolyta, she remains curiously static, seeming more a projection of a male problem than an interesting dramatic character."[69] But Emilia's unwavering consistency is a sign of valued self-knowledge in a play (and a period) in which shifting appetites are deeply stigmatized; certainly her "persuasion" for women in itself offers a check to the processes of male "projection." Rose describes Emilia quite incompletely as the "remote superior

68. Weller, "*The Two Noble Kinsmen,* The Friendship Tradition, and the Flight from Eros," p. 103.
69. Roberts, "Crises of Male Self-Definition in *The Two Noble Kinsmen,*" p. 141.

lady" of courtly love tradition.[70] Yet rather than being remote or superior, Emilia articulates a rebuttal of the Petrarchan system, asserting resistance to the gendered roles of courtly love. Rose places her along with Palamon and Arcite as "three ambivalent narcissists, for whom love becomes an isolated, compulsive experience."[71] On the contrary, Emilia's version of love is emphatically (homo)social, and her impending marriage is compelled, not "compulsive." Rose asks, "Is she merely a passive victim in regard to choosing a mate, or is she unwilling to assert her prerogative as a subject and make a choice?"[72] This is an impossible question, because Emilia has done nothing if not actively articulate her choice, throughout the drama, as a matter of her virgin "faith." To the exceptions raised against her "persuasion" of "true love 'tween maid and maid," she equably replies with model tolerance: "I am not / Against your faith, yet I continue mine" (1.3.91, 81, 96–97).

Indeed, Emilia's "*prerogative* as a subject" is exactly what is cancelled by Theseus's unbounded power over her. The drama traces this brutal cancellation of individual prerogative, which it connects to the political issue of "human title." Thus, the figure of Emilia in particular resists a construction of the play as focusing "exclusively on the conflicts of private life, conceived of as a separate domain" from the public sphere.[73] Instead, in juxtaposing the unboundedness of Theseus's absolute power with Emilia's articulated choice and its final subjection to Theseus's authority, the play actually proposes a longing for a form of life—public *or* private—from which the subordinating power of tyranny is absent. There, the individual might experience freedom of association as a means to self-fulfillment and Montaigne's *jovissance*. While *The Two Noble Kinsmen* associates marriage and heterosexual love with tyranny and compulsion, its representation of female "chastity" is coextensive with a full-blown argument for a female homosociality that represents this aspiration and, in doing so, carries even more poetic weight than the weaker and tainted male friendships in the drama.

Emilia's association with reason and wisdom, her sense of moderation, and the manner in which she intelligently takes part in efforts to persuade Theseus to mercy all combine with the absence of any hint of monstrosity to code this Amazon astonishingly positively. As Bawcutt notices, "Emilia

70. Rose, *The Expense of Spirit*, p. 219.
71. Ibid., p. 222.
72. Ibid.
73. Ibid., p. 216.

is shown as a serious and intelligent girl."[74] Emilia's seriousness is clear from her attempt to restrain Theseus from rash oaths and from her firm advocacy of the rule of reason. Exhibiting the Renaissance virtues of probity and "decorum," she is a proponent of martial defense (when appropriate) (1.1.128) and of compassion over perverse cruelty (when appropriate) (3.6.239, 242). All these positions are morally very serious; here they are propounded in a female voice. Only Emilia questions Theseus's illegitimate manner of rule.

In this same voice, Emilia sounds her critique of the gender mechanics of courtly love. In Emilia, the "female beloved" speaks up to announce that she has a critical consciousness that does not consent, exposing the Petrarchan system itself *as* projection. When Palamon and Arcite are caught dueling, Arcite pleads with Theseus, "Duke, ask that lady / Why she is fair, and why her eyes command me / . . . to love her" (3.6.168–70). Hippolyta similarly blames Emilia's face: "that face of yours / Will bear the curses . . . of after ages / For these lost cousins" (3.6.186–88). The follower of Diana finally responds: "In my face, dear sister, I find no anger to 'em, nor no ruin"; instead, she argues, *"the misadventure of their own eyes kill 'em"* (3.6.188–90, emphasis mine). This rejoinder is a fresh yet practical analysis of the Petrarchan situation from the "beloved's" point of view and in her voice; in another play, perhaps, it would be a comic moment. After horrified pleading against her implication in the violence of the duel as a necessary resolution to the situation—"Shall anything that loves me perish for me?" (3.6.241)—Emilia continues to protest the Petrarchan role she is accorded through the balance of the play. She laments "that my unspotted youth must now be soiled / With blood of princes and my chastity / Be made the altar" of death (4.2.59–61). She prefers that "neither for my sake should fall," (4.2.69) but also hopes in her address to Diana that "If well inspired, this battle shall confound / Both these brave knights" and she might "continue in [Diana's] band" (5.1.166–67, 162). She refuses to be an inspirational presence at the combat itself, exclaiming, "O, better never born, / Than minister to such a harm!" (5.3.65–66) Thus *The Two Noble Kinsmen* offers a woman who, rather than being remote and silent, is present, articulate, and in the fray, repudiating continually the gender and affective roles graven in the Petrarchan system.

What is the form of *frauendienst* that Emilia offers instead? She provides a fully developed articulation of an Amazonian position, situating herself exclusively among women affectively and socially. She not only con-

---

74. Bawcutt, introduction, *The Two Noble Kinsmen*, p. 24.

nects chastity with a preference for female society; her idea of her reputation and her identity is drawn from and maintained within the company of women. Emilia's first speech would be perfectly unremarkable if made by a male knight, but it is a woman speaking. The Third Queen, invoking *virginity,* has called upon Emilia to be the Queens' advocate. In stark contrast to Theseus, Emilia responds, "No knees to me. / What woman I may stead that is distressed / Does bind me to her" (1.1.35–37). Her performance of chivalric service results in a specifically female loyalty, and this first exchange links virginity to a social bond *between* women. Emilia describes herself as "a natural sister of our sex" (1.1.125).

Emilia's sisterhood, according to Hippolyta, rises to the level of a "persuasion," and we begin to hear its history. Emilia makes a case for the primacy of same-sex affection—even though she begins by assuring Hippolyta that "reason" supports that Theseus will place his marriage bond above friendship.[75] When Emilia begins to recount the history of her youthful friendship, Hippolyta knows immediately what is coming: "'Twas Flavina," she interjects (1.3.54). The celebratory reminiscence proceeds in the profound language of Montaigne's most emotional passages:

> I
> And she I sigh and spoke of were things innocent,
> Loved for we did, and like the elements
> That know not what, nor why, yet do effect
> Rare issues by their operance, our souls
> Did so to one another.
>
> (1.3.59–64)

Emilia here echoes the sense of sublimity and mystery with which Montaigne supplements Ciceronian rhetoric, suggesting an imperative not only within the soul but also beyond it, driving it without its conscious involvement.[76] Interestingly, her narrative does not suggest that likeness was the *source* of the friendship. Instead, sameness seems to have been, in a way, its *goal,* as the two copy each other, adopting the other's patterns and striv-

75. Weller interestingly argues that Hippolyta, too, may be unsure of herself in this respect. "In rebuking Emilia's praise of single sex friendship, [Hippolyta] also seems to rebuke something in herself that Emilia's words have sympathetically evoked. . . ." (*"The Two Noble Kinsmen,* The Friendship Tradition, and the Flight from Eros," p. 99).

76. "In the amitie I speake of, [mindes] entermixe and confound themselves one in another. . . . If a man urge me to tell wherefore I loved him, I feel it cannot be expressed, but by answering; because it was he, because it was myself. . . . There is beyond all my discourse . . . I know not what inexplicable and fatall power. . . ." (Montaigne, "Of Friendship," p. 149).

ing for resemblance.[77] Flowers, bodily ornament—conventional female
signs—are circulating, here, between women themselves. Even the casual
actions and careless habits of dress of one become the serious ambition of
the other:

> The flower that I would pluck
> And put between my breasts—O, then but beginning
> To swell about the blossom—She would long
> Till she had such another, and commit it
> To the like innocent cradle, where phoenix-like
> They died in perfume; on my head no toy
> But was her pattern; her affections—pretty,
> Though happily her careless wear—I followed
> For my most serious decking.
>
>   (1.3.66–74)

Emilia brings her rapturous but delicately erotic lines to a close with a
rhetorical turn, offering that "this rehearsal" has an "end." She concludes
with the proposition that "true love 'tween maid and maid may be / More
than in sex dividual" (1.3.81–82). The final locution is unusual, and it is
clear that hers is a dramatic proclamation, ushered in by a transport of passion, as Emilia discloses in conceding that her "rehearsal" is "old emport-
ment's bastard" (1.3.80). Hippolyta's first comment is to tell Emilia "you're
out of breath" before she reflects on Emilia's "high-speeded pace" to convert a declaration for homosociality into one against heterosexuality. She
surmises that Emilia "shall never . . . love any that's called man" (1.3.83–
85).[78] Emilia is sure she shall not, and the events of the play fully bear her
out. On the death of Arcite, she acknowledges him as a "right good man,"
still saying nothing about love (5.4.97).

The language used to describe Emilia's situation here is based on notions of choice, conviction, or "determination" (to quote Queen Elizabeth's

77. This pattern of increasing resemblance is also seen in Ben Jonson's "To the Immortal Memory and Friendship of that Noble Pair, Sir Lucius Cary and Sir H. Morison":
"Two names of friendship, but one star," the two young men "approach[ed] so one the
t'other, / Till either grew a portion of the other: / Each styled, by his end, / The copy of
his friend" (lines 98, 109–12). *Ben Jonson,* ed. Ian Donaldson (Oxford: Oxford University
Press, 1995).

78. Almost comically, Pirithous will repeatedly observe, with admiration, that Palamon and Arcite are "men" in a series of one line speeches. Observing Arcite in the tournament: "Upon my soul, a proper man"; (2.4.16) and upon the duel, "O heaven, what more
than man is this!" (3.6.156-157) and "These are men!" (3.6.265).

own term for it).[79] Her position is not centered in acts or in essences, but is articulable as a faith or a profession. It further rises to the level of an argument, proposing its thesis. In Hippolyta and Emilia's final exchange on the subject of Emilia's "rehearsal," Hippolyta calls Emilia's position an "appetite," a "persuasion," and Emilia refers to it as a kind of doctrine, a "faith" (1.3.89, 91, 97). The scope of this "faith" extends beyond particular friendships or "object choice" narrowly construed; Emilia invariably evaluates situations in terms that can only be described as woman centered. When the others commend Arcite at the tournament, Emilia says, "Believe / His mother was a wondrous handsome woman; / His face methinks goes that way" (2.4.19–21). When Theseus vows that Palamon and Arcite must die, Emilia fears becoming the "scorn of women": "the goodly mothers that have groaned for these, / And all the longing maids that ever loved 'em, / If your vow stand, shall curse me" (3.6.250, 245–47). Trying to choose one of the kinsmen in order to prevent violence between them, Emilia links Arcite's beauty to homosexual models and Palamon's looks to his mother. She compares Arcite with Ganymede and his brow with Juno's. As for Palamon, his melancholy appearance is "as if he had lost his mother" (4.2.28). All the affective lines in this speech avoid heterosexual models. But Emilia remains "guiltless of election," either between the kinsmen or for marriage, in her long address to Diana. Instead, she entreats Diana to give her to whichever man loves her best "or else grant / The file and quality I hold I may / Continue in thy band" (5.1.160–62).

The address to Diana highlights the question of jurisdiction that Theseus has been shown to confound. For Emilia's appeal to Diana finds her already appointed to marry an undetermined husband. Nevertheless, Emilia still holds out the possibility that she will be given to neither kinsman. Strangely, the servant of Diana, rather than betraying her oath of chastity or falling in love, is instead separated from her vow by a decree of the civil power. Emilia here has no desire to break off her alliance with Diana; no impulse of "nature" has eroded her vows. The play dramatizes the degree to which Diana's mythic power is eclipsed by Theseus's absolute sovereignty. On the verge of her betrothal to the unknown victor, Emilia describes herself as "bride-habited, / But maiden-hearted" (5.1.150–51). This split in subjectivity results not from her ambivalence, but instead arises as a wound to subjectivity stemming from Theseus's power to com-

79. Elizabeth I, "Queen Elizabeth's First Speech before Parliament," in *Elizabeth I: Collected Works*, ed. Leah Marcus, Janel Mueller, and Mary Beth Rose (Chicago: University of Chicago Press, 2000), pp. 56–58, 57.

pel. Emilia's "faith" retreats to the interior realm of the heart under Theseus's authority to compel her body into marriage.

In considering the construction of the "heart" as an interiority produced for Emilia by the regime of marriage in the public sphere, there is
one scene-within-a-scene that appears to have been completely neglected
in criticism. For Emilia's recollection of friendship with Flavina, though
passionate, is not the only evidence the drama offers regarding expressions
of Emilia's "prerogative" in contexts free of Theseus's control. While the
story of a past love with Flavina is nostalgic, one episode in *The Two Noble
Kinsmen* shows its "maiden-hearted" heroine "merry-hearted" in the play's
present tense. In the scene so much considered for the collapse of friendship between Palamon and Arcite, where from their prison window they
observe (but, like the criticism, do not hear) Emilia and her Woman, the
two women engage in a rich exchange. This exchange and its location suggest that serious female association is linked to a proprietary space and is
not just a matter for nostalgia. The trajectory of this suggestive exchange
is obscured by interlineation with Palamon and Arcite's dialogue. Perhaps
performance could make it very clear. Quoting the extracted conversation
in full makes its course very evident:

> EMILIA: This garden has a world of pleasures in't.
> What flower is this?
>
> WOMAN: 'Tis called narcissus, madam.
>
> EMILIA: That was a fair boy, certain, but a fool
> To love himself; were there not maids enough?
> Or were they all hard-hearted?
>
> WOMAN: They could not be to one so fair.
>
> EMILIA: Thou wouldst not.
>
> WOMAN: I think I should not, madam.
>
> EMILIA: That's a good wench;
> But take heed to your kindness, though.
>
> WOMAN: Why, madam?
>
> EMILIA: Men are mad things.
> Canst thou work such flowers in silk, wench?
>
> WOMAN: Yes.
>
> EMILIA: I'll have a gown full of 'em and of these.
> This is a very pretty colour; will't not do
> Rarely upon a skirt, wench?

WOMAN: Dainty, madam.

EMILIA: Of all flowers,
Methinks a rose is best . . .
It is the very emblem of a maid;
For when the west wind courts her gently,
How modestly she blows, and paints the sun
With her chaste blushes! When the north comes near her,
Rude and impatient, then, like chastity,
She locks her beauties in her bud again,
And leaves him to base briars.

WOMAN: Yet, good madam,
Sometimes her modesty will blow so far
She falls for it; a maid,
If she have any honour, would be loath
To take example by her.

EMILIA: Thou art wanton.
The sun grows high, let's walk in. Keep these flowers;
We'll see how near art can come near their colours.
I am wondrous merry-hearted, I could laugh now.

WOMAN: I could lie down now, I am sure.

EMILIA: And take one with you?

WOMAN: That's as we bargain, madam.

EMILIA: Well, agree then.

                                            (2.1.172–207)

Like Donne's lovers' chamber, like Palamon and Arcite's prison, "this garden" in which the women are alone "has a world of pleasures in't." The garden, a proprietary female space, composes a plentitude. The reflections on Narcissus, a possible commentary on the validity of Palamon and Arcite's friendship, introduce the concept of "hard-heartedness" in maids' response to men. Emilia proceeds to warn her "wench" to limit the "kindness" she shows to them, since "men are mad things." (This judgment is being confirmed simultaneously by Palamon and Arcite's descent into the "madness" of love.) Emilia's question "were there not maids enough?" takes on a certain dramatic irony, as well, in its identification of maids as the objects of love. The conversational shift to weaving in silk incorporates and echoes two elements already seen in Emilia's Flavina narrative: flowers and dress, blossoms and patterns, suggesting the intimacy of women in a dressing chamber. The references to work and art in producing the silk gown strengthen the sense of plenitude, showing that the feminine space inhabited by the women is a creative economy. Ironically, this "world of pleasures" is perfectly consistent with the urgings of conduct books that women, in the quarters presumably not set aside for their pleasure, should engage in useful pursuits like sewing and embroidery.

Emilia and her Woman continue their commentary on flowers, oblivious of being observed, as Emilia proposes the rose as the "very emblem of a maid" on account of its chastity. It is now the Woman's turn to warn the Lady: the rose is an unsafe metaphor, risky for a "maid," because it eventually opens and falls. Here the exchange takes perhaps its most interesting and unexpected turn. Emilia, having raised the issue of "hard-heartedness" in connection with a warning against unchastity (as an over-kindness to men), now teases the Woman, "Thou art wanton." On this note, she proposes that they withdraw into their quarters with "Let's walk in." The suddenly "wondrous merry-hearted" Emilia feels she could laugh; the Woman's response that she could "lie down" completes the allusion to a card game called "laugh and lie down" that both the Penguin and Oxford annotations consider a proverbial expression with sexual meanings.[80] Sexual meanings indeed, but this bantering conversation begs the question of just what sort of sexual meanings are in play. The familiarity of the usages "thou" and "wench," the "merry" flirtatious tone of the otherwise markedly serious Emilia, and the by now obvious inference that Emilia, at least, cannot be referring to a sexual "bargain" with a man—all these converge to suggest that these final lines refer to a sexual encounter between Emilia and her Woman. The ambiguity of the lines—are they hypothetical? Do they refer to some (future) "bargain" with a "mad" man?—is substantially dispelled by Emilia's "now" and her imperative tense in "Well, agree then." One is left with a sense that an "agreement" is concluded— that, indeed, may already have been established ("That's as we bargain, madam").

Amity's Amazonian Logic

The Two Noble Kinsmen's Emilia, then, offers a rebuttal to Renaissance commonplaces about the impossibility of female friendship. She appears onstage with a marked preference for her own sex, a preference that places homoerotics within the scope of female friendship, while making no sim-

80. Shakespeare, *The Two Noble Kinsmen,* Penguin edition, p. 195; Oxford edition, p. 115.

ple equation between the two. The status of "Emilia's choice" with respect to her impending forced marriage is unknowable, but the location of such a choice in a proprietary female space suggests that it is likely to be un-affected.[81] While Emilia's probable sexual transaction with her Woman di-verges from Montaigne's model—in admitting sexuality, in traversing class lines, and in the element of "bargaining" it contains—it nevertheless sug-gests a form of female association that fits smoothly with conventional Re-naissance patterns of female household seclusion or governance. Although domestic and interior spaces are widely associated with women, they are never investigated as the plural, female community which, in the larger households so often described, they must always have been. In Emilia here, as she becomes quieter and quieter under Theseus's ducal prerogative, the possibilities and nuances inherent in the Renaissance configuration of the female household just make it into articulation, obscured but recon-structible as a fragmented scene-within-a-scene. Emilia's "Let's walk in" gestures toward a Renaissance space in which female "chastity" finds ex-pression as a feminine economy, a social arrangement of women "among themselves."[82] This zone is constructed as a space beyond the inroads of a very negatively coded form of political tyranny, at least for a time.

Strikingly, in *The Two Noble Kinsmen,* the great figure of this resistance to tyrannical power is not the paradigmatic friendship-gendered-male so popular with writers of the period. Instead, friendship's partisan is a lady knight who revises the definitional prejudices of the male model regarding both gender and sexuality. In effect, Emilia's advocacy constitutes a "friend-ship theory" that does Montaigne one better. By embodying Montaigne's penultimate criterion of volitional association, Emilia shows how his effort to exclude women and sexual love from the field of friendship actually im-pinges upon and limits the sense of real choice that he exalts when he says, "our owne voluntarie choice and libertie hath no production more prop-erly her own, than that of affection and amitie" (p. 146). Emilia's case ar-gues the radical position that curtailing the range of self-specified, affective association is an act of tyrannical subjugation that violates reason.

An Amazon, articulately dedicated to a friendship that includes homo-erotics, figured as the voice of reasoning autonomy and the critique of ab-solutism? It appears that Shakespeare and Fletcher here were perfectly

81. For the spatial and affective arrangements of the noble household, particularly in reference to distances of both kinds between wives and their husbands, see Laurence Stone, *The Family Sex and Marriage in England, 1500–1800* (New York: Harper, 1979), p. 81.

82. Luce Irigaray, "Commodities among Themselves," in *This Sex Which Is Not One,* trans. Catherine Porter (Ithaca, N.Y.: Cornell University Press, 1985), pp. 192–97.

capable of overriding gender conventions and sexual silences, motivated by a need to effectively trope opposition to the intrusive power of tyrants, of absolute monarchy, of persons possessed of "greatness." Chastity, pluralized, strengthened as female friendship, and linked to a proprietary zone of affectionate autonomy, embodies the play's only contestation of political subjugation and irrational rule. The fabulous intensity with which "chastity" is urged for women in the Renaissance context was, no doubt, predominantly a device of control and authority. But perhaps a small part of the reason that chastity absorbs so much interest and attention is the way it, exactly like ideal friendship, could metaphorize anxious (male) relations to sovereign political power, to the unappealable incursions of those "appointed" to rule. *The Two Noble Kinsmen* raises this possibility even as it deploys a fully articulated Amazonian position as the gendered, homoerotic voice of individual prerogative under siege. What it shows is that the even the strongest conventions regarding gender, sexuality, and friendship could rewrite themselves when governed by a stronger urgency: the frightening blend of personal and political power embodied in the Renaissance conception of authority.

PART TWO

THE SUBJECTED SOVEREIGN

FOUR

Ungoverned States: Friendship, *Mignonnerie,* and the Private Monarch

❧

For the royal subject, friendship proposes an idealized world apart, a world magnifying that subject's "sovereign prerogative" as an individual. A notion of likeness between friends ensures parity; a sense of engagement somehow both avoids dependent status and enhances individual integrity; an absolute power of self-disposition grounds both the consensual basis of friendship and the full authority to end it. These utopian visions comprise private friendship's *jovissance.* Montaigne calls this associative form the most perfect product of "our genuine libertie" as volitional beings.[1] Unpredictably refracted through the lenses of gender, speech, anticommercialism, chastity, homoerotics, and sedition, friendship discourses show a mode of self-governance that, within each gender or status, may be parlayed into consensual governance, a governing with or by someone else in a state of parity. To envision this desired state is to propose a sweeping alternative to the normal politics of contingency, subordination, and dominion. While Derrida finds the dilemmas of autonomy and heteronomy played out under the auspices of "the tradition of a certain concept of friendship," Renaissance permutations of that tradition require that a third term be admitted: homonomy, or rule by an other who is like.[2] Such a slightly pluralized autonomy theoretically enables a new idea of consensual governance, a rule that does no violence to the selves beneath it since it is based in parity. In a Tudor regime in which the institutions of hierarchical government derive from a concept of ordained or appointed public

1. Michel de Montaigne, "Of Friendship," in *The Essayes of Montaigne: John Florio's Translation,* ed. J. I. M. Stewart (New York: Modern Library, 1933) pp. 153, 146. All subsequent references to Montaigne are to this edition and will appear in the text.

2. Jacques Derrida, "The Politics of Friendship," *The Journal of Philosophy* 85, no. 11 (November 1998): 632–44, 634.

"offices," friendship outlines a personal order of prerogative, choice, and election for the (royal) subject. In a performative sense, invention and assertion establish certain capacities we may term private in the rhetorical forum of "one soul in two bodies."

But classically informed friendship tropes are not the only double-bodied body with which Renaissance writers concern themselves. Two twinned figures of sovereignty offer competing theorizations, one taking shape as "privat" and the other as "publicke." While friendship celebrates the doctrine of "one soule in two bodies," Tudor kingship theory traced a parallel formulation and imagined the king as "one Person in two Bodies." In the much-noted decision entitled "Calvin's Case" (recorded in the *Reports* collected by Edmund Plowden under Elizabeth I), this now familiar legal formula held that

> the King has in him two Bodies, viz. A Body natural, and a Body politic. His Body natural is a Body mortal. . . . But his Body politic is a Body that cannot be seen or handled. . . . These two Bodies are incorporated into one Person, and make one Body and not divers.[3]

This theorizing of the nation's legal incorporation by means of a monarch's body essentially employs the sovereign as a metaphor for sovereignty. Despite the assertion of the unity of the natural and the immaterial bodies here, the ongoing relations between these two bodies proves to be a constant worry in early modern political culture.

As distinct versions of sovereignty, the constitutional theory of the king's two bodies and the friendship trope of a second self bear an uncanny resemblance to each other. But what relation holds between these coexisting paradigms? As we have seen in chapter 1, Renaissance discourses idealizing friendship seem less concerned with articulating a protorepublican or antimonarchical position than with evincing the structuring difference between the private person and the public figure through friendship's dispensations. If classical *amicitia* served as a vehicle to organize the private subjects's sovereign aspirations, a maximization of his autonomy, how does it signify for the king as the powerful figure of public authority? As we shall see, the rules of *amicitia* run afoul of the monarch's proverbial and mythic singularity, his public function to represent polity in generic rather than particular terms, and his concomitant duty to sublimate his affective life to the good of the realm. A monarch so engaged to a particular friend can

3. Edmund Plowden, *Commentaries or Reports* (London: n.p., 1816), quoted in Ernst Kantorowicz, *The King's Two Bodies: A Study in Medieval Political Theology* (Princeton, N.J.: Princeton University Press, 1957), p. 7.

only be, from the constitutional perspective of the realm's priority, a captured sovereign—a sovereign subject(ed) to an interest directly at odds with his political purpose. While kings could (and good kings must) have their counselors, Renaissance texts insistently return to the difference between a monarch's private or personal friend and this official, advisory role.

What this difference indicates is that *amicitia* is a power specifically attaching only to "private persons," as we see that term deployed. A private person has no seat in the "rooms" or "offices" constituting the early modern sense of governance through inhabitable "places" or conditions, a sense evident, for example, in Francis Bacon's essay "Of Great Place."[4] Private status designates the privation of such a legally conferred "dignity" *(dignitas);* a public being is one endowed with a public role or dressed in "robes of office." This sense of words like *honour* or *worship* is not at all limited to monarchs; it addresses all those personages Tiptoft describes as "in thastate publique."[5] The effects of this "estate" or status in early modern appropriations of friendship theory are thus not limited to the king's case, though his plight will seem particularly severe. Friendship logics reverse the customary sense of endowment and deprivation we associate with the usual dispensations of public status and privacy. Powers accorded in friendship, however counterintuitively, exceed magisterial and royal powers—and amity is one capacity denied to the sovereign.

When a king tries to undertake *amicitia,* he can only produce *mignonnerie,* as I shall term this phenomenon at the juncture of friendship and (mis)rule.[6] *Mignonnerie* presents the political scandal of a monarch's unsuppressed private self, with the individuated and self-centered body natural eclipsing the body politic, whose "Nature and Effects" were to have transformed (altered or repressed) the private body and its interests. Whereas the "two bodies" within the "one Person" of monarchy are described by Bacon as "inseparable, though distinct,"[7] *mignonnerie* displays the individuated body as separate—or separating—from "the Body that cannot be seen or handled." The king thus removes to a sphere of private interest while maintaining his access to the public treasury. This alterna-

4. Sir Francis Bacon, "Of Great Place," in *The Essayes or Counsels, Civill and Morall,* ed. Michael Kiernan (Cambridge, Mass.: Harvard University Press, 1985), pp. 33–36.

5. Cicero, *De amicitia,* trans. John Tiptoft (London: William Caxton, 1481), fol. 18v.

6. Rather than coin "minionry," I use *mignonnerie.* See F. Godefroy, *Dictionnaire de l'ancienne langue française,* vol. 5 (Paris, 1888; reprinted by Kraus Reprint Corp., 1961), p. 328. See also E. Huguet, *Dictionnaire de la langue française du seizième siècle* (Paris: Didier, 1961), 5:266.

7. Kantorowicz, *The King's Two Bodies,* p. 365.

tive, even monstrous, exclusionary polity subverts the entire purpose of the monarch's constitution for the public good, that is, what we might call the public interest. In John Ford's *Perkin Warbeck* (1634), it is the historical Henry VII who articulates proper sovereignty: "No undeserving favorite doth boast / His issues from our treasury; our charge / Flows all through Europe proving us but steward / Of every contribution."[8] A king dedicated to a private subject is no longer "wed" to the realm.[9] Although friendship might figure sovereignty from a subject's perspective, then, the monarch as English writers theorized him could not enter into this privileged, exclusive relationship without calling his sovereign condition into question.

"So Great a Difference Is There in Degree"

The central importance of equality to perfect friendship in Aristotle and Cicero rendered affectionate linkage across boundaries of rank an imperfect approximation at best. Aristotle proposed that "amitie consists in equality and similarity," but "when a wide disparity arises between two friends in point of virtue or vice, or of wealth, or of anything else; they no longer remain nor indeed expect to remain friends."[10] Cicero seems to admit a limited differentiation of rank between friends, and the rhetoric of Tiptoft's *De amicitia* invokes an approximation of equality between unequals: "they that ben souerayns, [superiors] in the nyghnesse of frendship and ioyne good wylle, sholde make them self egall with them, that ben lower than they, so as they that be bynethe theym, have no cause to sorowe." A dynamic of proximity and distance inheres in the term *nyghnesse,* suggesting how friendship entails nearings and approximations across status differentials. Indeed, an inference of social leveling could be made from Cicero's claim that "they that are the soueraynes, owe to submytte theym self in frendsyip [sic], and in maner exalte theym, whiche ben lower than them self."[11] But Cicero's language here can only threaten

8. John Ford, *Perkin Warbeck,* ed. Donald Anderson (Lincoln: University of Nebraska Press, 1965), 4.4.50–53.

9. Thus when Elizabeth I reportedly claimed marriage to the realm, her language not only represented an improvisation upon gender; it aptly figured the degree of commitment required of the ethical monarch. The relation to the realm is preemptive of other "loves."

10. Aristotle, *Nicomachean Ethics,* trans. Horace Rackham (Cambridge, Mass.: Harvard University Press, 1926), bk. 8, pt. 8, sec. 4–5.

11. Cicero, *De amicitia,* trans. Tiptoft, fols.. 18v and 20v. The Latin passages in the translation by William Armistead Falconer (Cambridge, Mass.: Harvard University Press, 1923) read: "maximum est in amicitia superiorem parem esse inferiori" (pp. 178–79) and "quam ob rem, ut ei, qui superiores sunt, submittere se debent in amicitia, sic quodam modo inferiores extollere" (pp. 180–81).

the ideology of degree that is vocalized, for just one example, in Shake-speare's *Troilus and Cressida,* where Ulysses defends its social function as a guarantor of justice, order, virtue, and reason. He warns, "Degree being vizarded, / The unworthiest shows as fairly in the mask" (1.3.83–84). The focus on likeness and parity in *amicitia* reacts to and confutes this power-ful role afforded to degree in the social imagination.

Writing of the special affective situation between a patron/employer and his secretary, Angel Day makes the following concession in 1592:

> the limits of *Friendshippe* . . . are streight, and there can bee no *Friend* where an inequality remayneth. Twixt the party commanded & him that commaundeth, there is no societie, and therefore no *Friendship* where resteth a *Superiority.*[12]

Aemilia Lanyer's "Description of Cooke-ham" (1611) directly addresses this difficulty of reconciling rank within a friendship ideal, first challeng-ing the notion and then lamenting its truth. Lanyer's country-house poem recollects the pleasures of a past relationship between the poet and her sometime benefactors, Margaret Clifford, Countess of Cumberland, and her daughter, Anne Clifford. Consistent with the anticommercial ideology of an *amicitia* above what Elizabeth Cary's *Tragedy of Mariam* terms the "base mechanic traffic that doth lend,"[13] Lanyer specifically situates virtue as both the foundation and result of companionate love between women of disparate rank. While there is no doubt that other, more economic realities shaped and strained Lanyer's relations with her patrons,[14] what is interesting here is the way Lanyer's poem strives to represent the bond of virtue as defeated by the strange imperatives of a class difference that will drive these friends apart. To be near the great, to have access to them; to be "great with" the great appears as a fleeting pleasure terminated by the im-peratives of "greatness" itself.

12. Angel Day, *The English Secretorie* (London: P. Short, 1599), p. 118.

13. Elizabeth Cary, *The Tragedy of Mariam, the Fair Queen of Jewry,* ed. Margaret Ferguson and Barry Weller (Berkeley and Los Angeles: University of California Press, 1994), (4.6.289).

14. Barbara Lewalski discusses the patronage aspects of Lanyer's career, and she situ-ates "A Description of Cooke-ham" with respect to Ben Jonson's "To Penshurst" (*Writing Women in Jacobean England* [Cambridge, Mass.: Harvard University Press, 1993], p. 219). See also Ann Baynes Coiro, "Writing in Service: Sexual Politics and Class Position in the Poetry of Aemilia Lanyer and Ben Jonson," *Criticism* 35 (1993): 357–76. The poem here describes the poet's affective situation in telling terms; it is one of "reverend love" (line 122). The last line of the poem describes how the Countess's "virtues" shall always "[tie] my heart to her by those rich chaines" (line 210).

"A Description of Cooke-ham" alleges profound feelings of love and links them to virtue, just as idealized male friendship does: Montaigne called friendship "this yoke" "guided by vertue" (p. 150). The Countess is abstracted as "Grace" and "Virtue";[15] in Lady Anne's "fair breast true virtue then was hous'd" (line 96); and these "virtues lodge in [the poet's] unworthy breast" as well (line 208). Despite Lanyer's grounding of the companionate past the women enjoyed in loving virtue, degree represents its final limit. Her poem summons up a physical world that registers human events and feelings, in accord with its generic status as a farewell to a place. The poem's logic thus proceeds by a poetics of proximity and distance. The women's approach inspires the house and environs: "Oh how (me thought) against you thither came, / Each part did seem some new delight to frame!" (lines 17–18) A litany of the effects on Cookeham's natural and architectural features follows from the ladies' presence (lines 18–92). The landscape reflects the noblewomen's departure in a similarly lengthy inventory (lines 133–46, 177–204). But this otherwise conventional anthropomorphizing of landscape and house does more than reflect the poet's sorrow at separation: its dynamic of physical *proximity* enables an account of the social, vertical *distance* that will insinuate itself into friendship. Metaphors of physical closeness are reversed and literalized as social or class distance.

This social differentiation proves fatal to the women's association by requiring physical separation. James Holstun's argument that period representations of women together take on the form of recalling an inevitably past moment could well be invoked here, and it would supply a different focus for the nostalgic structure of the poem.[16] But Lanyer offers her own reasoning about the inevitability of the women's parting, and it has less to do with what Holstun terms "lesbian elegy." The poet's reflections on separation instead entail an astonishingly direct complaint about the imperatives of social station, of estate:

> Unconstant Fortune, thou art most to blame,
> Who casts us down into so lowe a frame:
> Where our great friends we cannot dayly see,
> So great a difference is there in degree.
>   (lines 99–100, 103–6)

---

15. Germaine Greer et al., *Kissing the Rod: An Anthology of Seventeenth-Century Women's Verse* (New York: Farrar Straus Giroux, 1989), p. 46, lines 2, 7. Citations from the poem are from this anthology.

16. James Holstun, "'Will you rent our ancient love asunder?': Lesbian Elegy in Donne, Marvell, and Milton," *ELH* 54 (winter 1987): 835–67.

The separation is directly attributed to degree, a distance between those framed as "lowe" and the "great" that constitutes an ultimately unbridgeable gap—even where the purest of virtues are alleged. Intermittently a lament and critique, the poem conjoins passionate feelings of betrayal by the "great" with critical doubts about the validity of the system of degree separating the women. The lines thus flow in logical fits and starts:

> Many are placed in those Orbes of state,
> Parters in honour, so ordain'd by Fate;
> Neerer in show, yet farther off in love,
> In which the lowest always are above.
> But whither am I carried in conceit?
> My Wit too weak to conster of the great.
> Why not? although we are but borne of earth,
> We may behold the Heavens, despising death;
> And loving heaven that is so farre above,
> May in the end vouchsafe us entire love.
>   (lines 107–16)

"Orbes of state" designate not so much a public "sphere" as an orbit or trajectory properly pertaining to a personage of status ("state"), a partaker or sharer of "honour." The powerful affirmation of the low poet's authentic love and its baffled disappointment show the collision of friendship and degree, the two incommensurate paradigms of self-formation structuring the erratic pattern of the speaker's thoughts. First affirming the superiority of the "lowest" love, then succumbing to self-doubt as to her skeptical treatment of worldly greatness, then rallying with a rhetorical "Why not?" that can only resolve itself by a recourse to the elsewhere of heaven: so the poet finds impossible any reconciliation of friendship and degree, of private love and "Orbes of state." Only an invocation of heaven and death can compensate rhetorically for the otherwise vast gulf degree creates. "So great a difference is there in degree": indeed, a difference in degree, for friendship purposes, is in fact a difference in kind.

Renaissance texts reveal a rich but now obsolete vocabulary of cross-class companionship, indicating that degree was not quite as successful at preventing emotional class-crossings as Lanyer's poem suggests. The abundance of period terms—*minion, creature, catamite, familiar, copesmate, parasite, favorite, delicate, copartner, ingle* or *ningle, privado, placebo, fere,* and doubtless others—indicates enormous attention to the friendly (and sometimes erotic) relations that traverse the divides of hierarchical difference. By the very process of merger and likening we have seen friendship to build itself on, friendly affect threatens just the kind of "vizarding" of degree that figures in Ulysses' warning. Instead of a friendship originating in likeness, one finds a relationship threatening to produce it by blurring the roles of those who began as superior and inferior, whether the pair entails a person of "place" and a subordinate or an actual sovereign and subject.

These designations actually only name the socially inferior partner, and they link companionate affect with moral fault: weakness, lawlessness, deceit, eroticism, appetitiveness, even misrule. The notion of a "royal favorite" implies both royal whimsicality and partisanship or faction. The term *familiar,* ranging from those within the hierarchically arranged household to the notorious otherworldly companion to the English witch, enjoyed a specific period resonance as a private, secretive, or even criminal intimacy.[17] *Privado* suggests a confidential, communicative relation like that entailed in the classically derived ideal, but also a degree of privacy or covertness that jars with ideal friendship's basis in patent virtue.[18] *Placebo* ("I will be pleasing" in Latin) centers on flattering speech and named a parasite. In book 2 of *The Faerie Queene,* Edmund Spenser uses the "minion" figure to embody lawlessness and moral abandon:

> Fast by her side did sit the bold *Sans-Loy,*
> Fit mate for such a mincing mineon,
> Who in her loosenesse tooke exceeding joy;
> Might not be found a franker franion,
> Of her lewd parts to make companion."[19]

In Ben Jonson's *Volpone* (1606), the "delicates of a rich man" are glossed as favorites, and the word's culinary sense suggests an unregulated appetitiveness on the rich man's part.[20] Strikingly, these titles all name the lower partner of the pair. The exchange between the Chief Justice and Falstaff in *Henry IV, Part 2* (1598) affirms this one-sidedness. When the Justice exclaims, "Well, God send the prince a better companion!" Falstaff's retort— "God send the companion a better prince!" (1.2.188–90)—reverses the

17. See the Jacobean statute (1604) making a compact with an imaginary being a felony: it is illegal to "use practice or exercise any invocation . . . of any evil or wicked spirit, or . . . consult, covenant with . . . any evil or wicked spirit to or for any intent or purpose." Reprinted in Barbara Rosen, ed., *Witchcraft* (London: Edward Arnold, 1969), p. 57.

18. See the *Oxford English Dictionary* definition of *privado:* "*Obs.* An intimate private friend, a confidant; the favorite of a ruler."

19. Edmund Spenser, *The Faerie Queene,* ed. A. C. Hamilton (New York: Longman, 1977), bk. 2, canto 2, line 37.

20. Ben Jonson, *Ben Jonson's Plays and Masques,* ed. Robert Adams (New York: Norton, 1979), p. 42 (3.3.5).

sense but preserves the roles. The social superior is not named in his affective capacity.

While the nomenclature consistently hails one party, it raises an inference of moral fault on both sides. The higher partner appears excessively susceptible to appetite that renders him dependent, and the lower one is presumed to have questionable motives that he pursues by deceit, self-abasement, or manipulation. The now-archaic lexicon for these "private" relations spanning increments of degree reveals a concern about personal affect within the idea of order that degree supplied in Renaissance configurations of polity and authority. The languages of ongoing friendship between greater persons and those beneath them destabilize that order along with the identities it accords. Indeed, in the context of sexuality, Alan Bray has cogently shown that just such a transgression or mixing of degree could convert the otherwise conventional signs of acceptable and sentimental male friendship into the basis for a sodomy charge.[21] As I have argued in chapter 3, a further aspect triggering this allegation is the violation of a more general likeness principle I have called homonormativity, a positive principle ordering ideas about desirable unions.

As Bray also shows, alliances that seem "mercenary" (as any between those of different economic circumstances are liable to seem) rather than "personal" (friendships of "utility," in classical terms) are likeliest to become the objects of sexual and moral suspicion. As Montaigne points out, friendship's law of common property automatically implicates vertical relations in some form of leveling commerce, "all things being by effect common betweene [friends]; wils, thoughts, judgements, goods, wives, children, honor, and life" (p. 150). So he disqualifies "vulgar and customarie" friendships for the element of profit they suggest:

> All those amities which are forged and nourished by voluptuousnesse or profit, publike or private need, are thereby so much the lesse faire and generous, and so much the lesse true amities, in that they intermeddle other causes, scope, and fruit with friendship, than it selfe alone. (p. 145)

Part of the reason, of course, that need and profit represent proscribed bases for friendship hinges on their presumed introduction of the incentive for calculation that produces false friends. Where rank is a source of difference, one finds shape-shifting flatterers and "parasites" who impersonate friendship and end as betrayers. The plotting parasite effects control over the "great" person, who in turn becomes the vulnerable, dependent

---

21. Alan Bray, "Homosexuality and the Signs of Male Friendship," *History Workshop Journal* 29 (1990): 1-19, 10.

partner in a direct reversal of order and degree. Some examples will show how specific these imputations could be.

In *Volpone,* Jonson develops a case of parasitic falsity that brings these effects into full display, with particular emphasis on simulations of friendship. Volpone, a *clarissimo* of Venice, and his "parasite" Mosca become partners in an escapade to deceive an array of would-be inheritors of Volpone's wealth, though in fact Mosca plans to trick Volpone as well. The compact between the two shows a culpability on Volpone's part that has erotic dimensions. He finds it hard to contain his delight with Mosca's duping of others: "Excellent Mosca! / Come hither, let me kiss thee" (1.3.79); "I cannot hold; good rascal, let me kiss thee" (1.4.137). The passion Volpone "cannot hold" suggests a failure of self-possession in the Stoic sense; as we have seen, friendship discourses disgrace this subjection (to passion or to power) as inconsistent with a sovereign self. Volpone's passion expresses itself most explicitly in act 5: "My witty mischief, / Let me embrace thee. O that I could now / Transform thee to a Venus!" (5.3.102–4) Volpone's escalating exuberance marks his waning self-possession.

The (false) embrace of Mosca and Volpone finally goes too far. As a part of their plot, Volpone gives Mosca his nobleman's garb as a *clarissimo* (5.3.105), in violation of Venetian laws requiring dress in accordance with rank. Dress bore an enormous weight in setting social places, and Stephen Orgel has wryly noted that "for all the pulpit rhetoric about the evils of [sexual] cross-dressing, sumptuary legislation said nothing about the wearing of sexually appropriate garments. It was concerned with violations of the sartorial badges of class."[22] "Vizardings" of degree warranted a special level of legislative attention. In Jonson's play, Volpone himself takes on the habit of a common soldier (5.3.115). In his oblivious admiration of Mosca, Volpone ironically exclaims, "'Fore heaven, a brave clarissimo; thou becom'st it! / Pity thou wert not born one" (5.5.3–4). As we shall see in chapter 6, friendship's leveling likeness undermines this very system of "birth." Mosca's scandalous disguise and transformation to a nobleman (5.12.48–51) represents a transgression of rank and degree made possible by the parasite's creation and maintenance of an intimate relation with a *clarissimo.* The law cuts this scenario short. The judges in the final scene order "Disrobe that parasite" and charge Mosca as "the chiefest minister" in "these lewd impostures." For having "abused . . . / [the] habit of a gentleman of Venice, / Being a fellow of no birth or blood," Mosca is whipped

22. Stephen Orgel, *Impersonations: The Performance of Gender in Shakespeare's England* (Cambridge: Cambridge University Press, 1996), pp. 96–98.

and perpetually imprisoned (5.12.103, 108–12). Toying with affections, toying with degree: these are related problems for judicial intervention.

The imposture of high birth in rank-traversing relationships seems a risk even where affection is not pretended. In Thomas Nashe's *The Unfortunate Traveller* (1594), Jack Wilton, the title traveler, is a footloose English soldier when he links up as chief "servant" with a (fictionalized) Henry Howard, Earl of Surrey. Wilton compares the Earl to a prince and to God: he is "a prince in content because a poet without peer," and "God hath bestowed his perfectest image on poets[;] None come so near to God in wit."[23] From this lofty elevation, this "right noble lord" (p. 237) allows Wilton "to share half stakes with him in the lottery of travel" (p. 238), a prospect redolent with prodigality. A wild venture is suggested by the reference to stakes and lottery; a sojourn in Italy proverbially betokens a departure from "English" morality. In a very short time, the kind of role reversal plotted unilaterally in *Volpone* is contracted:

> By the way as we went my master and I agreed to change names. It was concluded betwixt us that I should be Earl of Surrey and he my man, only because in his own person, which he would not have reproached, he meant to take more liberty of behavior. As for my carriage, he knew he was to tune it as high or low as he list. (p. 246)

By this ruse, the earl expects to become anonymous, to sever his person from his earldom in the name of certain "liberties." Wilton expands: "I was master . . . and my master the Earl was but my chief man, whom I made my companion" (p. 248). Their game of imposture, in which the Earl, "God be with him, . . . could counterfeit most daintily" (p. 250), lands them in legal trouble. They are apprehended for *coining*, having spent counterfeit money received in a bribe. The political resonance of coining spelled out, for example, in Richard Baines's libel of Christopher Marlowe, is fully confirmed here. The Earl and Wilton's costumings violate the markings of class. Their transgressions against "estate" and its economic moorings lead to their arrest as plotters of "mischievous conspiracies against [the] state" (p. 251). Dissembling the truths of status adds up to trafficking in false coin: a virtual treason.

Wilton at this point raises the stakes of the role reversal by stealing Surrey's title: "The state of an Earl he had thrust upon me before, and now I would not bate him an inch of it." This assumption of an identity or "state"

23. Thomas Nashe, *The Unfortunate Traveller,* in *An Anthology of Elizabethan Prose Fiction,* ed. Paul Salzman (Oxford: Oxford University Press, 1987), p. 237 (subsequent references will appear in the text).

Wilton calls "an art . . . to separate the shadow from the body." Wilton, like *Volpone*'s scheming parasite, exploits the weak spot in conventional Elizabethan political thought: that persons (natural bodies) are not absolutely commensurate with the socioeconomic status or office they "embody." Wilton's imposture is cut short when the Earl finally catches him: "My soul, which was made to soar upward, now sought for passage downward" (p. 258). He "resigns" his "earldom," announcing, "Lo, into my former state I return again" (p. 259).

The comic resolutions of *Volpone* and *The Unfortunate Traveller* emphasize an order ultimately preserved against the moral and economic inroads made by shape-shifters. Disassociated from virtue, these companionate relations are instead linked to counterfeiting, dissembling one's social station, low economic or prodigal motives, and perhaps an excess of desire—all specific features against which ideal friendship is always articulated. Disparity of rank creates a presumption of moral baseness on both parts, and threatens to reverse the proper order of degree by creating opportunities for masking, counterfeiting, and "misrule."

Friendship and the Private Prince

"Great persons," of course, could still find an "equal" of the kind demanded by *amicitia*. Jonson's ode to Lucius Cary and Henry Morison, for example, extols "that Noble Pair" and the exemplary function their friendship had: "You lived to be the great surnames / And titles by which all made claims / Unto the virtue." [24] But the prince faced a more difficult problem. Aristotle places rulers alongside the gods in having a degree of superiority that disables friendship. He offers the case of a "friendship" between a man and a god as a disparity so great that it renders friendship impossible:

> This is most manifest in the case of the gods, whose superiority in every good attribute is pre-eminent . . . we cannot fix a precise limit in such cases, up to which two men can still be friends; the gap may go on widening and the friendship remain; but when one becomes very remote from the other, as God is remote from man, it can continue no longer.

By analogy, Aristotle argues that "the same point is clear in the case of kings. Persons much inferior to them in station do not expect to be friends with kings." [25]

---

24. Ben Jonson, "To the Immortal Memory and Friendship of that Noble Pair, Sir Lucius Cary and Sir H. Morison," lines 113-115, in *Ben Jonson,* ed. Ian Donaldson (Oxford: Oxford University Press, 1995).

25. Aristotle, *Nicomachean Ethics,* bk. 7, pt. 7, sec. 5.

Developing ideologies and theories of kingship raised these issues to a national magnitude as they elevated the Renaissance prince to a loftier monarch. Producing an especially acute vertical distance, this elevated role yielded a formidable solitude beyond the encompassing reach of any twinning "friendship" paradigm. David Starkey has suggestively described the emergence of a new species of monarchy, especially the implications of this shift for the positioning of the monarch among his closest associates. At the beginning of the fifteenth century, "a member of the royal entourage was known as a 'household man'; at the end, as a 'courtier.'" The engine of this change, Starkey argues, was a development in the nature of monarchy: "an early Lancastrian king presided, as a first among equals, over the 'joint-stock enterprise' of war with France; the Yorkists and still more the early Tudors elevated themselves unapproachably above even the greatest of their Lords."[26] This differentiation put a new premium on protocols of access, "nyghnesse," and proximity to the monarch.

The concept of such lofty elevation, however unevenly attained in practice, precipitates a new problem: while status as a *primus inter pares* seems to allow for personal comradeship, the "absolute" monarch figured as a virtual genus apart. (Indeed, the Latin root *ab-solus* designates not only a scope of rule, but also a state of disengagement.) The quasi-legal theorization of the king's two bodies had been profoundly shaped by "mythic fictions," in particular the evocative fiction of the phoenix.[27] The emblematic qualities of the magical bird—its virginity, sexlessness, and perpetual resurrection—achieved an extraordinary resonance in the age of Elizabeth, but one aspect is most interesting here. The conundrum of the phoenix came to serve as a metaphor for monarchical "being" that gave a figural solution to the problem of political continuity and corporate perpetuity. There is always only one, there is never not one, and that one has the unique burden of representing at once the sole individual and the entire species. While classically derived friendship provided a structure of contemporaneous doubling (Cicero's friend was an *alter idem*), the only possible plurality for the phoenix-monarch is a diachronic mirroring, a reiteration through time (Tertullian's reborn phoenix as an *alius idem*, "another the same").[28] The monarch, in whom individual and species coincide, could only find parity with antecedents and successors—never in syn-

26. David Starkey, *The English Court: From the Wars of the Roses to the Civil War* (London: Longman, 1987), p. 3.
27. Kantorowicz, *The King's Two Bodies*, pp. 388–401.
28. Ibid., p. 391, n. 254.

chronic time. This construction of the monarch as peerless collides directly
with classically derived friendship's defining image of twinned parity between friends.

John Lyly's *Campaspe* (1584) and Robert Greene's anglicizing variation,
Friar Bacon and Friar Bungay (circa 1590) play out the issues regarding the
private friendships of princes. The dramas each notably involve a friendship between a ruler and his subject. Both these rulers' friends are markedly
virtuous—no questions arise regarding their integrity or motives. But
both narratives precipitate a crisis of authority between the "friends" that
reveals how their formal political relation as sovereign and subject remains
the primary one. "Twixt the party commanded & him that commaundeth,
there is no societie, and therefore no *Friendship*," [29] and the friendship
mode can always be converted back *by command* to its underlying reality of
political dominion.

Campaspe, "played beefore the Queenes Maiestie on newyeares day at
night" in 1584, offers Elizabeth I a model ruler in Alexander the Great.[30]
The mastery of passion portrayed in Alexander's defeat of love here takes
on clear resonance in an address to a "virgin" queen. The preservation of
masculine integrity against the inroads love would make upon it emblem-
atizes princely integrity, which, as an ability to rule, was gendered masculine (regardless of the monarch's sex).[31] What is of particular interest here
is private friendship's role in relation to the ruler's self-governance. While
friendship tropes are initially invoked, their operation is soon repudiated
on the specific grounds of incommensurate status.

The conquering Alexander has fallen in love with the Theban Campaspe; he enters with his legendary martial companion, Hephestion. In con-
fessing his plight to his friend, Alexander deploys the language of merged
being (sharing good fortune and bad) and the trusting self-expression central to ideal friendship:

29. Day, *The English Secretorie*, p. 118.

30. John Lyly, *Campaspe and Sapho and Phao,* ed. G. K. Hunter and David Bevington
(Manchester: Manchester University Press, 1991), pp. 1, 34. Textual references are to this
edition. For a discussion of the dynamics of flattery in this address to Elizabeth, see David
Bevington, "John Lyly and Queen Elizabeth: Royal Flattery in *Campaspe* and *Sapho and
Phao,*" *Renaissance Papers* (1966): 57–67.

31. This aspect of masculinity is discussed in chapter 2 as supporting friendship over
marriage. For rule as a gendered power, see Janel Mueller, "Textualism, Contextualism, and
the Writings of Elizabeth I," *Tampere English Studies 4: English Studies and History* (1994):
11–38, 33.

Well, now shalt thou see what small difference I make between Alexander and Hephestion. And sith thou hast been always partaker of my triumphs thou shalt be partaker of my torments. I love, Hephestion, I love. (2.2.20–24)

The recipient of this confidence reacts with sorrow. His response reckons up the divergence of their opinions but proceeds, signaling a hope that his roles as subject and friend coincide: "might my words crave pardon and my counsel credit, I would discharge the duty of a subject (for so I am) and the office of a friend (for so I will)" (2.2.28–30). But the doubling of subjection and friendship requires an ominous differentiation of tenses; Falstaff will echo this troubled phrasing when he claims, "I have done the part of a careful friend and a true subject" (*Henry IV, Part 2*, 2.4.301–2). At first, Alexander urges Hephestion to speak freely, an instance of the "liberty of speech" signaled in chapter 1 as a mode of friendly communication: "Speak, Hephestion, for whatsoever is spoken, Hephestion speaketh to Alexander" (2.2.31–32). Thus invited, Hephestion embarks on a long, sober speech against the tyranny and effeminacy of love. But when Hephestion rests his case, Alexander sharply contradicts his own second-self language and invokes his regal majesty to renounce Hephestion's advice:

> Little do you know, and therefore slightly do you regard, the dead embers in a private person or live coals in a great prince, whose passions and thoughts do far exceed others in their extremity as their callings do in majesty. An eclipse in the sun is more than the falling of a star; none can conceive the torments of a king unless he be a king, whose desires are not inferior to their dignities. (2.2.91–98)

Their hierarchical status difference—a "private person" and a "great prince"—precludes the merger of affects and experiences that ideal friendship prescribes. Alexander first *permits* him to speak, but ultimately commands his silence: "no more, Hephestion" (2.2.130). Alexander's actions follow Machiavelli's, not Plutarch's, recommendations: a prince should "[bring] wise men into his council and [give] them alone free license to speak the truth—and only on those points where the prince asks for it, not on others, . . . when *he* wants advice, not when other people want to give it."[32] By the play's final lines, the conqueror himself repudiates love with apparent equanimity and, perhaps, some irony: "it were a shame

32. Niccolò Machiavelli, *The Prince*, ed. Quentin Skinner and Russell Price (Cambridge: Cambridge University Press, 1988), p. 82.

Alexander should desire to command the world if he could not command himself . . . when all the world is won . . . either find me out another to subdue or, of my word, I will fall in love" (5.4.168–74).

Greene's *Friar Bacon and Friar Bungay* transfers Lyly's story to a pastoral, markedly English setting, and he drastically alters the final account of love's meanings, perhaps commenting on Lyly's unromantic play.[33] The friendship theme is caught up in these changes, but its idiom and final trumping by political relations remain the same. The crown prince, Edward, plots to seduce Margaret, a country maid from Fressingfield. Edward's friend and hunting companion, Lacy, Earl of Lincoln, agrees to court her on the prince's behalf, though Edward's father is arranging a marriage for him as a part of English international diplomacy. Predictably, Lacy and Margaret fall in love. This dilemma troubles Lacy's logic. Recognizing his own feelings, Lacy debates with himself on the relationship between duty and desire:

> Recant thee, Lacy, thou art put in trust.
> Edward, thy sovereign's son, hath chosen thee,
> A secret friend, to court her for himself,
> And dar'st thou wrong thy prince with treachery?
> Lacy, love makes no exception of a friend,
> Nor deems it of a prince but as a man.
> Honor bids thee control him in his lust;
> Lacy, thou lov'st, then brook not such abuse,
> But wed her, and abide thy prince's frown.[34]

Trust and treason underscore Lacy's political relation to Edward, his binding duty; love and honor suggest a view from which the prince is but "a man" whose immoral purpose lowers him beneath Lacy's virtue; friendship, finally, suggests that Lacy, as a "secret" or discrete and trusted fiduciary, should protect the prince from himself. Reminiscent of the confusion Lanyer's speaker registers when she questions degree, these disparate imperatives confound the conjunction of friendship and authority for Lacy as a subject, a man, and a friend.

Prince Edward's angry reaction teems with familiar tropes of mirroring

---

33. Charles Hieatt documents the connections between Greene and Lyly and discusses Greene's "sentimentalization" of the plot. See his "A New Source for *Friar Bacon and Friar Bungay*," *The Review of English Studies* 32, no. 126 (May 1981): 180–87.

34. Robert Greene, *Friar Bacon and Friar Bungay,* ed. Daniel Seltzer (Lincoln: University of Nebraska Press, 1963), p. 34 (scene 6, lines 54–64, emphases mine).

friendship. Comparing their friendship to Alexander and Hephestion's legendary bond and calling Lacy and himself "private friends," Edward protests,

> Did I unfold the passions of my love,
> And lock them in the closet of thy thoughts?
> Wert thou to Edward second to himself,
> Sole friend, and partner of his secret loves?
> And could a glance of fading beauty break
> Th' enchained fetters of such private friends?
>   (scene 8, lines 26–31)

But Edward's rage has recourse to another set of metaphorical weapons. He reacts with a haughtiness similar to Alexander's and addresses the betrayal in terms of treason, a resonant allegation coming from a prince:

> Base coward, false, and too effeminate
> To be corrival with a prince in thoughts!
> From Oxford have I posted . . .
> To 'quite a traitor 'fore that Edward sleep.
>   (scene 8, lines 32–35)

Edward's anger, like Alexander's desire, ultimately gives way to a state of princely equilibrium. Decrying the unseemliness of being caught up in "lovers' leagues," he echoes Alexander: "The Prince of Wales has conquered all his thoughts" (scene 8). The same scene finds Edward prepared to go and meet the wife selected for him as a part of his performance of royal duty. As in *Campaspe,* princeliness assigns both the limit of friendship and the duty of self-restraint and sublimation. The prince's "other self" is his political subject bound to obedience. The prince's self, itself, is subject, too, to the demands of a sovereignty requiring absolute identification with office.

Mignonnerie in English

The classically derived friendship ideal, on the private side, represents a utopian version of polity, proposing the friendship pair as a world in which there are, as it were, two sovereigns.[35] The notions concentrated in Mon-

---

35. In Cicero's model, both friends entered friendship with full autonomy and had unilateral power to end it. See, for example, *De amicitia,* trans. Falconer, pp. 140–43 and 128–29 ("sublata enim benevolentia amicitiae nomen tollitur").

taigne's oxymoronic phrase "soveraigne amitie" (p. 150) reflect this sense of counterpolity. Likewise, Cary's assertion that "[n]either sovereign's nor father's hate / A friendship fix'd on virtue sever can"[36] envisions a world apart. The language of *The Two Noble Kinsmen* suggests friendship as a zone exclusive of a tyrannical sovereign's power to intrude, using the imagery of "a World" to describe both the two kinsmen's friendship in prison and Emilia's garden economy.[37] Such idealizations of friendship locate it in a separate realm of freedom and plenitude.

In these cases, as a part of friendship's dramatis personae, a monarch (usually a tyrant) can be found. While friendship ideas comprise an independent alternative to engagement with unilateral authority, a king's personal friendship threatens the basis of that authority directly—from within—when that king refuses to accept the constraints of office as we have seen Alexander and Edward accept them. The special case of the monarch presents a difference in degree that is indeed a difference in kind. For a king, *amicitia* can only default to *mignonnerie,* at once a form of friendship and (mis)rule, creating a constitutional problem for him as a monarch and for the polity he is to represent. In its own way, *mignonnerie* also proposes an alternative mode of governance; but rather than constructing a private world for two private persons, it insinuates itself into established rule. Instead of creating a politically risky "elsewhere,"[38] the minion's alliance captures the monarch himself. Such a captivated monarch transfers his primary allegiance from crown and realm to a specific subject instead. The humanists' virtually unanimous recommendation of friendship to princes notwithstanding, a sixteenth-century king could not enter that private "soveraigne" bond without becoming an icon of "improper sovereignty."[39] *Mignonnerie* represents the threat of government turned, not upside down, but inside out; of common-weal turned to private-weal as a result of the monarch's subordination of public office to private love.

Thus considered, the figure of the minion embodies a double impropriety, fixed precisely at the theoretical crossroads of classically derived

36. Cary, *The Tragedy of Mariam,* p. 92 (2.2.113–14).

37. William Shakespeare and John Fletcher, *The Two Noble Kinsmen,* ed. Eugene M. Waith (Oxford: Clarendon Press, 1989), 2.1.172.

38. Montaigne's concern to demonstrate la Boétie's obedient citizenship and his assessment of Tiberius Gracchus and company shows the delicacy with which his essay skirts the issue of sedition.

39. I borrow this phrase from Rebecca Bushnell, *Tragedies of Tyrants: Political Thought and Theater in the English Renaissance* (Ithaca, N.Y.: Cornell University Press, 1990).

friendship and an ethical monarchy that defines royal identity through its differentiation from self-serving tyranny. The minion's existence, on the one hand, contradicts the principles of virtuous, mirroring friendship by proceeding from "fondness" (with its implications of folly) rather than reason or virtue, by encompassing a status inequality, and by embracing the taint of utility that Montaigne tried adamantly to exclude from "unspotted" friendship (p. 145). On the other hand, the minion inhabits and literalizes the ambiguous personal aspect of Renaissance authority that inhered in the theory of the king's two bodies, thereby illustrating the incompatibility of the notion of a private monarch with a kingship often theorized as personal monarchy. By making all too evident the particular, individual, private emotions of the king—attributes that are proper to his natural person or body and symptoms of an incomplete sublimation of royal affect to the realm—the minion illustrates a limit in the double-bodied metaphor. While amity may look like sovereignty from a private point of view, the sovereign cannot enter its engagement without calling into question his sovereign condition.

Considering what to call "Companions" to "Princes," Francis Bacon instructs that "[t]he Moderne Languages give unto such Persons the Name of Favorites, or Privadoes: As if it were Matter of Grace, or Conversation," and he proposes that using the term *friend* in this context represents a borrowing of "the Word which is received between Private Men."[40] With all his attentiveness to the friendship terminology of "The Moderne Languages" and to the need for borrowed language from a private register, Bacon does not mention what has perhaps become the most marked period name for a prince's companion: "minion." By the seventeenth century, the term had acquired its now familiar opprobrious sense. But *minion* did not always signify in a moral register, and even by Bacon's time it did not exclusively suggest moral fault.

The *Oxford English Dictionary* offers several intensifying variations on its meaning: "a beloved object, darling, favorite"; "one specially favoured or beloved; a dearest friend, a favorite child, servant, or animal . . . often *fig.*, as in minion of fortune"; and finally, "*esp.* a favourite of a sovereign, prince, or other great person; *esp.* opprobriously, one who owes everything to his patron's favour, and is ready to purchase its continuance by base compliances, a 'creature.'" Among the *OED*'s examples, an early Scottish instance of 1501 directly contradicts the idea of "base compliances" in asso-

---

40. Bacon, *The Essayes or Counsels, Civill and Morall,* p. 82.

ciating the minion, instead, with reliable truth: "the kingis min[y]eoun roundand [whispered] in his eir, Hecht [High] Veritie."[41] When Marlowe used the word in Mortimer Senior's famous speech in *Edward II* (1593) ("The mightiest kings have had their minions: / . . . / And not kings only, but the wisest men"),[42] the list of illustrative cases, however controversially, assimilates the "minion" to an ideal of virtuous, heroic partnership. These cases indicate that *minion* could be applied in a morally neutral sense—or indeed to an admirable personage, even into the seventeenth century. But the balance of the *OED* evidence shows a mounting contemptuous sense for the word. It is fitting that this ambivalence should emerge within the same time frame in which the absolutist theory of kingship underwent such great expansion. Changes in the conception of the monarch inevitably affected conceptions of the personage or "creature" whose being derives from him.

In his analysis of fifteenth-century Burgundian and French culture, Johan Huizinga assembles evidence for a *mignon* who was actually a valued part of the proper accoutrements of a knight or prince, as a matter of good form and public approval. Huizinga describes "a form of sentimental friendship, that was expressed through the word '*mignon*'" and claims that "the royal *mignon* is a formalized institution that persisted through the whole sixteenth century and part of the seventeenth."[43] Emphasizing the *mignon*'s formal role in official events at court, he assesses such a friendship as one that "the favorite accounts toward his honor and . . . he himself advertises," adding that "the king has always a *mignon en titre,* decked in the same clothes as he is, on whom he leans during receptions." While Huizinga compares *mignonschap* with courtly love in terms of their equivalent symbolic importance, his evidence accords it a much greater material reality in day-to-day affective practices. Thus, "two friends of similar age, though of different ranks . . . dress themselves alike, sleep in the same room, and sometimes in the same bed." The practice admits even a kind of gender parity, since "in the same manner, queens also have a trusted friend, who dresses as she does and is called *mignonne.*" *Mignonnerie* manifests itself in dress, titles, and public performances, each highlighting its

41. Also noteworthy among the *OED* evidences is Donne's naming of John "the minion of Christ on earth."

42. Christopher Marlowe, *The Works of Christopher Marlowe,* ed. C. F. Tucker Brooke (Oxford: Oxford University Press, 1966), 1.4.390, 394.

43. Johan Huizinga, *Herfsttij der Middeleeuwen: studie over levens- en gedachtenvormen der veertiende en vijftiende eeuw in Frankrijk en de Nederlanden* (Tjeenk Willink & Zoon, Haarlem, 1921), pp. 88–90, my translations; all references are to this passage.

role in Huizinga's formalized, even ritualized world of visible high culture in the late middle ages, effectively poeticizing vertical difference into an engagement proper for display.

The chivalric propriety of displayed *mignonnerie* as such wanes, however, in relation to the emerging notion of a loftier monarch that Starkey describes. In his *Union of the Two Noble and Illustre Famelies of Lancaster and York* (1548), Edward Hall recounts an incident involving the Privy Chamber of Henry VIII. He provides an extended picture of *mignonnerie* from an early Tudor perspective and links the English court to the Continental milieu encompassed by Huizinga's *mignonschap.* Just as Bacon would later do, Hall takes an almost philological interest in what such royal companions should be called. Stressing the minion name, the Tudor chronicler also begins to link it with improper sovereignty. As Starkey recounts, Henry VII had altered the structure of the royal household by instituting (circa 1495) the Privy or "Secret" Chamber. While his own servitors had been lowborn and without influence (the head groom was "a mere gentleman" and his subordinates were "hardly even that"), under his successor the demographics of the Privy Chamber personnel changed. Henry VIII, instead, "filled the apartment with high-born favourites and boon companions."[44]

These minions in Hall's account (Nicholas Carew, Francis Bryan, and "diverse other young Gentelmen")[45] conduct a mission to the French king, Francis I, and Hall's narrative strikingly connects prejudices against French ways in general with disapproval of French royal misconduct in particular. After completing their mission, the English minions "remayned in the Frenche court," where "they with the Frenche kyng roade daily disguysed through Parys, throwyng Egges, stones and other foolishe trifles at the people, whiche light demeanoure of a kyng was much discommended and gested at." National identity and morality are at stake in Hall, because when the minions returned to England "they were all Frenche, in eatyng, drynkyng and apparell, yea, and in Frenche vices and bragges . . . so that nothing by them was praised, but if it were after the Frenche turne."[46] From the proper dressing-alike that Huizinga describes, we have come to a place where such a likening can only be a disguise.

In recounting a later episode, Hall treats Henry VIII in a somewhat

44. Starkey, *The English Court,* pp. 47, 4.
45. Edward Hall, *The Triumphant Reigne of Kyng Henry the VIII,* ed. Charles Whibley (London: 1904), 1:144, 175.
46. Ibid., p. 175.

more politic manner than he had Francis I.[47] The English king seems less than fully responsible for *mignonnerie,* having only assented to it by an excess of generosity ("gentlenes and liberalitie"). By this point, however, the "minions" were perceived not only as indecorous, but also as a threat to ordered government and kingly dignity: "certain young men in his privie chamber, not regarding his estate or degree, were so familiar and homely with hym, and plaied suche light touches with hym that they forgat themselves." As Hall relates, when asked by the council to redress "al these enormities and lightnes," the king "committed it to their reformacion." So Henry's companions were banished from court, "whiche discharge . . . greved sore the hartes of these young menne whiche were called the kinges minions."[48] Starkey's assessment of this episode is less circumspect than Hall's. Declaring that the young men "were universally known as the king's 'minions,'" he glosses this name as "politely to be translated as 'pretty boys.'"[49] While such a translation does anything but clarify the meaning of *minion,* Hall's history does link the name to indecorous behavior and improprieties with respect to "estate or degree." The minions' familiarities across the vertical distance of degree made them seem to "forget themselves," that is, their place, and to threaten a higher place.

The minion himself as a social "shape shifter" threatens both contemporary forms of civil service, bypassing not only aristocratic place ("estate or degree"), but also the evolving system of Tudor "meritocracy." As Wallace MacCaffrey reports of a later royal favorite, the earl of Leicester, "the meritocrats loathed the favourite as a dilettante; the aristocrats with equal fervour, as an *arriviste* adventurer."[50] The minion was thus a disturbance in several senses, but the real threat posed by his association with

47. Lord Sandys and Sir Thomas Lovell comment on this episode in Shakespeare and Fletcher's *Henry VIII* (1613), with a similar deflection of blame away from Henry and onto the minions and their French affectations. They refer to "the new proclamation" for "the reformation of our travelled gallants / That fill the court with quarrels, talk and tailors" (1.3.17, 19–20).

48. Hall, *The Triumphant Reigne of Kyng Henry the VIII,* p. 145.

49. Starkey, *The English Court,* p. 79. Jonathan Goldberg's *Sodometries: Renaissance Texts, Modern Sexualities* (Stanford, Calif.: Stanford University Press, 1992) explores the possible sexual meanings in this episode (pp. 47–48). Huizinga, for the earlier period, is clearly too categorical in his differentiation of *mignonschap* from *Griecsche vriendschap,* especially when he claims that sodomy was somehow both unknown and abhorred (p. 89).

50. Wallace MacCaffrey, *Elizabeth I* (London: Edward Arnold, 1993), p. 92. While Elizabeth never compromised her authority in her affections for Leicester and Essex and obviously did not forfeit her status as a monarch over them, these relations did trigger the kind of political, sexual, and court scandal I attribute to *mignonnerie.*

negligent rule was to the king's status as a sovereign ruler as such. Hugh Latimer's *Sermon of the Plough* (1548) offers an ecclesiastical parallel, linking *mignonnerie* to a clerical dereliction of duty: "They pastyme in their prelacies . . . with theyr daunsyng minyons."[51] The "familiar . . . enormities" of Henry VIII's minions seem to Hall "not mete to be suffred for the kynges honor"; the individual king who has strayed must therefore be restored to the royal *dignitas* by "reformacion." *Mignonnerie,* by capturing the straying king personally, posed a constitutional conflict, for both the king's immediate advisors and the monarchy itself, as embodied in a king who always has the capacity to act "unkingly."

A King Is Not "His Own"

Cicero claimed that autonomy and independence were prerequisites to the very capacity for friendship.[52] From the point of view of the political subject, the sovereign might be said to possess these qualities most acutely; ideas of sovereign power and prerogative express notions of agency in its strongest form. But public and private forms of agency entail differently constructed agents and different capacities. Commentators on the constructions of sovereign and subject, however, have focused on the power dynamics *between* them. E. M. W. Tillyard's *Elizabethan World Picture* describes a vertical hierarchy now viewed as an elucidation of ideology: sixteenth-century thought posited a monarch whose absoluteness and completeness represented the ultimate human degree in the pyramid of worldly power and the first rung of the ladder below divinity. The monarch's authority and the subject's being were dynamically interrelated, mutually guaranteed in this scheme.

Criticism has divided over the effectiveness of the monarchy's power, while still addressing this interaction. Stephen Greenblatt's new historicist formulation emphasizes the unilateralism of the sovereign-subject relation: "one of the highest achievements of power is to impose its fictions upon the world and one of its supreme pleasures is to enforce the acceptance of fictions that are known to be fictions."[53] Despite the references to pleasure

51. Hugh Latimer, "The Sermon of the Plough," in *Sermons by Hugh Latimer,* ed. George Elwes Corrie (New York: Johnson Reprint Corp., 1971), pp. 54–71, 60.

52. "For to the extent that a man relies upon himself and is so fortified by virtue and wisdom that he is dependent on no one and considers all his possessions to be within himself, in that degree is he most conspicuous for seeking out and cherishing friendships." Cicero, *De amicitia,* trans. Falconer, pp. 141–43.

53. Stephen Greenblatt, *Renaissance Self-Fashioning from More to Shakespeare* (Chicago: University of Chicago Press, 1980), p. 141.

and fictions, the model of power here is one acting to "impose" and "enforce." Louis Montrose, on the other hand, even as he proposes a mutual manipulability, is primarily interested in subjects—their power to react to power and to shape it. When Montrose argues that "in fact the ruler and the ruled are mutually defining, reciprocally constituted," he is perhaps less concerned with mutuality and more concerned to demonstrate the "controlling power of the writing subject over the representation he has made," that is, to specifically argue the efficacy of poetry and to see "writing as a mode of action."[54] His claims of a subversive power for poetry conceive a stronger, "central" power against which it struggled. Christopher Pye's deconstructive reading in *The Regal Phantasm,* though it configures royal power as theatrical and illusionistic, dependent in a sense on spectacle, nevertheless treats that theater of illusion as an efficacious agent.[55]

These debates about the measure of a sovereign's and a subject's shaping powers again suggest a struggle *between* them, a contest in which one or the other competing fiction might predominate. Friendship's differential constructions of these personages, though, makes it possible to consider the placement of sovereign and subject within one single, shared fiction. From this perspective, "affect" appears not as a link between them, but instead as a part of what separates them. Its performance leads to opposite effects for sovereign and subject. Friendship (unlike, for example, Petrarchan love in the reign of Elizabeth) thus declines to conjoin the participants in a myth of nationality. Instead, friendship makes the subject a king and the monarch a subject, by entitling private persons to affective prerogatives denied the king. This royal privation, an experiment in defining the public good or public interest bureaucratically, informs the final lines of Shakespeare's Sonnet 29: "For thy sweet love rememb'red such wealth brings / That then I scorn to change my state with kings."

For Tudor-Stuart culture concerned itself with both the theorization of a monarch and also his interpellation, constituting a special subjectivity to serve its own purpose of creating a specifically public power. The 1598 rhetoric of James I provides a drastic example of allegedly irreducible difference between public and private personage in this highly anti-Parliamentarian argument:

54. Louis Montrose, "The Elizabethan Subject and the Spenserian Text," in *Literary Theory/Renaissance Texts,* ed. Patricia Parker and David Quint (Baltimore: Johns Hopkins University Press, 1986), pp. 320, 332.

55. Christopher Pye, *The Regal Phantasm: Shakespeare and the Politics of Spectacle* (London: Routledge, 1990).

And if it be not lawfull to a priuate man to revenge his priuate injury upon his priuate aduersary . . . how muche lesse is it lawfull to the people, or any part of them (who are all priuate men . . .) to take vpon them the use of the sword . . . against the publicke Magistrate, whom to onely it belongeth.[56]

"Priuate men" assembled remain just that; according to this logic, not even their representative organization rises to the level of a "publicke" body, which title belongs to the magistrate, namely the king and his delegates. While Greenblatt emphasizes the power to impose fictions, the king is an individual (a natural body) designated to *inhabit* the supreme fiction, to voice the script implied by the period commonplace that princes live their lives on stages. In a letter explaining a shortcoming in her patronage, Elizabeth I subscribes herself "one even wholly yours (if she can be such a one that scant is found to be her own)."[57] The intersection of amity and theories of kingship presents a perspective from which the sovereign monarch appears constrained and limited, burdened and subject to imperatives of office that overwhelm the kind of private autonomous self-disposition requisite for friendship.

The king's status as *res publica* (public matter or property) emphasizes his serviceability to the commonweal. This creates an extraordinarily privileged chattel, doubtless, but one profoundly and legally not "his own." The serviceable monarch's full dedication was required in a sphere defined in the maxim *quod omnes tangit* as one which touches or affects all.[58] Kantorowicz often notes that the Tudor flowering of the king's two bodies doctrine presented an original variation. In sixteenth-century England, the monarch's "superhuman" theorization proceeds by a specific logic. Royal identity is conferred by the *superaddition* of the "Body politic," which Kantorowicz terms the "superbody," to the "Body natural." Focusing on this language of embodiment, he distinguishes the uniquely "English 'physiologic' concept of the King's Two Bodies."[59] My purpose here is to explore some implications of this resolutely "bodied" metaphor for the individual

56. James I, *The Trew Law of Free Monarchies* (1598), in *Political Writings,* ed. Johan P. Somerville (Cambridge: Cambridge University Press, 1994), p.78.

57. "A Precious Token of Her Highness's Great Wit and Marvelous Understanding," an edited transcription from British Library MS Additional 46367 (a journal of Sir John Harington's) by Donald Foster of Vassar College. I thank Professor Foster for bringing this letter to my attention.

58. This maxim defining a realm of public concern is discussed in Kantorowicz, *The King's Two Bodies,* p. 361.

59. See ibid., p. 20, and p. 20, n. 35; see also pp. 382, 406, 446–48, and 505.

monarch himself, as writers tried to shape him. The particular relation of
the two bodies *within* this "one Person" is of interest. What are the implications of "a state that inheres in the sovereign,"[60] of "personal" monarchy,
for the "state" or internal organization of that sovereign, especially in terms
of reckoning public and private character? And what does this internal relation mean for friendship purposes?

The basic formulation of the king's two bodies is familiar enough:
the king

> has a Body natural, adorned and invested with the Estate and Dignity
> royal; and he has not a Body natural distinct and divided by itself from
> the Office and Dignity royal, but a Body natural and a Body politic to-
> gether indivisible; and these two Bodies are incorporated in one Person,
> and make one Body and not divers . . . by . . . Consolidation.[61]

Within this double-bodied figure, the Body politic, the "superbody," is a
specific kind of mythic and figural construct of social or public concerns:

> the Body natural (if it be considered in itself) is a Body mortal. . . . But
> his Body politic is a Body that cannot be seen or handled, consisting of
> Policy and Government, and constituted for the Direction of the people,
> and the Management of the public weal.[62]

What is intriguing about this language is the fate of the natural body, and
any "private self" that might attach to it, after its "Consolidation" with the
body politic. For not only is the body politic "more ample and large"[63]
than the body natural; it also has the capacity to wipe out "Imperfections"
(i.e., imbecility, minority, sex) of the natural body.[64] Thus, not only does
the Body natural now "partake of the Nature and Effects of the Body politic," it also is "altered . . . to . . . another Degree."[65]

60. This is Montrose's expression from "The Elizabethan Subject and the Spenserian
Text," p. 311.

61. "The Case of the Duchy of Lancaster," in Plowden, *Commentaries or Reports,*
p. 213, cited in Kantorowicz, *The King's Two Bodies,* p. 9.

62. Plowden, *Commentaries or Reports,* p. 212, cited in Kantorowicz, *The King's Two
Bodies,* p. 7.

63. Plowden, *Commentaries or Reports,* p. 220a.

64. *See* Kantorowicz, *The King's Two Bodies,* p. 11, n. 9, which also quotes Bacon to
the effect that the assumption of the crown could wipe out a prior attainder.

65. *Willion v. Berkley* (argued in Common Bench in the third year of Elizabeth's
reign), in Plowden, *Commentaries or Reports,* p. 238, cited in Kantorowicz, *The King's Two
Bodies,* p. 11.

These formulations quickly became commonplaces in popular and political speech,[66] and they coincided with an already established ethical discourse of dutiful monarchy. As is evident in the speeches of Elizabeth I, the legal limbo of any freestanding private self found its parallel in the notion that any zone of royal privacy is fully charged out to claims of the good of the realm. Elizabeth's consistent expressions throughout her reign reflect an internalization of this effect. In her accession speech itself, she begins by charging her secretary, Sir William Cecil, "that without respect of my private will, you will give me that counsel that you think best."[67] To take on royal "Estate" is to bracket one's "private will."

In 1576, during the Parliamentary wrangles over her nonmarriage, Elizabeth distinguishes the status of "private persons" from that of "prince's state," just as we have seen Lyly's Alexander and Greene's Edward do. She offers her own astonishing image of the conflict between royalty and privacy in a counterfactual fantasy, imagining what it might be like "if I were a milkmaid with a pail on mine arm, whereby my private person might be little set by."[68] The milkmaid image here effects a neat reversal: instead of a private person imagining herself as queen, the public speech of this public being offers up a metaphor for private status. If she were a milkmaid, the logic goes, the queen would actually have had a sphere of privacy; instead, as an ethical monarch, her position must be one of willingness to yield up a self on the kingdom's account. She continues, dramatically portraying the degree to which her privacy must yield to her people's welfare:

> for your behoof there is no way so difficile that may touch my priva[cy] which I could not well content myself to take, and in this case as willingly to spoil myself quite of myself as if I should put off my upper garment when it wearies me.[69]

66. See Kantorowicz, *The King's Two Bodies*, p. 405, and p. 405, n. 310.

67. Elizabeth I, "Queen Elizabeth's First Speech," in *Elizabeth I: Collected Works,* ed. Leah Marcus, Janel Mueller, and Mary Beth Rose (Chicago: University of Chicago Press, 2000), pp. 51–52.

68. Elizabeth I, "The Queen's Speech at the Close of the Parliamentary Session, March 15, 1576," in ibid., pp. 167–71, 170. Shakespeare's *Richard III* (1593) echoes this image when the much-abused Queen Elizabeth avows, "I had rather be a country servant maid / Than a great queen with this condition" (1.3.106–7). See also Cary's *Tragedy of Mariam,* where Mariam laments, "Yet had I rather much a milkmaid be, / Than be the monarch of Judea's Queen" (1.1.57–58), and Shakespeare's *Antony and Cleopatra* (4.15.73–75) for this proverbial comparison.

69. Elizabeth I, "The Queen's Speech at the Close of the Parliamentary Session," p. 170.

This milkmaid image for imagining an impossible private condition appears again ten years later in Elizabeth's first speech to the 1586 Parliament on the problem of Mary Queen of Scots as she disclaims all active ill will toward the transgressing Mary:

> if . . . we were but as two milkmaids with pails upon our arms; or that there were no more dependency upon us, but mine own life were only in danger, and not the whole estate of your religion and well-doings; I protest . . . I would most willingly pardon and remit this offense.[70]

This fanciful dream of private status echoes other iterations of the sentiment. *Gorboduc,* played before Elizabeth in 1561, argues the tragic consequences when a king tries to retire from a lifetime of ruling "for the publique wealth and not for priuate ioye," lamenting how such service "wast[es] mannes lyfe, and hasten[s] crooked age."[71] Shakespeare's Henry IV soliloquizes his envy of that nameless, socially insignificant person who is visited by sleep in a way no king can be: "Deny it to a king? Then, happy low, lie down! / Uneasy lies the head that wears a crown" (*Henry IV, Part 2,* 3.1.30–31). In Beaumont and Fletcher's *A King and No King,* Arbaces sighs, "I would I might be private: / Meane men enjoy themselves."[72] The wistful pathos of these musings aside, their idiom reflects discursive constructions of public and private as a matter of being or personage rather than spheres of operation.

Although Elizabeth strenuously resisted intrusions from Parliament on the question of her marital status, and despite the enormous public pressures brought to bear on her single state, she never bases her refusal on what we might call private choice. That would not constitute a viable position. While Montrose characterizes her stance as a defense of "her maidenly freedom and royal prerogative,"[73] Elizabeth's own formulations disclaim any conjunction of personal freedom with political prerogative. She argues instead that singleness is the rational best choice specifically in regard to the

<hr>

70. Elizabeth I, "Queen Elizabeth's First Reply to the Parliamentary Petitions Urging the Execution of Mary, Queen of Scots, November 12, 1586," in *Collected Works,* pp. 186–96, 192.

71. Thomas Norton and Thomas Sackville, *The Tragedie of Gorboduc* (London: William Griffith, 1565), 1.1.171–72.

72. Francis Beaumont and John Fletcher, *The Dramatic Works in the Beaumont and Fletcher Canon,* ed. Fredson Bowers (Cambridge: Cambridge University Press, 1970), 1.1.298–99.

73. Montrose, "The Elizabethan Subject and the Spenserian Text," p. 309.

public charge that is monarchy, referencing the imperatives of the "present state."[74] Thus royal prerogative looks nothing like a utopian private form of maximal agency; it designates instead an (admittedly unappealable) sphere of allotted jurisdiction. This jurisdiction, in turn, is defined by an extremity of obligation. The imperatives of a duty to the realm in Elizabeth's paradigm finally indicate a complete dedication of the private self to her subjects' good:

> Beside your dutiful supplies for defense of the public—which, as the philosophers affirmed of rivers coming from the ocean, return to the ocean again—I have *diminished my own revenue* that I might add to your security, and been content to be a taper of true virgin wax, to *waste myself* and *spend my life* that I might give light and comfort to those that live under me.[75]

The successful performance of ethical monarchy, on Elizabeth's own showing, depends upon this complete self-expenditure. Elizabeth's rhetoric suggests not only that the good of the realm takes precedence in a conflict between its imperatives and the monarch's personal desire, but that a full valuation of the needs of the commonweal entails the price of royal self-depletion.[76]

The lonely, phoenixlike solitude of the king that is a virtual platitude in reflections on kingship in no way connects with a sense of privacy central to discourses of *amicitia* as autonomy and a related absolute power of self-disposition. While the monarch might have the power to take title to other people's lives, within ethical theories of rule he lacked title to himself. As historian John Guy phrases this irony, "the monarch's person was the regime's most spectacular asset."[77] One way to mark the later passing of this order is in Milton's 1649 justification of regicide, where he characterizes Charles I's physical self or natural body as "the mere useless bulk of his person."[78] Viewed through friendship's lens, this counterintuitive differentia-

---

74. Elizabeth I, "The Queen's Speech at the Close of the Parliamentary Session," p. 170.

75. Elizabeth I, "The Queen's Final Speech before Parliament, December 19, 1601," in *Collected Works,* pp. 346–51, 347.

76. William Flesch's work on monarchy's *expenditure* of power applies the theoretical work of Marcel Mauss and Georges Bataille to the Renaissance context: *The Limits of Generosity: Shakespeare, Herbert, Milton* (Ithaca, N.Y.: Cornell University Press, 1992).

77. John Guy, *Tudor England* (Oxford: Oxford University Press, 1988), p.14.

78. John Milton, *The Tenure of Kings and Magistrates,* in *John Milton,* ed. Stephen Orgel and Jonathan Goldberg (Oxford: Oxford University Press, 1990), p. 277.

tion of powers between sovereigns and subjects accords a certain privileged meaning to private life, and it undergirds the Renaissance commonplace that a friend is worth more than a kingdom; we will see the limitations of this settlement between public and private domains in Falstaff's case in chapter 5. But the absolute monarch, within this theory, is a monarch absolutely. Indeed, as Timothy Reiss paraphrases it, "the private being of the king, says Montaigne, is secondary and ought to be suppressed."[79] The sovereign's exclusion from the range of private pleasures and powers Montaigne calls friendship's *jovissance* so indicates what is being sought in the protobureaucratic theorization of public power: a "body" without any residual affective interests or imperatives of its own.

The exercise of a king's private will, unsubordinated to the good of the realm, "unkings" the king; indeed, it locates him within one of the worst Renaissance categories of moral failure: tyranny. As elucidated by Sir Thomas Smith in his 1583 treatise on government, tyranny and kingship are paired modes of rule distinguishable by the "maner" of "the obtaining of the authoritie, the maner of administration thereof, and the . . . marke whereunto it doth tend."[80] The "marke" of the tyrant's administration is his personal interest; in each context, the tyrant is the ruler who functions by his own will, for his own pleasure, and against the interests of the commonweal. The tyrant's unsuppressed private self subjugates royal office to itself: he "hath no regard to the wealth of his people, but seeketh onely to magnifie himself and his, and to satisfie his vicious and cruell appetite."[81] The "tyrannicall" "maner of . . . rule" proceeds in accordance with the "will" of tyrants or *by the private Counsell and advise of their friends and favorites* onely, without the consent of the people."[82] Here, in the context of defining tyranny in opposition to kingship, the figure of the king's friend or favorite appears. Unlike a publicly affected counselor, he proffers advice, private in origin and private in purpose, from a private place created by a monarch ruling in the private mode.

While the late-medieval paradigm of *mignonnerie* may have constituted a "proper" amity for a prince, sixteenth-century developments rendered it

79. Timothy Reiss, "Montaigne and the Subject of Polity," in Parker and Quint, *Literary Theory, Renaissance Texts,* pp. 115–49, 119.

80. Sir Thomas Smith, *De Republica Anglorum,* ed. Mary Dewar (Cambridge: Cambridge University Press, 1982), p. 53.

81. Ibid., p. 55.

82. Ibid., p. 54, and p. 54, notes 2 and 3 (emphasis mine).

not only archaic but doubly improper for a king. Friendship theory and its faith in decorous parity, along with monarchy theory's interpellating exaltation of the sovereign and demand for the subordination of his private self, converged precisely to one effect: affectively speaking, they rendered the proper sovereign *solitary*.

FIVE

The False Prince and the True Subject:
Friendship and Public Institutions
in *Edward II* and *The Henriad*

❧

The precepts of ethical monarchy devise a sovereign self to fulfill a unique function: the personal representation of the body politic. This calls for a king's identification with commonweal at the cost of any competing private imperative; in other words, it is a call for what we might name "disinterestedness." The cultural construction of royal identity captures the monarch's natural body and consumes whatever privacy (as a possessory interest in the self and its actions) may be "proper" to it, all in order to trope formally a vision of general polity. Sixteenth-century kingship so formulates a doctrine of the "public figure," a conception with, at once, popular currency and legal effect—as it still has in contemporary Anglophone legal contexts. In the forum of U.S. Constitutional law, for example, this tradition of nomenclatures is intact. Supreme Court decisions have differentiated the responsibilities of the media regarding the defamation of "public officials," "public figures," and "private persons" respectively, and such considerations entail an adjudication of what such persons may legitimately expect in the way of privacy.[1]

Two narratives put the stakes of the cultural fashioning of public bodies/kings under the sharpest glare: the *institutio regis* told as a tale of risk and mishaps (a tale that might go wrong) and the tale of a king's literal undoing or royal *demise* (which encompasses forms of "unkinging," among which death is only one variation).[2] Kinging and unkinging show

---

1. See *New York Times v. Sullivan,* 376 US 254 (1964) and its subsequent elucidation in *Curtis Publishing v. Butts,* 388 US 130 (1967) and *Gertz v. Robert Welch, Inc.,* 418 US 323 (1973).
2. Ernst Kantorowicz discusses the strange and specifically royal meanings of the term "demise." He quotes the case of *Willion v. Berkeley,* defining "demise" as "a Removal of the

the mechanisms of royal identity at work. The texts to be considered in this chapter, Marlowe's *Edward II* (1592) and Shakespeare's *Henry IV, Parts 1 & 2* (1597, 1598), address exactly these moments in monarchical construction—and in each case they use the question of the king's company, his friendships, to do it.

The prescriptive language of royal duty directs a monarch's sublimation of private interests in his required identification with the realm. The jurisprudential rules developed in Tudor case law held that the superaddition of royal estate to the king's natural body effected this ontological change, at least legally. The body politic, being "more ample and large" than the body natural, had the capacity to perfect the "Imperfections" (i.e., imbecility, minority, sex) of the natural body.[3] Despite these normative arguments, however, dramatic representations of unkinging explore the persistence of some personal characteristic or private desire, unsublimated to those suprapersonal interests that the king's natural body was conscripted to represent. These "debilities," from the standpoint of ideal monarchy, have failed to disappear with the attachment of royal estate, but instead linger to erode that estate. There are diverse forms this residual self could take: in *The Tempest,* Prospero had abandoned his public duty for a reclusive attachment to the private world of books; in *King Lear,* the king's folly subordinates the coherent unity of the realm as an opportunity for the private trial of daughters' love.

In the case of a male king, the marriage contract is ordinarily consistent with the maintenance of a sovereign condition (Elizabeth's canniness about the gendering of this issue barely needs mentioning). But "love" and its passions are another matter. Abandonment to passion, as Montaigne argued, subjects the lover to appetite and shatters his sense of proportion. In *Campaspe,* Alexander asks Hephestion, "Is love a vice?" and Hephestion directly affirms, "It is no virtue."[4] When Alexander admits he has fallen in love, he concedes it is "a thing far unfit for a Macedonian, for a king, for Alexander."[5] Hephestion's speech expounds on the shame and effeminization of love, as we have seen; and the language of subjection takes on a special cogency in the case of a king, in whom self-command appears even

---

Body politic . . . from one Body natural to another" (*The King's Two Bodies: A Study in Medieval Political Theology* [Princeton, N.J.: Princeton University Press, 1957], p. 13, n. 13).

    3. Kantorowicz, *The King's Two Bodies,* pp. 9–11; see especially note 9.

    4. John Lyly, *Campaspe and Sappho and Phao,* ed. G. K. Hunter and David Bevington (Manchester: Manchester University Press, 1991), 2.2.18–19.

    5. *Campaspe,* 2.2.24–25.

more crucial. Love, he argues, turns Alexander into a "subject"; he asks, "Shall it not seem monstrous to wise men that the heart of the greatest conqueror of the world" should be subject to "the weakest creature of nature?"[6] Love eviscerates the masculine self-mastery that undergirds the moral authority of rule, making it uniquely insidious for the sovereign. The king in love and the king ruled by a woman (as in *Macbeth* [1605] or *Cymbeline* [1609]) are thus variant cases of "monstrous [female] *regiment.*" Beaumont and Fletcher's later *A King and No King* (1619) literally plays out love's disestablishing effects for a king. Arbaces, passionately in love with a woman understood to be his sister, exclaims, "I would I might be private: / Meane men enjoy themselves."[7] As Rebecca Bushnell describes, "the 'king' is converted into a private citizen, thus licensing his desire."[8] This king gets his wish. Only king by mistake, he is licensed by the sudden onset of privacy.

How does friendship compare with love as affecting the king's condition? Friendship, in the affective, world-abandoning, self-sufficient sense that the idealizing discourses propose, represents a unique crisis distinguishable from love in the way it differs so markedly between sovereign and subject. A subject's self-disposition into "soveraigne amitie" expresses the height of individual autonomy: "our owne voluntarie choice and libertie . . . hath no production more properly her owne."[9] For the monarch, though, such a wholesale self-disposition sets off an ontological crisis. His entrance into an exclusive personal bond with one subject above all others (which "dissolveth all other duties, and freeth all other obligations" [p. 151]) also dissolves his royal condition. While in the case of love the sovereign might subordinate himself to passion, to a woman, all that is necessary for the same disestablishing effect in friendship is that he allow or create an equality (an honorable act in all others) between himself and his friend.

In these diametrically opposed effects, friendship differentiates the capacities of sovereign from subject. While friendship as a predominating affective bond precipitates a constitutional collapse for one, it "sovereigns"

6. Ibid., 2.2.61–64.

7. Francis Beaumont and John Fletcher, *The Dramatic Works in the Beaumont and Fletcher Canon,* ed. Fredson Bowers (Cambridge: Cambridge University Press, 1970), 1.1.298–99.

8. Rebecca Bushnell, *Tragedies of Tyrants: Political Thought and Theater in the English Renaissance* (Ithaca, N.Y.: Cornell University Press, 1990), p. 167.

9. Montaigne, "Of Friendship," in *The Essayes of Montaigne: John Florio's Translation,* ed. J. I. M. Stewart (New York: Modern Library, 1933), p. 146. Subsequent references are to this edition and will appear in the text.

the other. It appears as a special power of self-disposition and expression that only the private person can exercise. While this allocation of powers appearing through friendship's lens seems to privilege private life, the commonplace asserting that a true friend is always worth more than a kingdom shows that this allocation, is, of course, also a compensatory action. Falstaff's case in the *Henry IV* plays will indicate why this power should not be overly sentimentalized. It can be a legitimate power only by removing to a realm apart from court and political life, as a capacity pertaining to an exile. And for the sovereign? His exclusion from this private *jovissance* of affective agency shows how formulas for an adequately "public" power began by disendowing a "natural" body, by creating a body without impulses.

This chapter considers the ways *Edward II* and *The Henriad* explore and intensify the discourses of *mignonnerie* and ethical monarchy developed in chapter 4, in which friendship theory's ideal parity and monarchy theory's construction of a publicly affected singular being converge to bar the monarch from friendship in its utopian form. The dramas present reversed cases of friendship's disestablishing effects. *Edward II*'s dramatization of *mignonnerie* as a process that severs Edward from kingship reflects friendship's unkinging power. Where friendship rules, kingship fails, and participation in friendship exacts the price of sovereign status. Marlowe's play provides no real moral high ground from which the king's "subjection" (to passion, to Gaveston, and of the realm) is fully castigated. Instead, the crisis is driven by Marlowe's interest in how Edward's tragic psychology is inextricably caught between two contradictory interpellative discourses: the idealizing tradition of friendship and the normative rules of ethical monarchy.

The *Henry* plays also concern themselves with an irksome desire to be equal that persists in the monarch's affective psychology. But the successful repression of a monarch's "private" self; his denial of private, friendship relations; Falstaff's spatial relocation; and Henry V's final, uncompanioned isolation in a case history of the *institutio regis* combine to use the terms of friendship to plot an action that reverses Marlowe's. Shakespeare's dramas enforce a royal psychology compliant with the dictates of an ethic that renders friendship unavailable in its exclusive, affective—and private—form.

Considered together, these dramas comprise the paired gestures of kinging and unkinging, and they cast these events in the idiom of friendship. If *Edward II* is a straightforward depiction of the disastrous convergence of friendship and monarchy, the *Henry* plays will be seen to add new complexities to their divergence, by reversing a range of expectations about sovereignty and subjection, truth and dissimulation, and calculation and love. As evidence of the vitality of "amitie" in these differential proceedings, Shakespeare has his Machiavellian Prince Hal choose *mignonnerie* as the most scandalous thing for the Heir Apparent to embrace. The simulation of friendship transpires with a sinister ease, as warnings to princes tirelessly advise; Hal's perverse appropriation of this detail from princely advice tracts ironically inverts the normally accorded roles of seducer and seduced. By tracing such a separately fashioned sovereign and subject, friendship discourses mark off public and private powers in a mythical narrative of polity's founding moment.

Particularizing Edward's Errors

Many critics have discussed *Edward II*'s representation of the king's mode of rule and the political implications of Marlowe's position. Much of what has been said about the play is consistent with the analysis here, but the perspective friendship affords focuses the conflict as one between two logics of being for Edward: private friendship and public sovereignty. This perspective also shows the inevitability of *mignonnerie* in Edward's attempt to voice both scripts. The conflict enacts what is at once a constitutional and an affective crisis, since the head-on collision of these uncannily reversed modes dramatizes friendship's power to unking the king.

Though far apart in time and method, Laurens Mills and Alan Bray equally foreground the place of classical friendship in *Edward II,* seeming to agree that it offers something of which Edward is constitutionally capable. Mills proposes that *Edward II* should be interpreted "as a friendship play, rather than as a chronicle history," and he traces the presence of "Elizabethan friendship ideas" in the drama, which apparently had been overlooked until that time.[10] With respect to the notion of communal property, for example, he views Edward as "fulfilling . . . [a] condition of the classical views on friendship."[11] Mills does suggest that Edward's excessive devotion to "private pursuits" is inappropriate for a king and forebodes political catastrophe.[12] By making this a question of degree and not kind, however, he does not indicate how friendship itself, as an impossible task for a public body, actually relates to Edward's demise.

Bray's reading of *Edward II* also considers the idealized version of Elizabethan friendship but focuses on its contradictory "something other," ex-

---

10. L. J. Mills, "The Meaning of *Edward II*," *Modern Philology* 32 (1934–35): 11–31, 29.

11. Ibid., p. 20.

12. Ibid., p. 28.

amining the "curious symmetry between the Sodomite and the masculine friend." [13] In Bray's words, "the Elizabethan sin of Sodom . . . was never far from the flower-strewn world of Elizabethan friendship and it could never wholly be distinguished from it." [14] Accordingly, Marlowe describes "what could be a sodomitical relationship" but "places it *wholly within* the . . . conventions of Elizabethan friendship, in a tension which he never allows to be resolved. The image . . . is *simultaneously* . . . that of friendship" and its suspect double, sodomy.[15] Bray emphasizes the coexistence of "flower-strewn" friendship with sodomitical relations, but, like Mills, he does not address the implications of Edward's royal status for his essaying of the friendship form.

Jonathan Goldberg, on the other hand, differs with Mills and Bray on the status of friendship in *Edward II*. While Mills emphasizes its defining presence and Bray reads it to coexist irreducibly with sodomy, Goldberg claims that "Marlowe is defending sodomy" at the express expense of "idealized friendship or some spiritual relationship or some self-integrative principle of identity." [16] Arguing that Edward "institutes a sodomitical regime" and that "sodomy is the name for all behavior in the play," Goldberg reads Marlowe as definitively positioning his play as an instance of erotic and political "sodometry." [17]

Mills, Bray, and Goldberg are not specifically concerned to distinguish the situation of the sovereign within the general discourses they describe (friendship, friendship/sodomy, and sodomy, respectively). But elsewhere, in accounting for the statement by James I that sodomy was a crime warranting death—the king's own notoriously homosexual displays notwithstanding—Goldberg makes the point that "sodomy was so fully politicized that no king could possibly apply the term to himself." [18] The impossibility of the king's voicing sodomy converges with his incapacity to perform in friendship's idiom. Although much is at stake in differentiations of friendship and sodomy generally, in the king's particular case it is a difference that no longer signifies.

13. Alan Bray, "Homosexuality and the Signs of Male Friendship in Elizabethan England," *History Workshop,* no. 29 (spring 1990): 1–19, 2.

14. Ibid., p. 16.

15. Ibid., p. 10 (emphasis mine).

16. Jonathan Goldberg, *Sodometries: Renaissance Texts, Modern Sexualities* (Stanford, Calif.: Stanford University Press, 1992), pp. 123–24.

17. Ibid., p. 123.

18. Jonathan Goldberg, "Sodomy and Society: The Case of Christopher Marlowe," *Southwest Review* 69 (1984): 371–78, 376.

Although it is difficult to say whether Marlowe is defending *anything* in *Edward II*, the drama seems acutely attentive to the unavailability of what Goldberg calls a "self-integrative principle of identity," most particularly in the case of a desiring king. Marlowe's interest in a subjectivity under the pressure of conflicting demands aligns his play with the turn-of-the-century vogue of Senecan tragedy, or "closet drama." As we have seen in the instance of *The Tragedy of Mariam,* the ruminative, philosophical aspects of this genre reflect on the dilemmas of such competing discourses of responsibility as religion, family loyalties, ethics, gender roles, and political fealty. Closet drama's signature conundrum involves the private subject's position under tyrannical authority, often deliberating on the question of obedience to unjust laws. In these tragedies, the subject's "interiority" tends to be created by a violent psychological exile from the political, legal, or public sphere. Rarely taking up one side or the other, closet drama usually elucidates the dilemma situation. The Marlovian innovation here inverts these norms by focusing on the king's particular dilemma, tracking the effects of his public role and showing him, in effect, tyrannized by the impossible conjunction of private affect and royal duty. The interiority that Edward calls "the closet of my heart" (5.3.22) is the accidental effect of a torsion within the idea of kingship.

In juxtaposing the repeatedly invoked tropes of "spiritual" friendship with their contestation by Edward's enemies, Marlowe serves up a dilemma of perspective on the friendship question by directing a collision between these public and private meanings. Edward's condition as anointed king critically determines this dilemma. Since the principles of *amicitia* can only take effect as *mignonnerie* for Edward, his opting for friendship reads as an attempt to implement a private condition. The king wants to act like a private person by choosing exclusive, utopian friendship; his enemies, ironically, are those who want him to be a king.

In this clash, Marlowe pits the king's idealizing rhetoric for his relation to Gaveston against those of the barons, whose sense of *mignonnerie* is, not surprisingly, pejorative. All the "flower-strewn" language of twinning and merged economies of the self comes from the king. On their reunion, he exclaims to Gaveston, "Why shouldst thou kneel? Know'st thou not who I am? / Thy friend, thy self, another Gaveston" (1.1.141–42); at Gaveston's banishment he declares, "thou from this land, I from my self am banish'd" (1.4.118). Even after Gaveston has been killed, Edward maintains this doubled-soul language, referring to his "sweet favorite" as "my dearest friend, / To whom right well you knew our soul was knit" (3.3.41–42).

But while Edward speaks virtuous friendship's idiom, those around him consistently refer to Gaveston as the king's "minion." Even Mortimer Senior, who attempts to justify the king, citing Alexander, Hercules, Achilles, and even Socrates and Cicero as legitimating precedents, employs a decidedly unclassical term when he claims that kings will have their "minions" (1.4.400ff.). Edward cannot fathom the scorn in Mortimer's clipped, one-line observation that "the king is love-sick for his minion" (1.4.87). This king never specifically intends the scandal of *mignonnerie*. Unlike the calculating Hal, Edward never shows awareness of what proper sovereignty entails, nor does he complain of any alienation inscribed within that role.

Any king's effort to enact friendship according to its classically derived script, as I have just argued in theoretical terms, will look like *mignonnerie* so long as the king remains a king. In Edward's case, this becomes especially evident when he implements the friendship doctrine of communal property. From the start, Gaveston announces that Edward has proposed his sharing of "the kingdom with thy dearest friend" (1.1.1–2), a farming out of the realm that could not more blatantly signal a monarchical fault. But it does adhere precisely to the normative notion (from Cicero to Montaigne) of shared property in friendship: "Wants thou gold? Go to *my* treasury" (1.1.166), Edward advises Gaveston. Much has been made of this king's wrong, "personal" sense of absolutism in treating the royal treasury as his own. Here we see how friendship's doctrinal virtues direct this fall from kingly virtue.

"Soveraigne amitie" and ethical monarchy, as perfectly incompatible systems of propriety, demand precisely the opposite actions. After the favorite's banishment, Edward professes his willingness to exchange a king's revenue for him: "could my crown's revenue bring him back / I would freely give it . . . / And think I gained, having bought so dear a friend" (1.4.307–9).[19] The notion that a friend was worth more than a kingdom was proverbial; Montaigne, for example, recounts the anecdote of a soldier who would not swap his horse for a kingdom but would "willingly forgoe him to gaine a true friend" (p. 152). But for a private person to prefer a friend to a kingdom looks radically different from an anointed king's willingness to offer the kingdom (his public trust) to or on behalf of a private

19. As Mills points out ("The Meaning of *Edward II*," p. 180), Marlowe makes this point in *Tamburlaine,* part 1, in Tamburlaine's affirmation: "These are my friends in whom I more rejoice, / Than doth the King of Persea in his Crowne" (*Tamburlaine,* pt. 1, 1.2.436–7).

friend. *Edward II* makes clear that while this impulse might be proper as a subject's hypothetical declamation, it was not a king's prerogative.

A king's public trust subjects him to a different set of moral imperatives. When Edward is discovered literally sharing his throne with Gaveston (peopling it with two bodies), the barons spark with rage. Negotiating with them, Edward proposes that they

> Make several kingdoms of this monarchy
> And share it equally amongst you all,
> So I may have some nook or corner left
> To frolic with my dearest Gaveston.
>   (1.4.70–73)

Marlowe's language borders on parody here, for such a proposition exposes a reprehensible disregard for commonweal, as does the oxymoronic image of a frolicking king. Even the devastation of civil war fails to arouse this king's concern: "Do what they can, we'll live in Tynemouth here, / And so I walk with him about the walls, / What care I though the earls begirt us round?" (2.2.220–22) His taunt reveals this king's desire to inhabit a private world apart. The subtle extension of Ciceronian self-sufficiency into counterpolity takes on totally different implications voiced by Marlowe's Edward, whose all-enveloping interest in Gaveston echoes precisely the kind of separate, all-sufficient world of which friendship dreams. But such a gesture of withdrawal is always wrong on a king's part because he cannot recuse himself; its language is almost comic in a king's mouth. A minion presiding in the treasury and a king completely absorbed in some removed "nook or corner": what more inflammatory images could better dramatize the neglect and betrayal of political commonweal?

A king's very existence properly entailed attention to other "loves." As Mortimer Senior baldly phrases Edward's choice, "If you love us, my lord, hate Gaveston" (1.1.79). In the king's fleeting reconciliation (to his vocation, to his wife, and to the realm and its peers), proper monarchical love has its short-lived moment. Isabella, temporarily rejoined with Edward, exults, "now is the King of England rich and strong, / Having the love of his renowned peers," and Edward responds, "we will requite that love" (1.4.365–66, 382). These affirmations are not enough for the gloomy Mortimer, however, who lingers onstage to repeat his original complaint about improper friendship and improper monarchy: "that one so basely born / Should by his sovereign's favour grow so pert, / And riot it with treasure of the realm" (1.4.402–4). Here Mortimer's protest of the "pertness"

of a minion who solicits the prohibited "familiar" in a king echoes the counselors' protest we have seen Edward Hall record in Henry VIII's history.

As if Edward's opening of the national treasury to his friend's use were
not enough, his favoring of "one so basely born" makes him indifferent to
his royal estate but for its value in pleasing his favorite: "But to honor
[Gaveston] / Is Edward pleas'd with kingly regiment" (1.1.163–64). As it
becomes clear to him that "kingly regiment" interferes with his passionate attachment, he longs for retirement to a private condition in which
friendship would be possible. Fleeing from Mortimer's usurping forces and
hiding in a monastery with his "friends," Edward exclaims, "this life con-
templative is heaven— / O that I might this life in quiet lead! / But we
alas are chas'd" (4.6.20–21). Here Edward himself finally recognizes that
the effectively private capacity of friendship—and the zone of exile it demands—cannot be his.

The king must accept either his office or death. In equating the self
with the friend ("Comes Leicester . . . / To take my life, my company from
me?" [4.6.64–65]), Edward once more invokes a privilege only available
across the divide he finally perceives between himself and "private men"
(5.1.8). When Mortimer's men wash the king in ditch water, lowering him
beneath even the lowborn friend he tried to elevate, he admits,

> O Gaveston, it is for thee that I am wronged.
> For me, both thou and both the Spencers died;
> And for your sakes, a thousand wrongs I'll take . . .
>   for them I'll die.
>
> (5.3.41–43, 45)

Edward's embrace of friendship, as *mignonnerie,* precipitates a royal demise
in its fullest sense, for he is stripped of both his estate and his life—killed
off in *both* of "the king's two bodies."

Friendship Parties in *The Henriad*

As Mills proposed of *Edward II* in 1934, so I propose that *The Henriad*
can be read "as a friendship play" and not just "as a chronicle history."[20]
Informing the plays of Shakespeare's second tetralogy, we find the ethics
of ideal friendship, the seditious character of its monstrous case in a rebel
conspiracy, and the collision of *mignonnerie* with ethical monarchy. That

---

20. Mills, "The Meaning of *Edward II*," p. 29.

constellation, together with the truly enormous number of references to friends and companions in the plays (for the two parts of *Henry IV,* a concordance lists seventy-seven instances of variations upon "friend" and "companion"),[21] suggests that they should certainly be counted as "friendship plays" in the Shakespearean canon along with the more obvious *The Two Gentlemen of Verona* (1594), *The Merchant of Venice* (1597), and *The Two Noble Kinsmen* (1613). But the plays' treatment of friendship subjects the "flower-strewn" model to enormous pressure, even skepticism. Whereas, for Mills's purposes, a friendship-centered approach meant an alternative to focusing on statecraft or kingship, *Henry IV* (one play in two bodies) indicates rather the degree to which friendship discourses actually constitute kingliness—not as a model to be followed, as advice books to princes had argued, but as a practice for sovereigns to eschew. At stake in this royal turning from amity is a mode of imagining the parties to national polity.

In *Henry IV* the collision of *mignonnerie* (as improper friendship across disparity of rank) with sovereignty (as a cancellation of royal affect driven by "personal" desires) takes a strikingly different form than it did in *Edward II,* and the implications of this difference for polity are far-reaching. Instead of unkinging the king, *mignonnerie* appears in *Henry IV* as a part of the dissembling Prince Hal's own stagecraft, as he deploys it as his notorious (false) threat to his becoming a proper king. The threat is powerful because *mignonnerie* bears such an insidious relation to the national treasury and the commonweal, but the threat is contained because it is always only just that. At the same time, the plays situate Hal's fiction within an array of friendship forms that carefully encircle and exclude monarchical being. On one side of the solitary monarch is the alliance of "friends" who band together in rebellion; on the other is the emphatically "merry," convivial world of Falstaff and company. These two spheres are alike in emphasizing "friendly" association and in linking it to the furtherance of particularly "private" (here, politically improper) interests. Both kinds of interest clash, politically and affectively, with the solitary burden of monarchy and its proper orientation to the public good.

The bipartite nature of *Henry IV* has traditionally raised literary questions about its heterogeneity. Are they separate plays or a single one? Do the high and low plots stray too far apart? Is the mix of comedy and trag-

---

21. Marvin Spevack, *A Complete and Systematic Concordance to the Works of Shakespeare* (Hildesheim: Georg Olms, 1968) in nine volumes, vol. 2.

edy an unhappy one? Assessing the workings of friendship across this mix suggests that the dispensations in such a heterogeneity constitute a political vision in itself. The moral implications and affective economies of friendship circulate across the boundaries of the double-bodied *Henry IV,* and they have a fundamental place in the incommensurate pictures of the public monarch and the private self that Shakespeare's text offers. But Shakespeare's vision implies that these structures require certain reversals of expectation about friendship as truthful speech and genuine affect. These reversals have provocative implications for the general state of polity: the sovereign prince in this friendship play employs the *falsity* usually allocated to the minion as parasite; the prince and not the minion betrays his over-fond partner; and the prince's allegedly dangerous companion, as a "be-witched" "friend and a *true* subject," takes on an infinite vulnerability. This capacity for personal love, in turn, is finally assigned to and contained within an elsewhere of private life. The threat to sovereignty posed by *mignonnerie* is "a foil to set . . . off" (*2HIV,* 1.2.203) the "restoration" of proper associative relations legitimating Hal's regime.

The perspective offered here departs from a common critical tendency to view Hal in individual or developmental terms, extending from an idealizing "royalism"[22] that stresses political maturation to a psychoanalytic approach, describing Hal as a "prototypical male subject" in a "narrative of psychic development."[23] Such readings, whether celebratory or critical, frequently view Hal's "development" as an accrual of power, knowledge, (prudence) and selfhood.[24] Within a developmental view of Hal, Falstaff must be read in quasi-allegorical terms, though representing, in the words of John Dover Wilson, "a composite myth which had been centuries amaking."[25] So Falstaff has been seen, whether positively or negatively, to represent many things within a narrative about Hal: from Vice, Riot, and

---

22. So William Empson describes John Dover Wilson in "Falstaff and Mr. Dover Wilson," *The Kenyon Review* 15 (spring 1953): 213–62, 220. Their partisanship about the plays' hero obscures the ways Hal and Falstaff's differentiation as well as their ultimate distantiated relation are suggested.

23. Valerie Traub, *Desire and Anxiety: Circulations of Sexuality in Shakespearian Drama* (New York: Routledge, 1992), pp. 50–51.

24. E. M. W. Tillyard (*Shakespeare's History Plays* [London: Chatto & Windus, 1944], pp. 264–80) represents an antidevelopmental view, very correctly noting the absence of "mental conflict" in "Shakespeare's studied picture of the kingly type" (pp. 268–69).

25. John Dover Wilson, "The Falstaff Myth," in *Henry IV: Critical Essays,* ed. David Bevington (New York: Garland Press, 1986), pp. 117–38, 120.

Misrule[26] to childish regression,[27] alternative fatherhood,[28] the repressed
maternal body,[29] and sodomitical desire.[30] Falstaff variously appears as an
obstacle to be cast off, a catalyst, or a tutor or guide for Hal. At stake in
these determinations is what Hal's final "repudiation" of Falstaff means,
and the readings are similarly diverse: it shows a foregone conclusion,[31]
a necessary development,[32] a plot spinning out of control,[33] a moral or
human deficit in the prince,[34] a religious conversion,[35] or the restoration
of orthodoxy.[36] Considering these matters from friendship's perspective,
however, stresses the plays as a story of polity in two persons, a mytho-
graphic account of polity's founding moment as a joint *establishment* of
the public body and *relocation* of Falstaff and all he represents. The capacities attaching to private and to public personages now find themselves
physically distributed across the geographic spaces that start as exile and
will, perhaps, become "spheres."

Reading the relationship of friendship and monarchy has the further
interest of engaging directly with the identities so insistently given to Hal
and Falstaff in the plays. Beyond appearing as a "prototypical male subject," Hal appears as different in kind from all other (male) subjects. Hal
is always the Heir Apparent and the "true prince"; Falstaff names himself
"the prince's companion" and a "friend and a true subject." The protocols
of friendship in *Henry IV* centrally calibrate the plays' construction of

26. C. L. Barber, *Shakespeare's Festive Comedy: A Study of Dramatic Form and Its Relation to Social Custom* (Princeton, N.J.: Princeton University Press, 1959), pp. 192–221.

27. W. H. Auden, "The Prince's Dog," in *The Dyer's Hand and Other Essays* (New
York: Random House, 1948), pp. 182–208, 195.

28. Coppelia Kahn, *Man's Estate: Masculine Identity in Shakespeare* (Berkeley and Los
Angeles: University of California Press, 1981), pp. 48–81.

29. According to Traub (*Desire and Anxiety,* p. 550): "Falstaff represents to Hal not an
alternative paternal image but rather a projected fantasy of the pre-oedipal maternal, whose
rejection is the basis upon which patriarchal subjectivity is found." Janet Adelman, considering the absence of the mother rather than her central presence as a repression, sees Falstaff
as an alternative father in *Suffocating Mothers: Fantasies of Maternal Origin in Shakespeare's
Plays, Hamlet to the Tempest* (New York: Routledge, 1992), pp. 11–12.

30. Goldberg, *Sodometries,* pp. 145–75.

31. Tillyard, *Shakespeare's History Plays,* pp. 268–69.

32. Dover Wilson, "The Falstaff Myth," p. 122.

33. A. C. Bradley, "The Rejection of Falstaff," *Oxford Lectures on Poetry* (London:
Macmillan, 1909), pp. 247–73.

34. Jonas Barish, "The Turning Away of Prince Hal," *Shakespeare Studies* 1 (1965):
9–17.

35. J. A. Bryant, "Prince Hal and the Ephesians," *Sewanee Review* 67 (1959): 204–19.

36. Barber, *Shakespeare's Festive Comedy,* p. 217.

sovereign and subject; friendship's relative availability highlights the disparity between these categories of personage. The vantage of friendship also discloses a narrative in which Hal and Falstaff are equally crucial in their ultimate separation from each other in a final picture of "proper" political categories. Friendship's ultimate place in the diverging domains of sovereign and subject highlights the dynamics of polity—both at its institution and in its ongoing operation. For it is *polity* that actually *begins* at the end of part 2, at the very moment and in the very gesture criticism has considered an end to the engagement of Prince Hal and Falstaff.

Improper Friendship's Proper Places

Many critics have commented on *Henry IV*'s mixture of genres. C. L. Barber emphasizes Sidney's description of contemporary playwriting in *The Defense of Poesie:* they are "neither right comedies nor right tragedies, mingling kings and clowns."[37] W. H. Auden observes that "the world of historical reality which a Chronicle Play claims to imitate is not a world which [Falstaff] can inhabit."[38] Another perspective zeroes in on the double plot structure. William Empson, for example, argues that "the double plot method is carrying a fearful strain" at critical moments in the play.[39] Friendship urges another description of this heterogeneity, in terms of three domains distinguishable by the associative rules presiding within them. On the one hand is the world of treasonous rebellion, where conspirators repeatedly style themselves by the name "friend." On the other hand is Falstaff's sphere, centered on the enjoyment of company, whether in petty plotting or in carousing in a "good fellowship" that he rightly says Hal lacks (*1HIV,* 1.2.130–31). Against both of these networks of association, and directly threatened by them, stands solitary monarchy. Here, King Henry IV appears alone and speaks in soliloquy, facing treasonous overthrow; here, Hal keeps his own counsel and shams capture by *mignonnerie.* This associative typology organizes the arguably disparate realms of the plays, realms that in themselves actually thematize the very issue of "mingling kings and clowns."

Under the pressure of such politics, the tattered residue of Montaigne's twinned soul model appears as a lonely speech in which Falstaff laments a relationship between the prince and Poins. Falstaff regards them with sad

37. Ibid., p. 195.
38. Auden, "The Prince's Dog," p. 183.
39. William Empson, *Some Versions of Pastoral* (New York: New Directions, 1974), p. 46.

jealousy, treating likeness and identity ironically in terms of slightness of *weight*—a standard by which he is further excluded. The prince, he speculates, loves Poins "because their legs are both of a bigness . . . and such other . . . faculties as 'a has, that show a weak mind and an able body, for which the prince admits him. For the prince himself is just such another; the weight of a hair will turn the scales between their avoirdupois" (*2HIV,* 2.4.227, 231–37). On the heels of this speech, Poins and the prince arrive together in disguise, but Falstaff hails them at once: "Ha! A bastard son of the king's? And art not thou Poins his brother?" (*2HIV,* 2.4.264–66) The balance of the plays' friendship vocabulary, however, leaves "flower-strewn," classically derived models far behind. Friendship's register instead is laden with implications of *mignonnerie,* influence, partisanship, and rebellious alliance.

The parties to the "noble plot" (*1HIV,* 1.3.276) refer to their "confederacy" (*1HIV,* 5.4.38) in the nomenclature of friendship. Hotspur upbraids the writer of a letter warning him of the risks of rebellion: "What a lackbrain is this! By the Lord, our plot is a good plot as ever was laid; our friends true and constant: a good plot, good friends, and full of expectation; an excellent plot, very good friends" (*1HIV,* 2.3.14–17). The repeated interlocking of "friends" and "plot" associates friendship with seditious conspiracy. Members of the rebel compact address one another as "noble friends" (*2HIV,* 1.3.2), and "my friends and brethren in these great affairs" (*2HIV,* 4.1.6). The Archbishop of York seeks to expand the conspirators' circle with "I must go write . . . / To other friends" (*1HIV,* 4.4.40–41). Rallying with "Let order die," Northumberland urges, "get posts and letters, and make friends with speed. / Never so few, and never yet more need" (*2HIV,* 1.1.214–15). Worcester even presumes to instruct the king in friendship, proposing that his failures precipitated civil war. In doing so, he sees friendship as a partisanship that encompasses unlawfulness: "It pleased your majesty to turn your looks / Of favor from myself and all our house; / And yet I must remember you, my lord, / We were the first and dearest of your friends. / For you *my staff of office did I break* in Richard's time" (*1HIV,* 5.1.30–35, emphasis mine). Though the rebels may wave the banner of commonweal (for example, *1HIV,* 4.3.79–80), it is clear their rebellion stems from their own loss of royal favor. According to Worcester, the king had begun "to make us strangers to his looks of love" (*1HIV,* 1.3.287).

Falstaff, too, plays the part of a friendship commentator. In the midst of the robbery plot, when he realizes he is the object of a secondary intrigue, he exclaims, "A plague upon it when thieves cannot be true to one another!" (*1HIV*, 2.2.26–27) When the prince and Poins improvise on the plan and steal the stolen money from Falstaff, he accuses them: "You are straight enough in the shoulders; you care not who sees your back. Call you that the backing of your friends? A plague upon such backing! Give me them that will face me" (*1HIV*, 2.4.139–42). Falstaff's advocacy of loyalty in friendship finds further expression at Shrewsbury. Alone briefly with the prince, Falstaff says, "Hal, if thou see me down in battle and bestride me, so! 'Tis a point of friendship." Hal answers, "Nothing but a colossus can do thee that friendship. Say thy prayers and farewell" (*1HIV*, 5.1.121–24). Exalted friendship is reduced to the opposite against which its idealizing rhetoric strove throughout the sixteenth century: a mere "backing" in the name of particular interests.

In his insistence upon friendship principles (even if among thieves) as well as in his own general impulse toward company, Falstaff represents friendship as desire, as an affectively driven bond. As Auden writes, "it is Hal's company he wants, not [or at least not primarily] a pension from the Civil List." [40] Falstaff, not unlike Edward II, has a passion for friendship, a tendency to be "bewitched." Even as Poins plays a practical joke on him, Falstaff proclaims, "I have foresworn his company hourly any time this two-and-twenty years"; despite knowing better, he admits, "I am be-witched with the rogue's company. If the rascal have not given me medi-cines to make me love him, I'll be hanged. It could not be else: I have drunk medicines. Poins! Hal!" (*1HIV*, 2.2.15–19) His case with Hal is the same. "Bewitched by the rogue's company," Falstaff is truly a "desiring subject."

Upon news of Hal's coronation, Falstaff and company race off to London to attend him. Falstaff breathlessly assures himself that his dusty traveller's condition will recommend him to the new king:

This doth infer the zeal I had to see him. . . . It shows the earnestness of my affection— . . . my devotion— . . . As it were to ride day and night, and not to deliberate, not to remember, not to have patience to shift me— . . . But to stand stained with travel, and sweating with desire to see him, thinking of nothing else, putting all affairs else in oblivion. (*2HIV*, 5.5.13–27)

When Hal appears as Henry V, Falstaff passionately hails him as "My King! My Jove! I speak to thee, my heart!" (line 47) This address encompasses a whirling blend of relational languages. It descends from the absolute othernesses of king and "Jove" to "my heart," a compressed figure of iden-

40. Auden, "The Prince's Dog," p. 190.

tity that phrases Hal as the "other self" familiar from utopian idealizations of friendship. The address struggles to enclose the most extreme degree of difference with the most extreme possibility of identity, in the passionate moment when Falstaff seeks to be acknowledged.

Falstaff's understanding of friendship as a passionate affection that plays favorites and the traitors' version of friendship as rebellion operate at the direct expense of the commonweal. Falstaff's band of robbers set upon money due to the king: Gadshill calls out, "on with your vizards! There's money of the King's coming down the hill; 'tis going to the king's exchequer" (*1HIV,* 2.2.49–51). These plotters proceed against the public trust. The rebels' conduct is parallel. Not only do the rebel friends falsely invoke the name of commonweal, and not only do they commit treason in the name of self-interest, they also prepare to divide the realm among themselves. Cutting off other "unprofitable chat" (*1HIV,* 3.1.63), Hotspur, Glendower, and Mortimer literally carve the map by "indentures tripartite" (line 80), severing it "into three limits very equally" (line 73). Irritable Hotspur immediately quibbles that his "moiety . . . / In quantity equals not one of" the others', and they proceed to fight over diverting a river (*1HIV,* 3.2.96–97, 98–119). They are prepared to rend the body of the realm for their own private interest. The nobles "pray continually to their saint, the commonwealth, or rather, not pray to her, but prey on her" *(1HIV,* 2.1.76–78). "Friendship" in these settings is linked to a privileging of private over general interests—in other words, "interestedness"—as a form of parasitism upon the commonweal.

Friendship also circumvents the law in the dramas. The rebel friends' treasonous compact is a dramatic instance, but unlawfulness crops up in the low plot also. Falstaff approvingly witnesses the small-time, underhanded effects of friendship on a quotidian level. During Falstaff's visit to Master Shallow, a local justice of the peace in Gloucestershire, one Davy visits the justice to seek influence in a pending lawsuit against his friend. Shallow says Davy's friend is "an arrant knave, on my knowledge," but Davy responds that even "a knave should have some countenance at his friend's request . . . if I cannot . . . bear out a knave against an honest man, I have but very little credit with your worship. The knave is my honest friend, sir" (*2HIV,* 5.1.37, 39–44). One need not, in this scheme, be an "honest man" to be an "honest friend," *pace* Aristotle and Cicero.

Rereading the Solitary Hal

While the modalities of friendship in the realms of rebellion and the tavern are strongly implicated in private interests and partisan "backing,"

Hal's own engagement with the friendship relation remains to be considered. Critics may differ on whether Hal spends time with Falstaff because of friendship and love or because Falstaff entertains him while he bides his time, but they generally agree that there is warm affection *between* them. While there may be some textual support for this, there appears to be even greater support for an ironic distance that often rises to the level of abuse. The comic quality of this conduct need not occlude its cruelty. Perhaps the witty virtuosity of the Hal-Falstaff exchanges also makes it easier to gloss over the implications of the baldly stated plot Hal announces alone onstage in act 1 of part 1. This more-than-familiar soliloquy displays a haughty distance from Falstaff and company and a plot that explicitly instrumentalizes them in Hal's own secret campaign:

> I know you all . . .
> herein will I imitate the sun,
> Who doth permit the base contagious clouds
> To smother up his beauty from the world,
> That when he please again to be himself,
> Being wanted, he may be more wondered at
> By breaking through the foul and ugly mists
>
> . . . .
> By so much shall I falsify men's hopes;
> And . . .
> My reformation glittering o'er my fault,
> Shall show more goodly.
>
> (*1HIV,* 1.2.183 – 02)

These lines, so often invoked to show Hal's original intent to conform to princeliness, must also be assessed for their less glorious implications about his friendship with Falstaff. While it is often noted that Hal's prodigal period does not include any really bad acts (robbing Falstaff of stolen money and returning it to the victim can hardly be bad—indeed, it is "princely"), the soliloquy makes clear that the "offending" thing is his association. Hal's plan is to *seem* to embrace *mignonnerie* as a form of specifically royal misbehavior. In "falsifying" this threat, Hal appears to thwart the system of degree he is supposed to represent.

With this speech, Hal announces that, though only "Heir Apparent," he is already functioning in a kingly mode; already acting like the singular "sun," though his father still lives. For Hal is alone and self-contained, not only onstage, but in knowledge. His dissimulation is perfectly convincing to the world. The king considers Hal so worthless he would swap sons to be Hotspur's father instead; Hal's enemies do not fear him because they are

convinced of his folly; and the king's councillors fear that "all will be over-
turned" and that "nobles" shall have to "strike sail to spirits of vile sort"
under Hal's regime (*2HIV,* 5.2.19, 17–18). Falstaff, as Auden poignantly
assesses it, "believes" this fiction; he "believes that his love is returned, that
the Prince is his other self."[41] Hal is thus alone as any dissembler is alone
even in company, in a solitude the plays propose is proper to a king and in
which the technique of dissimulation is essential.

Hal's dissimulation of *mignonnerie* raises the banner of impropriety
from his very first appearance with Falstaff. Here Falstaff uses markedly indecorous familiarities with the Heir Apparent. He addresses him as "Hal,"
"lad," and repeatedly as "sweet wag" (*1HIV,* 1.2.1, 15, 21). In *Of Domesticall Duties,* William Gouge argues that husbands better maintain their
authority over wives by forbidding them to use diminutives or nicknames.
Gouge refers the reader to these rules about wives to instruct how masters
and servants should likewise employ proper forms of address in order to
preserve hierarchy.[42] Thus these first lines indicate Falstaff's improper
abandonment of the formalities of hierarchy for a "merry" familiarity.

Falstaff continues to imagine—though importantly in the placeless
hortatory subjunctive—the fabulous world of *mignonnerie* as a political regime of friendship ahead of him:

> Marry then, sweet wag, when thou art king, let us not that are squires of
> the night's body be called thieves of the day's beauty. Let us be Diana's
> foresters, gentlemen of the shade, minions of the moon; and let men say
> we be men of good government, being governed as the sea is, by our
> noble and chaste mistress the moon. (*1HIV,* 1.2.21–27)

The high artifice confounding day and night; the oxymoronic concept of
"gentlemen" of the "shade"; and the valiant reconfiguration of the inconstant moon as the mistress of a "good government" more properly helio-
centric—these all converge to raise the specter of alternative governance
and inverted rule. "Squires of the night's body" may evoke those minions
of Henry VIII, who constituted the early form of "the king's body service."
In proposing foresters, shadow, the moon, and the sea as somehow related
to "good government," Falstaff gives a first resonant example of what the
Chief Justice will later call his "manner of wrenching the true cause the
false way" (*2HIV,* 2.1.105–6).[43] In this way, Falstaff represents "misrule"

41. Ibid., p. 191.
42. William Gouge, *Of Domesticall Duties* (London: John Haviland and William
Bladen, 1622), pp. 282–83, 596–99.
43. See Goldberg's notion of "preposterousness" in *Sodometries,* passim.

not in himself, as an alternative ruler, but as a party to a *mignonnerie* that may capture the "proper" king.

Hal raises the stakes of his game when he proposes they extemporize a dialogue between the prince and his father. Falstaff's playing the part of the king suggests an inversion of order and degree: he "stands for" the king and pointedly introduces his Euphuistic royal performance with "Stand aside, nobility!" (*1HIV*, 2.4.358, 371) Falstaff proceeds "like one of these harlotry players" (lines 377–78) to impersonate royalty, and the first fault he finds with Hal relates directly to his associations: "Harry, I do not only marvel where thou spendest thy time, but also how thou art accompanied . . . pitch . . . doth defile; so doth the company thou keepest" (lines 380–81). Both the phrasing and the theme of defiling contact will be exactly taken up by the real Henry IV later in the drama.

Typically, Falstaff cannot stay "in character" or untrue to his persistent self. When he begins to speak in his own behalf, Hal "deposes" him (line 413) and plays the king himself. In that "guise," he argues an orthodox position against "converse" and companionship with "a devil . . . in the likeness of an old fat man" (lines 425–27), taking off on a long streak of abusive name-calling. When Falstaff again breaks character to defend himself, both "players" in the play are no longer playing, and ironically *this* theatrical improvisation supports, rather than undermines, the system of order and degree. Falstaff's impassioned self-defense, often quoted to show its generalized meaning ("Banish plump Jack, and banish all the world!") is first and foremost a personal plea:

> Banish Peto, banish Bardolph, banish Poins; but for sweet Jack Falstaff, kind Jack Falstaff, true Jack Falstaff, valiant Jack Falstaff, and therefore more valiant, being, as he is, old Jack Falstaff, banish him not thy Harry's company, banish him not thy Harry's company. (*1HIV*, 2.4.451–56)

In addition to his passion for company, Falstaff certainly expects the personal benefits that would presumably accrue to a future king's minion: "Rob me the exchequer the first thing thou doest, and do it with unwashed hands too" (*1HIV*, 3.3.175–76). The fat knight not only expects access to the public treasury, he also expects to be above law and to subvert law to his personal use. Upon hearing of Hal's accession, Falstaff plans to ride all night to London, crying, "Let us take any man's horses; the laws of England are at my commandment. Blessed are they that have been my friends, and woe to the lord chief justice!" (*2HIV*, 5.3.132–35) In Falstaff's enchanted picture of a minion's benefits, he pictures himself presiding over treasury and law, but also over a king as subjugated to passionate friendship as Ed-

ward II, who was "love-sick for his minion." Full of confidence, he exclaims, "I know the young king is sick for me" (lines 131–32).

Of course, this king is not lovesick, nor was he lovesick as a prince.
Though Hal has misled the Chief Justice into believing that Falstaff was
the prince's misleader (*2HIV,* 1.2.137), Falstaff is strictly correct when he
corrects the Justice with "The young prince hath misled me" (line 139).
What is ambiguous here is that while the primary sense of "misled" is to
have been led astray *morally,* the layers of Hal's regal deceptiveness mislead
others about the facts of his intentions or his emotions. Tillyard points
out the degree to which Hal has refined his dissembling skill, "relish[ing]
the ironic act of telling the truth in the assurance that he will thereby deceive."[44] In general, through the course of the dramas, in Barber's words,
"it is essential . . . that the prince should be misconstrued."[45] His sham
mignonnerie has fully fooled his father, who seeks "some private conference" (*1HIV,* 3.2.2) with his seemingly prodigal son. The powerful double
image of the two royal figures alone together serves as an occasion for discussing kingliness and what it comprises. In his speech to the straying
prince, Henry IV links vertical association to the cancellation of princely
status.

The king's address to his son perfectly echoes Falstaff's ventriloquized
"pitch doth defile" speech, while it expands into an analysis of how association across hierarchy transforms royal personhood and brings about its
demise. He urges Hal that "thou hast lost thy princely privilege / With vile
participation" (*1HIV,* 3.2.87). The king wonders whether he is being punished for his own "mistreadings" in the actions of his son, wondering how
else "such rude society, / As thou art matched withal and grafted to" could
"accompany the greatness of thy blood / And hold their level with thy
princely heart" (lines 14–17). He wonders how his son could possess
"affections" that alienate him from "court" and "blood" (lines 30–35), and
he describes how his own strict self-constraint and distance better served
"presence" and "state" (lines 56–57). This description of royal failure
echoes Sidney's disapproving view of "mingling kings and clowns":
Richard II "carded [mixed] his state; / Mingled his royalty with capering
fools; / Had his great name profaned . . . / . . . / Grew companion to the
common streets, / Enfeoffed him to popularity" (lines 62–63, 68–69).
The essence of royalty, in Henry IV's view, lies in preserving lofty distance.
The relation of the king's natural body to the body politic it was to repre-

---

44. Tillyard, *Shakespeare's History Plays,* p. 272.
45. Barber, *Shakespeare's Festive Comedy,* p. 196.

sent, then, is an abstract relation destroyed by too much literal or physical mingling between prince and people.

This sense of friendship as a proximity that defiles appears at every level of the plays' world. Falstaff had initiated this argument in his "pitch doth defile" speech as Henry IV; in the scene following Henry IV's lecture on the corrosive effects of "vile participation," Falstaff sounds the theme again: "Company, villainous company, hath been the spoil of me" (*1HIV*, 3.3.9–10). This is the point also of the Hostess's tale of being brought before the law:

> I was before Master Tisick, the debuty, . . . and, as he said to me, "I' good faith, neighbor Quickly," says he, "receive those that are civil, for," said he, "you are in an ill name." . . . "For," said he, "you are an honest woman, and well thought on; therefore take heed what guests you receive. Receive," says he, "no swaggering companions." (*2HIV*, 2.4.78–87)

Falstaff revisits this issue of companionship's effects in his commentary on the provincial world of Justice Shallow, reckoning it, too, as a structure of contagion. He observes that "their spirits are so married in conjunction with participation of society that they flock together in consent. . . . It is certain that either wise or ignorant carriage is caught, as men take diseases, one of another. Therefore let men take heed of their company" (*2HIV*, 5.1.62–64, 68–71). While the idea of defiling companions spans the dramas' social hierarchy, such defilement in the low plot involves a transformation in morals or character. At the level of royalty, the transformation is acute enough to trigger an ontological problem. In the words of Henry IV, the cost of "vile participation" is "princely privilege."

In Henry IV's conversation on princeliness with his son, Hal assures him not that he will change, but that he will "hereafter . . . / Be more himself" (*1HIV*, 3.2.92–93). Despite Hal's assurance and in light of his ongoing associations, Henry remains concerned throughout part 2. As Falstaff, in the person of the king, had wondered "How thou art accompanied" (*1HIV*, 2.4.381), so does Henry continue to inquire about his son's friends. Toward the end of the play, the ailing king dreads his son's imminent reign and discusses the prospects with his nobles and younger sons. First he asks the duke of Gloucester, "Where is the prince your brother? / . . . / And how accompanied?" (*2HIV*, 4.4.13, 15) Henry IV then embarks on the theme of brotherhood and outlines a wished-for sense of brotherly conduct among his sons. The king then asks his other son "why art thou not . . . with him?" and when told the prince is at London, he asks again, "And how accompanied?" (lines 50, 52) As the king's health worsens, concern over the prince's company becomes more pressing. This time he gets an answer: "With Poins and his continual followers" (line 53)—Poins, whom Falstaff has named in jealous irony "the prince's brother."

Criticism never considers Poins in his specificity, tacitly agreeing, perhaps, that "Poins is presumably as tiny and insignificant as a point."[46] Poins, however, has to be important in light of the dramas' concern with the shaping influence of those proximate to the prince. For while attention has been directed to the relationship between Hal and Falstaff, the dramatic action consistently places Poins closer to the prince, as Falstaff's disappointment shows. If Falstaff is set up as the show companion in Hal's defiling *mignonnerie*, the critically underestimated Poins really inhabits the space "near about the prince."

In contrast with the taunts Hal gives Falstaff in their first dialogue, he shifts to a tone of pleasant greeting when Poins enters: "Good morrow, Ned" (*1HIV*, 1.2.104). Poins then proposes the Gadshill robbery. When Hal demurs, Poins says to Falstaff, "Sir John, I prithee, leave the prince and me alone" (line 138). Poins, like Henry IV, can procure time alone with Hal by simple request, as the king similarly does later with "Lords, give us leave; The Prince of Wales and I / Must have some private conference" (*1HIV*, 3.2.1–2). The two secretly converse. Poins proposes they trick Falstaff, setting upon him in disguises after he has robbed the travellers. Poins addresses Hal with "sirrah," a form more decorously applied to one's social inferiors. In the execution of their secret plan, Hal and Poins communicate in asides ("Ned, where are our disguises? / Here, hard by. Stand close," and "stand close! I hear them coming" [*1HIV*, 2.2.69, 70, 89]). So Hal and Poins effect their own conspiracies.

This is not the last time Poins and the prince will "stand close," nor is it the last time they will operate under cover of disguise. Later in the act, the two enter together and Hal brags of prodigious offstage drinking. He claims, "I tell thee Ned, thou hast lost much honor that thou wert not with me in this action" (*1HIV*, 2.4.18–19).[47] This time Hal proposes a silly and even uncharitable jest to be executed by the pair. They proceed to overwhelm the tapster by multiplying their demands for drink, with the stage directions providing that "the drawer stands amazed" (after l.76). In part 2, this collaboration continues. After Falstaff warns Hal by letter to "be not

46. Murray J. Levith, *What's in Shakespeare's Names* (Hampden: Archon Books, 1978), p. 38.

47. In *Henry V*, in his battle address, Hal will similarly argue, "he to-day that sheds his blood with me / Shall be my brother . . . / . . . / And gentlemen in England now abed / Shall think themselves accursed they were not here" (*Henry V*, 4.3.61–63, 64–65).

too familiar with Poins," Hal and Poins decide to spy on his conduct in Eastcheap with Mistress Quickly and Doll Tearsheet. They agree to disguise themselves as drawers and wait on Falstaff's table. The prince's own observations express the shape-shifting implications of his multiply masked identity: "From a god to a bull? A heavy descension! It was Jove's case. From a prince to a prentice? A low transformation! That shall be mine, for in everything, the purpose must weigh with the folly. Follow me, Ned" (*2HIV*, 2.2.162–65). Analogizing a prince to a god, Hal's Ovidian reflections dramatize his feigned degeneration. His "low transformation" in petty plotting and inferior company is a "folly" attendant on his "purpose."

The prince proceeds to reflect on his association with Poins in an exchange that links hierarchical affection, human vulnerability, and weariness to a default of princely blood and being, wondering whether "belike . . . my appetite was not princely got" (*2HIV*, 2.2.9). While, from Poins's perspective, royal blood would treat simple troubles as trifles beneath a prince's notice, the prince suggests another kind of problem. Hal claims that he grieves over his father's ill health, but that his pretense of being enthralled to *mignonnerie* prevents him from plausibly expressing it. When the prince confesses weariness, too, Poins responds, "I had thought weariness durst not have attached one of so high a blood" (lines 2–3). Hal considers that "it discolors the complexion of my greatness to acknowledge it" (lines 4–5). When Hal asks, "Doth it not show vilely in me," Poins reprimands him that his expressions are unbecoming of a prince (lines 5–8).

Subsequently, the trifle that wrongly engages the prince shifts from the "small beer" of ordinary emotions like sorrow and tiredness to Poins himself: "What a disgrace it is to me to remember thy name! Or to know thy face to-morrow! Or to take note how many pair of silk stockings thou hast, viz. these, and those that were thy peach-colored ones! Or to bear the inventory of thy shirts" (lines 12–17). These lines reflect the closeness of living together and its intimate knowledges. Hal goes on to argue that his improper association with "vile company" renders his true expressions about his father unbelievable, making him seem "a most princely hypocrite" (line 50). In this reflective conversation, Hal not only actually names Poins as his "friend"; he also behaves in the friendship mode of truthful speech and honest confession. This is only possible, however, because Hal has created a situation in which his truths are unhearable—Poins is astonished that the prince "should talk so idly" (line 28). Ironically, the prince's idle talk is true. He admits to Poins that although "it is not meet . . . I could tell thee, as to one it pleases me, for fault of a better, to call my friend, I could be sad" (lines 36–39). The prince speaks to Poins with poignant directness here, and his speech has an honesty reminiscent of his opening soliloquy. Poins, whom Falstaff has called the prince's "brother" and Hal has called a "friend," is never assimilated at the close of the play; neither repudiated nor retained, he simply disappears.

Poins is not the only disappearing character whom the prince styles his friend. Hal announces, "I am . . . friends with my father" (*1HIV,* 3.3.174–75). This "friendship" indicates a likeness based on something more than lineal descent. In *Man's Estate,* Coppelia Kahn emphasizes the similarity between Henry IV and Henry V. To do so, Kahn points out the structural and thematic parallels of the two soliloquies in part 2, seeing Henry's famous "uneasy lies the head that wears the crown" speech and Hal's soliloquy addressing the crown as revealing likeness, paternity, and identity between father and son.[48] While this is undeniable, the cause of such identity, and indeed the subject of the two speeches, is the ideological construct of lonely, other-directed, and singularly burdened *monarchical* being, whether Lancastrian or otherwise. Royal identity generates the likeness or "friendship" between the pair more than the generic fact of paternity. Like the phoenix so often used to symbolize the generativity and longevity of monarchy, Hal is to Henry an *alius idem.*

In the world of *Henry IV,* the king and the Heir Apparent coexist uneasily, in a circumstantial dilemma that escapes expression in the phoenix metaphor. Hal's status as Heir Apparent is repeatedly invoked. As I have argued earlier, he shows himself throughout to be performing in a royal, solitary fashion. Hal is "ready" to be king, in terms of nature or competence, from the beginning, but the position of Heir Apparent is an anomalous one. Proximate to the crown, the heir disturbs it—Henry IV reflects upon this ominous power when he fears Hal might join the revolt against him (*1HIV,* 3.2.125–28).[49] Though Hal is far from such a rebellion, part 2 dramatizes the instability of a *pair* of phoenixes, in the scenes where, believing his father already dead, Hal takes up the crown and crowns himself (*2HIV,* 4.5.42). His father revives after Hal has left the chamber, and sees this action as one more frivolous act by a reprobate son. In their reconciliation, Hal assures his father that he had not desired the crown, but had reproached it. Shakespeare suggests the uneasy severability of sovereignty and person here, as the crown and the estate royal appear to float between the two Henries.

48. Kahn, *Man's Estate,* p. 76.
49. Elizabeth I often reflected on the dangers of being or designating a "second person."

Hal's self-crowning highlights the almost mystical ambiguities surrounding the transfer of sovereignty. Does he mistake his time or does he
break the law? When the moment passes, Hal enjoys an ironclad sovereignty, as is clear from his final exchanges with the Chief Justice. The Justice defends his earlier imprisonment of the young prince by a theory that
law and crown, as "the image of the King [he then] represented," super-
seded blood and "the immediate heir of England" (*2HIV*, 5.2.79, 71).
Hal's ready acceptance of the preeminence of law recognizes and affirms
the subordination of a natural body or private self whose ascendancy he
had exaggerated. The process is recalled in *Henry V,* where the new king
is described as having been cleansed of his past by an ascension to royal
estate, cancelling any imperfections and "leaving his body as a paradise"
(*Henry V,* 1.1.24–31).

Banishings and the Birth of Polity

Hal's offstage succession of his father represents no developmental process,
no *psychomachia,* no maturation. Instead, by action of law, his awaited
"transformation" into a king takes effect. It is essential to consider what
Falstaff is doing and where he is at exactly this moment. While Hal is becoming Henry V, Falstaff is not only far from court, but a night's ride from
a London to which he never really returns. Sojourning in Gloucestershire
with Shallow, Falstaff is being introduced to a world of private and provincial life. Tillyard urges that the Gloucestershire scenes round out a grand
theme of commonwealth, emphasizing epic inclusiveness.[50] But the world
of the court and the world of this rural, pastoral privacy are far apart, and
Falstaff is being effectively instructed which realm will be proper for
him from this point forward. This severance of worlds (held together so
uneasily throughout the plays, as so many have noted) urges that polity
rests upon a particular repudiation and banishment of the companionate
"friendship" modalities so fully tainted in the plays.

For Falstaff, who has represented a principle of companionship throughout, a pastoral provincial scene of merriment, feasting, and good fellowship
is proffered—away from court. He observes the universe of Shallow and
his friends with an anthropological interest (*2HIV,* 5.3.10–11), and seems
to discover this new world with surprise (lines 37–38, 69–70). The word
merry and its variants appear fifteen times in fifty-odd lines, often in song
(lines 17–69), sharply contrasting with the notion of "care," which has
been so heavily associated with the monarch. It is a world of male mutual

50. Tillyard, *Shakespeare's History Plays,* pp. 298, 301–4.

assurances, emphatically homosocial in its hail-fellow-well-met tone, its emphasis on smooth male relations ("This Davy serves you for good uses. He is your servingman and your husband" [lines 10–11]), and its condemnation of shrewish womankind (lines 32–36). Shakespeare stresses its natural and agricultural bounty, its production of apples and wheat. A merry world of male friendship far from court, it is, according to Falstaff's exclamation, "'Fore God . . . a goodly dwelling and a rich" (lines 5–6). But when a messenger "from the court" arrives, Falstaff instantly abandons his place in the bucolic scene to go to the new king. On sight, Hal, now Henry, banishes Falstaff from his accustomed royal presence "on pain of death" (*2HIV*, 5.5.64). For Falstaff, this sentencing to a private elsewhere is more than a simple repudiation by Hal. It extends to an exile that the next scene literalizes as imprisonment, when Falstaff and company are carried off, protesting, to the Fleet.

Ironically, as Falstaff is consigned to a private mode of being, rendered powerless, and excluded from government, the institution of polity also yields a constrained monarch, for whom the affectivity of the private realm has become fully improper. Friendship and its *jovissance* now lie outside his defined rights, competence, and powers. Instead of a pure attainment of the most extreme form of agency and power, one finds a figure denied access to the sovereign relation that friendship writers cast as a pinnacle of unsubordinated being. Hal had earlier reproached the crown as a thing that "dost pinch thy bearer," "the care on thee depending / Hast fed upon the body of my father. / . . . / . . . thou . . . / Hast eat thy bearer up" and "murdered my father" (*2HIV*, 4.5.28, 158–59, 163–64, 167). While Falstaff's girth emblematized his powers of consumption, royal being is represented here in terms of self-expenditure. The "care" imposed by the crown wastes the body of the king as the body politic subsumes the body natural by "Consolidation." Without "sweet company," the proper monarch reflects on his condition in sober isolation.

For Hal, this careful, caretaking, disciplined being depends upon a suppression of the show self he concocted. On his father's death, he proclaims, "in his tomb lie my affections" (*2HIV*, 5.2.124); banishing Falstaff, he claims, "I have turned away my former self" (*2HIV*, 5.5.59). While Barber has emphasized Hal's attainment of an "inclusive sovereign nature,"[51] and Tillyard has proposed that Hal's sojourn in the *demimonde* acquaints him with "the range of the human gamut,"[52] these critics grasped too quickly

---

51. Barber, *Shakespeare's Festive Comedy*, p. 195.
52. Tillyard, *Shakespeare's History Plays*, p. 276.

at a positive, humanist explanation of Hal's behavior. This is the view offered by Warwick that Hal "studies his companions" to gather important kingly knowledge of wrongful things to avoid later (*2HIV,* 4.4.67–98). But the loss of the power of friendship indicates the monarch's subordination to his public function of representing the common interest. When Hal moves from the "I know you all" in act 1 of part 1 to the "I know you not" in act 5 of part 2, the action involves not only a gain of authority but the forfeiture of a capacity to exercise prerogative over the self; this very action mythically and allegorically traces the *institutio polis.* As Francis Bacon writes, "there bee some whose lives are, as if they perpetually plaid upon a stage, disguised to all others, open only to themselves, but perpetual dissimulation is painful."[53] With public identity, a concomitant self-enclosure takes effect that precludes friendship's affective bond.

The monarch finds the unhindered self-expression associated with "soveraigne amitie" denied to him, since he is not to be "his own" in that exalted way. The delegitimation of private affectivity for the king is the precondition for imagining political society in institutional terms by metaphors of a personal body. Friendship is assigned to a realm of exiled privacy where it represents a subject's prerogative. In the English camp at Agincourt, Henry V testifies to the fate not of the feigned self he publicly cast off, but the "inner" self he must continue to disavow. There, like Henry IV, Henry V traditionally laments "the hard condition" of a king (*Henry V,* 4.1.219) and speculates about "What infinite heart's-ease / Must kings neglect that private men enjoy!" (lines 222–23) What for the subject was a false, flatterer's mode, dissimulation, becomes the precondition of a monarch's expression of any personal self. King Harry tells his attendants, "I and my bosom must debate awhile, / And then I would no other company" (lines 31–32). But he proceeds not to be without company, but to enter a company shorn of his regal status. Hal adopts a disguise one more time, in an uncanny parallel to the counterfeiting subjects-in-kings'-coats who drew off the king's attackers at Shrewsbury. He assumes the costume of a common soldier, cloaking his identity, to make his famous speech advocating the ordinary, private, emotional life of the king. "I think the king is but a man, as I am. . . . His ceremonies laid by, in his nakedness he appears but a man . . . his fears . . . of the same relish as ours are" (lines 98–106). Only on the condition of hiding his true status does the king have license to utter the truth of his "private" thought, the "ordinary" affects of

53. Sir Francis Bacon, "Of Frendship," in *The Essayes or Counsels, Civill and Morall,* ed. Michael Kiernan (Cambridge, Mass.: Harvard University Press, 1985), p. 80, n. 1.

his natural body. And when the other soldiers ask him to identify himself on this pilgrimage to privacy, twice he answers, simply, "a friend" (lines 36, 89).

Henry IV proposes that the founding moment of polity or common-weal is the moment that friendship, as a mode of affective partisan loyalty, is exiled from a public world of law and government. Here this institutional process also incorporates the specific betrayal of the private person of Falstaff. This presentation of friendship accords it not the slightest trace of the civic relevance it enjoyed in Cicero and clung to in Montaigne. On the contrary, the sovereign turns away from personal friendship. He embraces instead his place in council and his official "friends"—counselors like the allegorical Chief Justice who simply *is* his "office" (an "impersonal state functionary" in Barber's words) [54] and who will advise him how to enact his public trust. Friendship as personal affection takes a place within a private sphere cut off from court power. The constitution of the "private" sphere in Shakespeare's formulation proceeds, perhaps, from a need to rid personal monarchy from affective aberrations, to make government impersonal, neutral, procedural, and bureaucratic. Polity here involves a *mutual* disciplining, a diminution of both sovereign and subject. The subordinated sovereign is denied the power of any but the most generalized affectivities, and "soveraigne amitie" is a subject's prerogative solely within a new kind of "elsewhere" no longer fully reflecting choice—the elsewhere of banishment.

54. Barber, *Shakespeare's Festive Comedy,* p. 216.

Friendship's Offices:
True Speech and Artificial Bodies
in *The Winter's Tale*

What if a pair of friends are actually "a pair of kings"?[1] In the second scene of *The Winter's Tale,* two kings are in company at the court of Sicilia: Leontes, that kingdom's monarch, and Polixenes, the king of Bohemia. Both they and their attendants extol their longtime friendship. Royal affairs call Polixenes back from his extended visit, but Leontes and (more consequentially) his obedient queen cajole Polixenes into remaining longer. (The plot will soon turn on this act of persuasion, when Leontes sees enough in it to reprise Othello's mistake.) Once Polixenes has agreed to stay, he recounts their friendship's childhood beginnings. He uses immediately recognizable friendship language:

> We were as twinned lambs that did frisk i'th' sun,
> And bleat the one at th'other; what we changed
> Was innocence for innocence—we knew not
> The doctrine of ill-doing, nor dreamed
> That any did.
>
> (1.2.66–70)

Polixenes' portrait of friendship's origins accords it an Edenic force; lambs figure a maximal innocence that is made explicit in contrast with an eventual knowledge of "ill-doing." The twinned lambs recall the metaphors Shakespeare employed in *A Midsummer Night's Dream* to amplify Helena's outrage when Hermia seems to have betrayed her. Lamenting Hermia's apparent disregard for their "school-days friendship" and "childhood innocence," Helena conjures up their youthful condition as "two artificial

---

1. William Shakespeare, *The Winter's Tale,* ed. Stephen Orgel (Oxford: Oxford University Press, 1996), 5.3.146. Subsequent references are to this edition and appear in the text.

gods, / [Who] with our needles created both one flower, / . . . / As if our hands, our sides, voices, and minds / Had been incorporate."[2] Their life she reckons "like to a double cherry," with "two seeming bodies, but one heart" (3.2.209, 212). This is powerful evocative language. But not only does it arise in a moment of enmity. The image is also pointedly nostalgic, as James Holstun has shown us. In an essay unfolding the final interrogative of Helena's speech ("will you rent our ancient love asunder?"), Holstun considers the seemingly inevitable casting of "lesbian" eroticism in past time.[3]

What might such a nostalgic formation mean in a king's case? At one level, reviewing friendship retrospectively comports with a king's subsequent translation into a public being, one lacking the agencies of privacy by which such affective bonds might possibly and legitimately be forged, as discussed in the preceding chapters. Polixenes might be seen to lament the loss of this condition. Indeed, his language goes on to suggest this reading when he ponders the following hypothesis:

> Had we pursued that life,
> And our weak spirits ne'er been higher reared
> With stronger blood, we should have answered heaven
> Boldly, 'not guilty,' the imposition cleared
> Hereditary ours.
>
> (1.2.71–74)

Criticism normally glosses these lines and the earlier phrase "ill-doing" as the narrative of a fall into heterosexual knowledge. But it is crucial to see just how dependent this gloss is on Hermione's replies, when she teases him about holding such a view of the two kings' wives. Her lines, by their merry, bantering style, actually draw Polixenes toward a sexual sense.

While Hermione's playfully arch response to Polixenes is certainly not unwarranted by his language, his words *also* describe a transition from innocence to the higher position and status of kingship. Indeed, to be "higher reared / With stronger blood" rather economically describes the theoretical, legal, and hereditary aspects of this condition. His calling "ill-doing" a "doctrine" also suggests a more political sense for his words, one

---

2. William Shakespeare, *A Midsummer Night's Dream,* in *The Complete Works of Shakespeare,* ed. David Bevington (New York: Harper Collins, 1992), 3.2.202–4, 207–8. Subsequent references to plays other than *The Winter's Tale* are to this edition unless otherwise noted.

3. James Holstun, " 'Will you rent our ancient love asunder?': Lesbian Elegy in Donne, Marvell, and Milton," *ELH* 54(winter 1987): 835–67.

embedded in the realities of courtly administration, negotiation, and intrigue. His speculative "Had we pursued that life" echoes the counterfactual imaginings of other kings, real (Elizabeth I) and dramatic (the Henries), who wished they might "be private." As discussed in chapters 4 and 5, such hypothetical musings are a commonplace in kingship lore; Polixenes embodies this reflection in a recollected condition of "twinned" friendship. Thus his lines express a nostalgia for private status through friendship language, perhaps just as Helena's friendship lines comprise what Holstun calls a "lesbian elegy."

This reading draws further support from the play's preceding first scene, in which two attending lords discuss the monarchs they serve. We hear the same account of their pastoral childhood union, this time from Camillo, the trusted advisor of Leontes: "They were trained together in their childhoods, and there rooted betwixt them then such an affection which cannot choose but branch now" (1.1.21–23). The horticultural vocabulary (*trained, rooted, branch*) will be important again later, but here it suffices to note how it intensifies the sense of action or procedure in Helena's "double cherry" *incorporate(d)*. After this retrospective glance, however, Camillo elaborates the ways their mutual kingship has altered the practices of friendship between them:

> Since their more mature dignities and royal necessities made separation
> of their society, their encounters, though not personal, hath been royally
> attorneyed with interchange of gifts, letters, loving embassies, they have
> seemed to be together, though absent. (1.1.23–28)

The repetition of plurals and possessives effects an almost dizzying blur of identities and reflects Montaigne's swirling economies of self: "In the amitie I speake of, they entermixe and confound themselves one in the other, with so universall a commixture, that they weare out the seame that hath conjoyned them together."[4] We hear an echo of the letter-writing and absence trope central to friendship doctrines, economically expressed in Donne's line, "Sir, more than kisses, letters mingle souls; / For thus friends absent speak."[5] Nevertheless, the formal diplomatic language emphasizes the changed condition of the two friends. Burdened now by the overwhelming political demands and responsibilities of their respective king-

4. Michel de Montaigne, "Of Friendship," in *The Essayes of Montaigne: John Florio's Translation*, ed. J. I. M. Stewart (New York: Modern Library, 1933), p. 149. Subsequent references are to this edition and appear in the text.
5. John Donne, "Sir, more than kisses," in *The Complete English Poems*, ed. C. A. Patrides (London: Dent, 1985), lines 1–2.

doms ("dignities" recalls the technical term *dignitas*), amity must be at-
torneyed. The diplomats' language recalls the sense of kingly friendship's
impossibility that chapters 4 and 5 have proposed. But the drama of this
romance also depends on two new twists in the familiar friendship story:
not only is Polixenes equal to this king, he is also neither dead nor absent.

The generic situation of Shakespeare's late plays proverbially softens the
letter of the law, and friendship doctrines are no exception to the operations of romance. Indeed, the romances do much to focus on the private
lives of kings.[6] In doing so, their relation to political questions becomes, by
that very means, more emblematic and allusive. Lest the strange combination of analogy and alterity that I have described between friendship and
kingship, between notions of the private subject and the public being of
monarchy, remain too orderly, *The Winter's Tale* presents a perspective on
their blurring. This final chapter moves out from specifying period uses of
friendship as an ontology differentiating persons and powers. Instead, *The
Winter's Tale* presents an opportunity to explore friendship as a practice.
For, as we shall see, the Renaissance passion for friendship figures is not
without its methodologists. This play provides extensive practice-driven
homologies between friendship and polity, and those links especially depend on a conjoint sense of "craft."

What friendship makes legible in *The Winter's Tale* is not just an allegorical relationship, but also a happy confusion between statecraft and
friendship's functions at an emblematic level. As Kim Hall notes in passing, *amity* is a term applied principally to *nations*.[7] It often signifies, even
more specifically, a treaty or "friendly league" between nations and
peoples.[8] Expressing this focus on the nation, Henry Peacham's *Minerva
Britanna*[9] gives an image of *Vicinorum amicitia* ("the friendship of neigh-
bors"; see fig. 7). In a visual literalization of the rooting and branching

6. Comparing *The Winter's Tale* with earlier Shakespearean "dramas of royalty," Orgel
notes how "In fact . . . we will be struck by how little distinction is . . . accorded to the office of king" in the play (Orgel, introduction to *The Winter's Tale,* p. 6).

7. Kim F. Hall, *Things of Darkness: Economies of Race and Gender in Early Modern
England* (Ithaca, N.Y.: Cornell University Press, 1995), p. 56.

8. "Friendly league" is a common phrase, generally indicating the positive value of
such bonds in terms of unity and concord. But Elizabeth I framed this question in a
strongly different way. Defending the virtue of her isolationist foreign policy, she saw a subordination of the realm in such international contracts or "foreign friendships" (speech at
the Closing of Parliament, 15 March 1576, British Library Additional MS 33271, ed. and
transcr. Janel Mueller. I thank Professor Mueller for access to this transcription).

9. Peacham's book was entered in the Stationer's Register on 9 August 1611.

Figure 7. Henry Peacham, *Vicinorum amicitia,* from *Minerva Britanna or A garden of heroical devises* (London: W. Dight, 1612), p. 41. Photo courtesy of The Newberry Library, Chicago.

amity of Leontes and Polixenes, the emblem's gloss stresses "frendly league," "mutuall amitie," and "open signes of Frendship." As Leontes later laments, his rash suspicion of Polixenes and Hermione, having exiled his friend almost as violently as Falstaff had been, bereaves him of his "society, / *Amity too*" (5.1.134–35, emphasis mine). Friendship and sovereignty are so mutually emblematic in *The Winter's Tale* that it is impossible to say, finally, which allegorizes which. As twinned artificial bodies, friendship and polity (emblematized in kingship) each require a science or craft—"offices"—by which they may be maintained.

"Admonitions and corrections," Montaigne offers parenthetically, "are the chiefest offices of friendship" (p. 145). We have seen in chapter 1 how friendship doctrines identify sharp speech as the signature, evidentiary mark of a true friend, especially in contrast with the unctuous words of his counterfeit, the flatterer. Naturally, this liberty of speech serves as a crucial link to the functions of good political counsel. What also becomes evident in the readings that follow, however, is the degree to which frank, truthful speech alone is inadequate to fully perform these offices. Performances of friendship or statecraft also necessarily employ as much artifice—"false" writing—as "true speech." This chapter proceeds toward a reading of *The Winter's Tale* after generating a sense of "friendly methods" in the texts of Plutarch and Francis Bacon; texts, that is, that survey friendship prudentially.

This procedure responds, in part, to the diverse readings of the play by critics attentive to its gender dispensations. On the one hand, much has been said about the apparent reconciliation between genders in *The Winter's Tale,* especially through the linked acceptance of heterosexuality and of women it seems to indicate.[10] While Janet Adelman has decisively shown the centrality of fantasies of male parthenogenesis in Shakespeare, especially in the one-gendered "resolutions" offered or attempted by *Macbeth* and *Cymbeline,* Adelman herself sees *The Winter's Tale* as almost an exception to the systematic parthenogenic fantasy she details.[11] On the other hand, Valerie Traub has read the play as ultimately involving "a containment of female erotic power" proceeding from masculine anxieties about its potency.[12] The present reading of *The Winter's Tale* shifts the terms of this inquiry to suggest a different route through these issues. For it is by specifically imagining forms of relation beyond heterosexually reproductive ones that the play seems less wedded to misogynistic resolutions than we might otherwise expect. The relative acceptance of women it evinces is fueled by a different dynamic—one that is certainly generative but decidedly *not* based in procreation or eroticism. Thus, in Renaissance terms, gender can matter less. For friendship's practical modalities of speech and writing appear in *The Winter's Tale* not merely as alternatives to familial and biological relations: they appear as the sine qua non of the perpetuation, regeneration, and invigoration of the ongoing life—of the self *or* the state. Perhaps by virtue of a resultant freedom from the anxieties attending heterosexuality which Traub has described, both genders appear as friendship's practitioners.

10. See Carol Thomas Neely, "Women and 'Issue' in *The Winter's Tale," Philological Quarterly* 57 (1978): 181–94 (discussed shortly) for the most direct argument to this effect, though many scholars seem to assume it.

11. Janet Adelman, *Suffocating Mothers: Fantasies of Maternal Origin in Shakespeare's Plays* (New York: Routledge, 1992), pp. 235–36.

12. Valerie Traub, "Jewels, Statues and Corpses: Containment of Female Erotic Power," in *Desire and Anxiety: Circulations of Sexuality in Shakespearian Drama* (New York: Routledge, 1992), pp. 25–49.

Further, this inquiry into "friendship's offices" highlights a knowingly intersubjective theory of the self, one we might well call fiduciary or "custodial." As crucial to propagation and perpetuation as birth, the offices of friends extend, correct, and enable the life of the befriended subject. As we shall see, these offices can be specified as modes of speech and writing. The interpersonal wardship or stewardship thus envisioned in the intimate contexts of friendship discourses, in turn, shapes ideas of how to maintain a grander legal fiction: the artificial body of polity, reflected in the preservation of a kingly line. While the stewardship responsibilities of the king have previously been considered to preclude friendship, this chapter now turns to ways of theorizing a stewardship *of* the king in abstracted friendship terms. For friendship tropes powerfully inform political conceptions of the role of counsel. The political implications of the "liberty of speech" celebrated in both arenas may not constitute a form of crypto-republicanism (since it is legitimated by means of personal loyalty to a sovereign's "true" self or nature), but they represent a crucial early, intimate formulation of this political dynamic.[13] By the obliquity of intimate emblems, friendship discourses of free speech and entrusted lives enliven and extend the abstract doctrines of "good government."

Plutarchan Medicines: "The Soveraign Remedie"

References to Plutarchan texts are legion in the Renaissance; those invoking his *Lives* (first translated into English from French by Thomas North in 1579) are perhaps easiest to document. But the segment from Plutarch's *Moralia* discussing the discernment of flatterers also has a readily visible impact on period thought, whether by means of Latin editions, Elyot's summary version in *The Boke Named the Governour* (1531), Thomas Blundeville's 1561 translation (with a second edition in 1580), or in Philemon Holland's version published in 1603. "To discern a flatterer from a friend," as the title of this version announces, is a practical, how-to manual. Its emphasis on skills and technique powerfully supplements the more definitional and classificatory impulses considered thus far. As a key locus classicus enshrining frank speech or candor as an essential practice of friends, Plutarch's appeal was particularly enhanced for humanists (and reasoners of other kinds) by the portrait he gives: the friend takes shape as a prudential practitioner. In Holland's translation, "as in all things else, so

---

13. See Quentin Skinner, *Liberty Before Liberalism* (Cambridge: Cambridge University Press, 1998), for an indication of the relation between "liberty" concepts and Stoic notions of value; for a political genealogy of "free speech," see my discussion in chapter 1.

free speaking, is to have the perfection from a mean and mediocrity";
guided by the measure of such a mean, the practitioner locates all decisions
in specific occasions and judges with an eye to the practical results of his
"chastisements."[14]

Plutarch's παρρησια, translated in modern editions as "candor," is usually termed "liberty of speech" in Holland's version (passim, esp. pp. 87–
89). Holland's repetition of this term, distinguished of course from speaking "licenciously" (p. 87), trades on its proximity to a political meaning,
especially considering the political characters he discusses. As is usual in
friendship treatises, the illustrative cases include numerous references to
tyrants, kings, commanders, and their spontaneous reformation by friendship examples (most notably Dionysius and Agamemnon), as well as the
familiar political friendships of Harmodious and Aristogiton and Achilles
and Patroclus (pp. 88–89). Thus, many of Plutarch's instances invoke the
interpersonal relations of significant political actors, mixed with private
stories of individual business or family matters.

Invariably, Plutarch focuses on instances of speech or rebuke by these
friendship figures, indicating their exemplary value, both positive and
negative. One shows judiciousness, another goes too far:

> it was not an unproper or unelegant speech, wherewith a musician upon
> a time stopped King *Philips* mouth that he had not a word to say
> againe. . . . But contrariwise, *Epicharmus* spake not so aptly and to the
> purpose in this behalf. . . . And as badly answered *Antiphon.* (p. 89)

In a method clearly resonant for a nation of common-law thinkers, Plutarch thus characterizes the evaluations his prudent friend must make.[15]
He demonstrates, as he recommends, a practice of judging cases, timeli-
ness, circumstances, and probabilities of efficacy. Most consequential for
Renaissance configurations of Plutarch, the predominant metaphor for the
friend is that of a medical doctor.

---

14. Plutarch, *The philosophie commonlie called, the morals, written by the learned
philosopher Plutarch of Chaeronea. Translated out of Greeke into English, and conferred with
the Latine translations and the French, by Philemon Holland* (London, Printed by Arnold
Hatfield, 1603), p. 87. Subsequent references are to this translation and appear in the text.

15. My understanding of prudence here has benefited from the discussions in Victoria
Kahn, "Humanism and the Resistance to Theory," in *Literary Theory/Renaissance Texts,*
ed. Patricia Parker and David Quint (Baltimore: Johns Hopkins University Press, 1986),
pp. 373–96; and in Lorna Hutson, *The Usurer's Daughter: Male Friendship and Fictions of
Women in Sixteenth-Century England* (New York: Routledge, 1994).

"This liberty of speech, whereof I speak, is in the nature of a medicine," Plutarch argues, and, underscoring the importance of the mean, "if it be not given in time convenient, & as it ought to be, besides that it doth not good at all, it troubleth the body, worketh grievance, and instead of a remedy proveth to be a mischief" (p. 87). Plutarch extends the medical conceit with the arrival of the doctor figure:

> like as a Chirurgion, when he maketh an incision and cutteth the flesh of his patient, had need to use great dexterity, to have a nimble hand and an even. . . . So this liberty of speech unto a friend. (p. 89)

The recipient of this frank speech is "sick" of a "disease," in need of a "drug"; the admonitions and corrections, "like as the discovery and cure also of some filthy and foule disease," should be done discreetly (pp. 90, 92). Errors in frankness are compared to the cost of a physician's mistakes. Overzealous admonition of trivial faults results in a kind of drug tolerance: "frank reprehension (the soveraign remedie for grosse and main faults)" becomes ineffective, "much like unto a Physician, who hath employed and spent a medine [sic] that is strong and bitter . . . in small infirmities" (pp. 94–95). Finally, even the good physician's desire for appropriately limited measures (preferring "to cure the malady . . . by rest and sleep" [p. 95]) and his focus on postsurgical health become exemplary:

> we ought in this case to imitate good Physicians and Chirurgions: for when they have made incision or cut any member, they leave not the place in pain and torment still, but use certain fomentations and lenitive infusions to mitigate the anguish. (p. 96)

Plutarch's attending, prudent friend takes up, discursively, the life-and-death fiduciary role of a medical doctor. He functions as a physician by imitation, and his "soveraign remedie" is speech.

What kind of friend or self is it in the first place who is at such risk? Not, certainly, Cicero's figure, who is self-adequate and whose freedom from need determines his very eligibility for friendship. On the contrary, the figure in Plutarch's text strays from virtue; in fact, when Plutarch considers this self, "we find there an infinite number of defects, and many vanities, imperfections and faults" (p. 87). While Cicero's Laelius bluffly claims to leave behind ideal figures (to those philosophical Greeks), Plutarch authors an even more single-mindedly practical discourse addressing the self's quotidian realities. In place of Cicero's paragon of virtue and competence, we find a self—and a friend—who is in need of a doctor.

Indeed, Robert Burton's *The Anatomy of Melancholy* (1621) makes seamless use of these logics, discussing the role of the friend in the cure of melancholia. His model extends the Plutarchan doubling of doctor and friend into the context of a more explicitly medical tract. "When the patient himself is not able to resist or overcome these heart-eating passions," he writes, "his friends or Physician must be ready to supply that which is wanting."[16] The specific trigger for this need is the patient's own sudden powerlessness: confession of griefs to a friend is required when "our judgement be so depraved, our reason over-ruled, [our] will precipitated." This model of the medically weakened self in melancholia indicates the wider valences of counsel as a remedy. When such a self falls, as he naturally must, in Holland's words, into "misgovernment of himselfe" (p. 91), another self must come into service. Plutarch himself gives Alexander the Great as an example. Alexander, he recounts, found two things that convinced him he was no god, despite what other people said. Considering these things (sleep and "the use of Venus"), the example continues, "he found *he was worse than himself*" (p. 87, emphasis mine). The striking grammar here, severing a notional self from an actual one, arises again at the end of the discussion. In the revelatory moments of non-self (misgovernment or failing the notional standard of self),

> then will it be a fit time to speak unto a friend thus: . . . Lo what we your friends require of you: these are the duties and offices which are beseeming your person: for these hath nature made and framed you. (p. 95)

The self abandoning its place is replaced (and then re-placed) by the friend who scripts both a proper self and the route back to it. Here is a self, defined by duties and offices and the friend's direction; he presents an expressly collaborative and intersubjective discourse of self-formation. As a doctor, as a custodian, the friend is another self—when the self, itself, is not.

Bacon's Counsel and the Patched Body Politic

A friend who dictates the terms of a proper self and who labors to restore an errant personage to the place, "the duties and offices which are beseeming [his] person," has a new specificity in his friendship responsibilities. Especially in dramatic representations, as we shall see, the role of the political counselor moves *precisely* within the terms of such a logic. But this

---

16. Robert Burton, *The Anatomy of Melancholy*, eds. Floyd Dell and Paul Jordan-Smith (New York: Tudor Publishing Co., 1927), pp. 472–73.

convergence of public and private personas also appears in the expressly political reflections of Francis Bacon's *The Essayes or Counsels, Civill and Morall*. Bacon essentially co-articulates the doctrines of friendship and counsel, with "Of Frendship" and "Of Counsell" both appearing for the first time in the expanding amalgam of the *Essayes* in 1610–12.[17] These two essays comprise an almost continuous commentary. Both concern themselves with the production of an artificial, incorporated entity—an intersubjective form configured by two members, whether two friends or a king and counselor. In Burton's suggestive phrase, "Friends' *confabulations* are comfortable at all times."[18] These artificial bodies each compensate for similar problems; each makes similar new powers available.

First, Bacon's "Of Frendship" intensifies the key components of Plutarch's discussion of candor. The self is no longer simply liable to occasional error; a medico-scientific vision of the constant organic processes of the body serves as the basis of a metaphor for moral health. These processes, like the actions of a machine, are ongoing and always vulnerable to imbalances. Within this humoral theory, "a principall *Fruit* of *Frendship*," Bacon writes,

> is the Ease and Discharge of the Fulness and Swellings of the Heart, which Passions of all kinds doe cause and induce. We know Diseases of Stoppings and Suffocations, are the most dangerous in the body; And it is not much otherwise in the Minde. (p. 81)[19]

After listing *"Sarza . . . , Steele . . . , Sulphur . . . ,* [and] *Castoreum"* as remedies capable of "opening" various suffocating organs, he concludes that "no Receipt openeth the Heart, but a true *Frend*" (p. 81). The lack of this essential, virtual-body function provided by the friend results in either an impairment of understanding or, more strikingly, a kind of self-consuming cannibalism (they are, "if a Man would give it a hard Phrase . . . Canniballs of their owne *Hearts*"[p. 83]).

Friendship's "second fruit"—"Faithfull Counsell"—similarly appears

---

17. Francis Bacon, *The Essayes or Counsels, Civill and Morall,* ed. Michael Kiernan (Cambridge: Harvard University Press, 1985), p. cxvi. Subsequent references are to this collated edition (based on Bacon's final edition of 1625), unless otherwise noted, and appear in the text.

18. Burton, *The Anatomy of Melancholy,* p. 471, emphasis mine.

19. This fruit, based in a personal communication of the "affections," is the one Bacon denies to princes, who, "in regard of the distance of their Fortune from that of their Subjects and Servants, cannot gather this *Fruit*" (without the inconveniences attending the raising up of *"Favorites,* or *Privadoes"*) (p. 82).

as a dynamic form of bodily chemistry. Given the medical sense of *sovereign* in the period, Bacon's phrasing of *counsel* as "Healthfull and Soveraigne for the *Understanding*" is almost redundant. (Walter Dorke, in 1589, had similarly termed it a "soveraigne consolation as a most cordial medicine against any corrasive," and Burton claimed that "Collyrium is not so sovereign to the eyes as [friendship] is to the heart.") [20] One's fraught "Wits and Understanding doe clarifie and breake up, in the Communicating and discoursing with Another"; by such means, one "tosseth his Thoughts" into a better order (p. 84). The presence of the friend in this self-ordering is so crucial that Bacon appends the suggestion of an artificial substitute: "a Man were better relate himselfe, to a Statua, or a Picture, then to suffer his Thoughts to passe in smother" (p. 84). Here is friendship in its most prosthetic moment. It is at this point in the essay that Bacon registers Plutarchan rhetoric most overtly. One's self, muddled, straying, and unreliable, is the worst flatterer of all. And the antidote? "There is no such Remedy against the *Flattery* of a Mans Selfe, as the Liberty of a *Frend* . . . the best Receipt . . . is the Admonition of a *Frend*" (p. 85). The conjunction of liberty and admonition echoes the political suggestiveness of Holland's translation.

The final phase of the friendship essay assembles these reflections to offer an invigorated restatement of the double-bodied formula of friends as "other selves." Counsel is at the center of this restatement. In light of the intersubjective operations he has described, Bacon's emphasis underscores the way the friend makes possible a scope beyond the reach of one self alone. The incorporated entity is something bigger:

> a Man hath as it were two Lives in his desires. A Man hath a Body, and that Body is confined to a Place; But where *Frendship* is, all Offices of Life, are as it were granted to Him, and his Deputy. For he may exercise them by his *Frend*. (p. 86)

For a person to have "two Lives in his desires" bodes well for the degrees of *jovissance* proposed by Montaigne. But it is the structure of agency by which such powers are effected that is most dramatic here. The rationales for friendship echo not only theories of kingship and of political organization in general but even those of modern corporation laws: a supercession of the natural body's spatial and temporal limitations, an expansion of

---

20. Walter Dorke, *A Tipe or Figure of Friendship. Wherein is liuelie, and compendiouslie expressed, the right nature and propertie of a perfect and true friend* (London: Thomas Orwin and Henry Kirkham, 1589), sig. A3r; and Burton, *The Anatomy of Melancholy*, p. 471.

implementable "Offices of Life," and a protocol of deputation, proxy, or agency by which this larger body may enact "desires." It is this monumental logical extension of the "one soul in two bodies" notion that leads Bacon to his conclusion "that it was Sparing Speech of the Ancients, to say, *That a Frend is Another Himselfe:* For that a *Frend* is farre more then *Himselfe*" (p. 86). The friend is no mere replicant—his presence translates the self and the scene into a different mode of being.

As an aside in the friendship essay, Bacon raises the standard of complete, as against partial, recourse to counsel. Asking counsel "by Peeces," fragmenting one's affairs and disclosing only limited parts to different persons, is not only a "partial" (piecemeal) act; it also yields "partial" (interested and partisan) advice: "it is a rare Thing, except it be from a perfect and entire *Frend,* to have Counsell given but such as shalbe bowed and crooked to some ends" (p. 85). Such "Scattered Counsels" generate another Plutarchan physician's image, in which the requisite "entire" knowledge of the whole body prevents the administration of a "cure" that "overthroweth your Health in some other kind" (p. 86). Precisely this sense of an absolute, unqualified communication of one's affairs in full appears as the opening salvo in Bacon's essay "Of Counsell."

Proclaiming that the "greatest Trust betweene Man and Man" consists of counsel, it is the fullness of extent that distinguishes it from "other Confidences":

> In other Confidences, Men commit the parts of life; their Lands, their
> Goods, their Children, their Credit, some particular Affaire: But to such,
> as they make their Counsellours, they commit the whole. (p. 63)

The same rationale—the "tossing" of thoughts into better order—is given: "Things will have their first, or second Agitation; If they be not tossed upon the Arguments of *Counsel,* they will be tossed on the Waves of *Fortune*" (p. 63). But only briefly does Bacon consider the generic instance "betweene Man and Man." The overwhelming focus of the essay is to address princes on this score, extolling the virtues of counsel and describing the best methods to manage it. Most strikingly, despite the celebrations of fulsomeness, princes are repeatedly warned against it, and thus differentiated from private persons. Unlike the true friend, a king should not "communicate all Matters, . . . but may extract and select"; nor should he reveal "his owne Inclination too much. . . . For else *Counsellours* will but take the Winde of him; And instead of giving Free Counsell, sing him a Song of *Placebo*" (pp. 65, 68). (The notion of the flatterer as a "placebo" derives from the liturgical Latin "I will be pleasing" from Vespers in the Office of the Dead.)²¹ At every turn, Bacon's perhaps self-servingly abject moves stress nonreciprocity, incompletion, secrecy, and an asymmetrical understanding. The greatest strength of the prince lies in his knowledge of his servants' natures; contrarily, "the true composition of a *Counsellour,* is rather to be skilled in their Masters Businesse, then in his Nature" (p. 66). What kind of self and what kind of transformations to it result from this purposefully "scattered" practice of counsel?

The essay's most bizarre image begins to answer this question, offering an emblematic formula drawn from classical mythology: "Ancient Times doe set forth in Figure, both the Incorporation, and inseparable Conjunction of *Counsel* with Kings; and the wise and Politique use of *Counsel* by Kings" (p. 64). This "Figure" has two phases. First, there is the "marriage" of Jupiter with Metis, who "signifieth *Counsell:* whereby they intend, that *Soveraignty* is married to *Counsell*" (p. 64). Thus far, the figure is fairly straightforward, although marital imagery is more often associated with constitutionalist thought than with counselorship. But the unfolding narrative of these "marital" relations affords a striking, corporeal form for the connection between a counselor and a king. Metis becomes pregnant, but, in Bacon's words, "Jupiter suffered her not to stay, till she brought forth, but eat her up; whereby he became himselfe with Child, and was delivered of *Pallas Armed,* out of his Head" (p. 64). Bacon expounds this figure in terms of procreation—referring matters to counsel is "Impregnation," and conciliar deliberations are located in "the Wombe of . . . Councell"—but the gender configurations are multiple. Counselors have wombs; so does the Jupiter-prince figure. Counsel is consumed and converted; "Decrees and finall Directions" are compared to Athena herself.

This figure is literally, as Bacon technically describes it, "monstrous" (p. 64). This patchwork body echoes Elyot's refraction of Aristotle ("Aristotell in his politykes exorteth gouernors to haue their frendes for a great numbre of eeyen, earis, handes, and legges"); Montaigne reflects on it discussing his observations in "Of A Monstrous Child" ("this double body, and these different members, having reference to one onely head, might serve for a favorable prognostication to our King" [p. 640]); and even James I himself defends against it ("I hope . . . no man will . . . thinke that I . . . should be a Polygamist and husband to two wiues [i.e., Scotland and

---

21. Although the *Oxford English Dictionary* lists the first medical use of the term *placebo* only in 1785, Bacon seems to predict it here by his conjunction of metaphors. There are a variety of appropriations of the liturgical phrase for colloquial use: "to sing placebo," "to be at the school of placebo," to be "a placebo," and the use of Placebo as a proper name (i.e., in Chaucer's "Merchant's Tale").

England]; that I being the Head, should have a diuided and monstrous Body").[22] The resulting sovereign body is a Frankenstein-esque assemblage of parts, an amalgam achieved by cannibalistic logics rather than either parthenogenic or procreative ones.

Such figurings of the artificial "body" of sovereignty are common in the emblem books of the period. Recycling an image of the sovereign as *concordia* from Andreas Alciati's *Emblematum Liber* and reprinting engravings from Gabriel Rollenhagen's *Nucleus Emblematorum* (1611), George Wither's *A Collection of Emblemes, Ancient and Moderne* (1634) offers a striking visualization of the sovereign as a multi-armed figure emblematizing *"concordia insuperabilis"* (see fig. 5 in chapter 1). Suggesting the image "doth rather fashion out a *Monster*, / Than forme an *Hieroglyphicke*," the gloss relies on a logic of monstrous assembly. Stressing a managed conglomerate of *"Faculties,* or *Friends,"* the moral invokes prosthetic self-extension: the individual "fits them so; and, keepes them so together / . . . / As if so many *Hands,* they had been made; / And, in *One-Body,* usefull being had" (lines 2–3, 11, 13, 15–16).[23] The possession of "usefull being" echoes the kind of serviceable sovereign identity proposed in chapter 4; here the cultural process of creating this hybrid, grafted body emphasizes a "monstrous" artifice.

The Winter's Tale and the Offices of Friendship

With *The Winter's Tale,* we see the same imbrication of counsel and friendship doctrines evident in Bacon's writings. The relation of these salubriously entangled discourses to sovereignty as a "monstrous" form is crucial to the play's logic. Ruminations on counsel appear at the very center of *Gorboduc* as the inaugural "history play" in England, and continue not only throughout history play texts, but also in material that more emblematically deals with philosophies of governance—of self or state. After almost three hundred deliberative lines by three differing counselors, Gorboduc takes six lines to conclude, despite them, "In one self purpose do I still abide."[24] Leontes' disclaimer of counsel in favor of "prerogative"

22. Thomas Elyot, *The Boke Named the Governour,* ed. Foster Watson (London: J. M. Dent, 1907), p.193; and James I, "Speech to Parliament, March 19, 1604," in *Political Writings,* ed. Johan P. Somerville (Cambridge: Cambridge University Press, 1994), p.136.

23. George Wither, *A Collection of Emblemes, Ancient and Moderne* (London: A. Mathewes, 1635), p. 179.

24. Thomas Sackville and Thomas Norton, *Gorboduc, or Ferrex and Porrex,* ed. Irby Cauthen (Lincoln: University of Nebraska Press, 1970), 1.2.342.

echoes Gorboduc's, even as Shakespeare enhances the passionate instability behind it: [25]

> What need we
> Commune with you of this, but rather follow
> Our forceful instigation? Our prerogative
> Calls not your counsels . . .
> We need no more of your advice.
>   (2.1.161–64, 168)

But the highly Senecan, powerfully topical history play *Gorboduc* and the
romance *The Winter's Tale* take up the same problem.

Constance Jordan has made a comprehensive case for reading Shakespeare's romances explicitly in terms generally reserved for the histories:
"the *romances* speak the language of politics . . . they project the matter of
the histories on a scale both vaster and more subtle . . . their subject is the
fate of rulers, their states, and peoples." [26] Jordan's work squarely situates
the romances in the contexts of political thought in the Jacobean period.
Representations of counselorship in *The Winter's Tale* serve as important
supporting evidence for this claim. They also begin to show how romances
may well provide terms, in turn, for reading both the histories and Renaissance formulations of political organization in more overtly practical contexts: friendship discourses exert an enabling and shaping influence on
theories of political counsel. For *The Winter's Tale* presents a chiastic mixture of counselorship and amity, where friends are counselors, and where
counselors' political conduct employs the script of Plutarchan friendship.
Each allegorizes the other.

Tracing friendship's "offices" in the play, moreover, confirms many
scholars' sense of the oddity of *The Winter's Tale* compared with other
treatments of gender in Shakespeare's work, but begins to account for it
in new terms. For friendship forms such as those manifest in the texts of
Plutarch and Bacon determine the drama's resolution, and the degree to
which they do so radically de-emphasizes the role generally accorded to
forms of relation (sexuality, marriage, parenting) deriving from heterosexual reproduction. Jordan points out that the "romances are generically

---

25. For an excellent discussion of the Jacobean debates immediately surrounding the
term *prerogative,* see Stuart M. Kurland, "'We need no more of your advice': Political Realism in *The Winter's Tale,*" *Studies in English Literature* 31 (1991): 365–86, 367–68.

26. Constance Jordan, *Shakespeare's Monarchies: Ruler and Subject in the Romances*
(Ithaca, N.Y.: Cornell University Press, 1997), p. 12.

suited to a figured drama in which images of the family and the physical body of the monarch function as political metaphors."[27] But *The Winter's Tale* is unique among the romances in its combination of two features. First, it portrays a universe in which family metaphors in particular are incapable of sustaining dynastic integrity (in this respect, it is like *Cymbeline* or *The Tempest*). Friendship and counsel figure instead as crucially effectual "political metaphors." Second, this supercession of heterosexual reproduction (the proverbially cursed "woman's part" in *Cymbeline*) does not wholly depend on a misogynistic logic.[28] Of all Shakespeare's plays, *The Winter's Tale* is surely the least merely co-optive of the work of its female characters. But this does not add up to an "acceptance" of heterosexuality and the processes of sexual reproduction. In its kaleidoscopic refraction of friendship and counsel across gender, generation, and "office," the play displaces forms of biological reproduction (personal and dynastic). In its place we find the kind of generative writing, even "confabulation," evident in Plutarchan, intersubjective, custodial "friendship." As a political metaphor, then, it is a concoction bred of friendship and counsel that plays the determining role in this most amicable conclusion of a play widely cited as a highpoint in Shakespeare's dramas of reconciliation. The self and sovereignty are both the express charges of "other selves"; each experiences "new birth," delivered by means of the "artificial" methods of practicing other selves.

Commingled Friendship; Scattered Counsel

The nostalgia of the "twinned lambs" speech notwithstanding, the tropes of ideal friendship remain in force at Sicilia in the play's opening scenes. The elaborate dialogue[29] between Camillo and Archidamus in 1.1 employs the formal language of diplomatic hospitality to such excess that a virtual competition for indebtedness results, one reflecting the doctrine more

27. Ibid., p. 13.

28. Jeffrey Masten's work on "textual intercourse" also discusses nonheterosexual reproduction, considering play texts as fully collaborative textual products (*Textual Intercourse: Collaboration, Authorship, and Sexualities in Renaissance Drama* [Cambridge: Cambridge University Press, 1997]). Though Masten's work primarily traces these logics "between men" in the specific contexts of emergent institutions of drama, it has been "fruitful" for the more cross- or postgendered processes I am describing in *The Winter's Tale*.

29. For a decisive discussion of the incomprehensibility and density of the language of *The Winter's Tale*, see Stephen Orgel, "The Poetics of Incomprehensibility," *Shakespeare Quarterly* 42, no. 4 (winter 1991): 431–37.

simply stated in Cary's *Mariam:* "with friends there is not such a word as 'debt'."[30] The lords' previously mentioned celebration of kingly friendship ends with a line strongly predictive of Palamon and Arcite's ominous conclusion in prison: "I think there is not in the world either matter or malice to alter it" (1.1.31–32).[31] It will, of course, be altered beyond recognition in the scene to follow.

In 1.2, Polixenes extends the confounded economies typical of friendship discourses, describing an infinity of debt as he attempts to depart for Bohemia (1.2.3–9). While Leontes' desire to keep his friend's company is conventional enough, his insistence is not. Hence Leontes' first mistake in *The Winter's Tale* is not his rash hallucination of adultery between Polixenes and Hermione. It is instructive to turn to Cicero on this point to fully assess the import of Leontes' insistence that Polixenes stay. Cicero's *Laelius* proposes the following:

> Often . . . important duties arise which require . . . separation of friends; and he who would hinder the discharge of those duties because he cannot easily bear his grief at the absence of his friends, is not only weak and effeminate, but is far from reasonable in his friendship.[32]

It is this opening misstep by Leontes that sets the stage for others, and this sequencing will be repeated throughout the play. Later in the scene, Leontes speechlessly reflects the oppression of his own thoughts and so appears to others as if "he has lost some province, and a region / Loved as he loves himself" (1.2.365–66). This language suggests both losses, of Hermione and of Polixenes. Hermione, as wife, is easily discerned in the imperialist and geographic symbolics of Renaissance gender representations as a question of "dominions." But Polixenes registers equally as the loss in question, both in his frequent geographic designation as "Bohemia" and in the reflexive, "other self" poetics of the line. We may even hear in

30. Elizabeth Cary, *The Tragedy of Mariam, the Fair Queen of Jewry,* ed. Margaret Ferguson and Barry Weller (Berkeley and Los Angeles: University of California Press, 1994), 2.2.100.

31. Palamon concludes their friendship declamation with "I do not think it possible our friendship / Should ever leave us" (*The Two Noble Kinsmen,* 2.1.168–69).

32. Cicero, *De amicitia,* in *De senectute, De amicitia, De divinatione,* trans. W. A. Falconer (Cambridge, Mass.: Harvard University Press, 1923), pp. 184–85. The Latin reads: "saepe incidunt magnae res, ut discedendum sit ab amicis; quas qui impedire volt, quod desiderium non facile ferat, is et infirmus est mollisque natura et . . . in amicitia parum iustus."

it an echo of Edward II's statement to Gaveston upon his exile: "Thou from this land, I from my self am banished."[33] In a strange mingling of vocabularies, Leontes casts Polixenes in heirship terms, calling him "apparent to my heart" (1.2.175). The vocabularies of succession and friendship converge.

In the political crisis engendered by Leontes' fit of unreason, two further switching points between public institutional roles and private affections arise. The first involves heirship proper, and the second involves the figures serving in the offices of counsel. With the arrival of Leontes' heir, Mamillius, Leontes' suspicion of his wife reveals how close the doubled-self tropes of friendship are to the notion of children as (should-be) copies of their fathers. Referring to Mamillius's nose, Leontes considers how "They say it is a copy out of mine" (1.2.121). While the two kings were "as twinned lambs," Leontes and his son are "almost as like as eggs"—whose similarity was proverbial, according to Stephen Orgel's note on the line (129).[34] In the context of a royal family, of course, concerns about succession freight the image of the copy-child with matter beyond mere paternity. We have seen the uncanny relation of friendship's *alter idem* to kingship's *alius idem*, one doubling simultaneously and the other mirroring only across time. This scene brings the two formulas together closely enough to confuse them.

For there is not only an Oedipal rivalry but also a political one inherent in the position of the heir apparent.[35] This rivalry makes itself evident in the first scene of the play, when the attending lords cease to praise the mutuality of the kings' friendship only by turning to praise Leontes' heir and anticipating his succession with happiness (1.2.32–43). In the next scene, Leontes' mind turns just this corner, but the implications are more ominous. He moves seamlessly from doubting his friend to doubting his son.[36] Together, the political threat of the son-copy and the alleged sexual threat of the friend-copy both converge on Hermione. "You have mistook,

33. Marlowe, *Edward II* (1.1.118).

34. See also Montaigne's remark in "Of Experience": "The Greekes, the Latines, and wee use for the most expresse examples of similitude, that of egges" (*Essayes*, p. 962).

35. Indeed, such a rivalry suggests an odd propriety in Hal's self-cloaking in *Henry IV, 1 & 2*. Orgel provides useful discussion of the overtly political rivalry between King James and Prince Henry (Orgel, introduction to *A Winter's Tale*, p. 16).

36. For a detailed psychoanalytic reading of this crisis, see Stanley Cavell, *Disowning Knowledge in Six Plays of Shakespeare* (Cambridge: Cambridge University Press, 1987), pp. 193–96.

my lady, / Polixenes for Leontes," the angry husband charges (2.1.81–82). This transfer point also registers in Polixenes' description of his own son as "now my sworn friend and then mine enemy" (1.2.165). Ultimately, the death of the heir Mamillius and the exile of the friend are related, even substitutable, by-products of Leontes' mad misconduct.

But the laws of romance, of course, leave hope in play. When Leontes condemns the newborn Perdita, he exiles her "to some remote and desert place quite out / Of our dominions" (2.3.175–76). Sent to be a ward of chance and fortune, Perdita, Leontes' only political and biological heir and the extension of himself in time, leaves his "dominion" to be preserved within the custodial jurisdiction of Bohemia. Perdita harbors where the figures of friendship and counsel also find refuge. These figures custodially preserve and then restore the self and the state in Leontes' copy-child, whom Paulina (Hermione's ally and the wife of the Sicilian counselor, Antigonus) has termed "Although the print be little, the whole matter / And copy of the father," and whose like features Paulina exhaustively itemizes (2.3.98–107).

In the personage of the counselor Camillo, we find a related mingling of political and personal relations, here two roles (counselor and friend) in one person rather than one role refracting between two (heir and friend). Camillo's situation uneasily inhabits the two categories of private friend and political servant; Shakespeare carefully contrives to show the dangers of this blurring for the old counselor. In their first scene alone together, Leontes violently chides Camillo for either being negligent in his office or betraying Leontes' trust more intentionally. Leontes upbraids him, saying, "I have trusted thee, Camillo, / With all the nearest things to my heart, as well / My chamber-counsels, wherein, priest-like, thou / Hast cleansed my bosom" (1.2.232–35). "Chamber-counsels" evokes the sense of spatial and domestic reserve emerging from the institutional rise of the privy or withdrawing chamber, but Orgel glosses it in more personal terms as "intimate secrets." A privatized Leontes thus seems to invoke the affective language twice in the speech, instead of juxtaposing matters of the "heart" with matters "of office."

As he continues arraigning Camillo in the alternative, he names his counselor "a servant *grafted* in my serious trust" as a result of such confidences (1.2.243, emphasis mine). In this first explicit reference to grafting in the play, Shakespeare picks up the horticultural metaphors used to express the friendship between the two kings, which "rooted" and "branched." He intensifies the degree of artifice reckoned to inhere in the incorporation of two bodies into one in naming this technique.[37] The process of grafting, like the "double cherry" that grows "incorporate," yields another monstrous artificial body not far removed from Bacon's "monstrous" ingestion.

When Leontes proceeds to relate his erroneous view of Hermione, Camillo immediately and decisively checks his king with a sharp, perfectly Plutarchan sense of "becomingness" to the self: "'Shrew my heart, / You never spoke what did become you less / Than this, which to reiterate were sin" (1.2.278–80). An insistence that the (royal) self adhere to the standard of that self (i.e., not just to law or reason) voices the logic of Plutarch's doctor of subjectivity; indeed, Camillo goes on to urge Leontes to "be cured / Of this diseased opinion" (lines 293–94). The more unadulteratedly political case of Kent's addressing Lear sheds light on how political this intimate moment is. When Kent faces Lear's rebuke and exile for honesty, he too makes use of this language: "Kill thy physician, and thy fee bestow / Upon the foul disease."[38] If Kent may serve as the paragon of a counselor's performance, as Richard Strier has shown, Camillo is clearly in the same family.[39] Kent's banishment proceeds from true speech about Lear's madness; he proclaims he'll "shape his old course [i.e., honesty] in a country new" (1.1.188). This is in fact what *Camillo* does do in his optative exile to Bohemia. But the sense of service to which Kent adheres leads him to something quite different: disguised, he remains in Lear's jurisdiction and company, "for which I raz'd my likeness" (1.4.4).

Camillo's situation differs from Kent's in a key particular. He has been commanded to undertake a crime in the murder of Polixenes—"if I could find example / Of thousands that had struck annointed kings / And flourished after, I'd not do't" (1.2.353–55), he laments in soliloquy. Without underestimating the generic differences between the two plays, this affir-

37. For a wonderful treatment of "joinery" and its material implications for textual production, see Patricia Parker, "Rude Mechanicals," in *Subject and Object in Renaissance Culture*, ed. Margreta de Grazia, Maureen Quilligan, and Peter Stallybrass (Cambridge: Cambridge University Press, 1996), pp. 43–82.

38. Shakespeare, *King Lear*, in *The Complete Works of Shakespeare*, ed. David Bevington (New York: Longman, 1997), 1.1.164–65. Subsequent references are to this edition.

39. Richard Strier, "Shakespeare and Disobedience," in *Resistant Structures: Particularity, Radicalism, and Renaissance Texts* (Berkeley and Los Angeles: University of California Press, 1995), pp. 165–202. Strier strikingly connects the physician's metaphor with a radical text of political theory, George Buchanan's *De Jure Regni Apud Scotos,* which not only invokes the comparison, but similarly casts the prudential physician as one who "knows when and how to administer medicines" (p. 175).

mative unlawful order distinguishes Camillo's moral and legal situation. But Leontes' preceding speech makes additional reasons clear in a sobering, terse conflation of the languages of friendship and authority: "Do't, and thou hast the one half of my heart; / Do't not, thou splitt'st thine own" (lines 344–45). On this command's account, Camillo draws the inevitable conclusion, "I must / Forsake the court" (lines 358–59). Following the same trajectory as Falstaff and Gaveston and the reverse route from Kent, Camillo's way nevertheless involves continued service to his king.

For from this moment, we see the offices and attributes of friendly counsel give new meaning to Bacon's "Scattered Counsels" as they refract in an emblematic diaspora of good faith, just as, for example, Carol Thomas Neely describes sexual and marital issues "diffused" and "dispersed" among generations and continents in the play.[40] The doublings of self multiply. Camillo, counsel's figure, embarks to the king's true friend's kingdom in the role of counselor to Polixenes. As in his service to Leontes, the relation involves affective and official aspects. On the one hand, when Polixenes encounters Camillo under the changing circumstances in Sicilia, he notes, "Your changed complexions are to me a mirror, / Which shows me mine changed too; for I must be / A party in this alteration, finding / Myself thus altered with't" (1.2.376–79). The merged states involve seeing one's own fate in the face of another self. Polixenes relies on no political power to convince Camillo to inform him of a dangerous truth. Instead, he conjures him "by all the parts of man / Which honour does acknowledge" to advise him on his individual case in the prudential manner of statecraft: "Declare / What incidency thou dost guess of harm / Is creeping toward me; how far off, how near, / Which way to be prevented, if it be; / If not how best to bear it" (lines 397–401). This scripting of just how Camillo should advise him echoes the consultative counsel shown when, in *Othello,* the Duke and senators test emerging information about the Turkish fleet's approach—a scene demonstrating proper deliberation in statecraft.[41] Camillo's good-faith reply results in the beautiful poetry of Polixenes' invitation to friendship: "Give me thy hand; / Be pilot to me and thy places shall / Still [always] neighbour mine" (lines 442–44). The ambiguity of leadership here suggests the complexities of entrustment evident in friendship doctrines. Indeed, the disjunction beween "give me thy hand" (fiduciary, consoling) or neighborliness and "be pilot to me" (en-

40. Carol Thomas Neely, *Broken Nuptials in Shakespeare's Plays* (New Haven, Conn.: Yale University Press, 1985), pp. 166–209, 166.
41. Shakespeare, *Othello,* 1.3.

trusting, self-bestowing) recalls Montaigne's dramatic blurring of sovereignty and subjection.

Nevertheless, sixteen years later in Bohemia, the political fact of authority limits the volitional sense of what grew from a relation of honor and liberty in Sicilia. When Camillo wishes to return to Sicilia to die, Polixenes argues against it on grounds of his necessity to Bohemian affairs. Urging the matter of his son's errancy, Polixenes exhorts Camillo to be his "present partner in this business, and lay aside the thoughts of Sicilia" (which may refer to the place and to Leontes equally). Camillo's rote, obedient, servant's response chillingly belies its assertion of willingness: "I willingly obey your command" (4.2.50–52).

From this point, Camillo will take up the guidance of Florizel in the prince's breach with his father, and his rhetoric extends the multiplicities of self traced so far: "If you may please to think I love the King [Polixenes], / And through him what's nearest to him, which is / Your gracious self, embrace but my direction" (4.4.518–20). Camillo's master plan takes them all—himself, Polixenes, Perdita, Florizel, and more—back to Sicilia. There the lost copy-child heir, Perdita, returns to the penitent king from his copy-friend's dominion in the arms of that friend's copy-child. The straying heir Florizel (whose mother "did print your royal father off, / Conceiving you" [5.1.124]), though estranged from his own father, gains Leontes as "friend" to his "desires" (5.1.229–30). The "twinned lambs" resume their doubled being, too, all through this political counselor's services. Another self effects the restoration of four *further* other selves.

Camillo, of course, is not the only counselor in *The Winter's Tale.* Two others crucially complete the play's portrait of counsel: Antigonus and, more significantly, Paulina. Unlucky Antigonus receives the immoral order from the king that his newborn heir be "instantly consumed with fire" (2.3.133). Like Emilia's scene in *The Two Noble Kinsmen,* a ruler's rash decrees bring his more reasonable court to its knees: "On our knees we beg . . . that you do change this purpose. . . . We all kneel" (lines 150–52). Antigonus (having agreed to Leontes' bargain constraining him to any "adventure" to save the baby girl) is ordered on pain of death to abandon her in "some remote and desert place quite out / Of our dominions" (lines 175–76). Antigonus, a masculine Antigone facing a dilemma of obedience to two sets of law, makes the wrong choice to comply with Leontes' outrageous order. He may thus deserve to meet the death he finds on Bohemian sands. But the bear that famously devours him on the seacoast, an avatar of Leontes' rashness and brutality, is also an important visual trope from friendship lore. When Antigonus exits "pursued by a bear," he suffers

FIGURE 8. Arnold Freitag, *Fucatae amicitiae nota,* from *Mythologia Ethica* (Antwerp: Christopher Plantijn, 1579), p. 61. Photo courtesy of The Newberry Library, Chicago.

the proverbial fate of those abandoned by false friends. Stressing how only adversity reveals whether friends are true, Arnold Freitag's *Mythologica Ethica* (1579) gives a visual and animal form to this friendship test, one originally stemming from Aesop (fig. 8). While the false friend runs off to hide up in a tree, the unfriended victim is left to the savagery of a ravenous bear, a creature Thomas Nashe calls "the most cruellest of all beasts."[42] The image, picked up in Henry Peacham's *Minerva Britanna* (fig. 9), thus encodes the dangers risked should a friend prove false. While critics have puzzled over its violence and incongruity, the bear scene in *The Winter's Tale* literally enacts these popular visual emblems of friendship betrayal in specifying the fate of Antionus.

However, Antigonus makes bad choices in his dilemma. Camillo describes it precisely, in language expressing the same crisis that Cary's

42. Thomas Nashe, *The Unfortunate Traveller,* in *An Anthology of Elizabethan Prose Fiction,* ed. Paul Salzman (Oxford: Oxford University Press, 1987), p. 235.

FIGURE 9. Henry Peacham, *In amicos falsos,* from *Minerva Britanna or A garden of hero-ical devises* (London: W. Dight, 1612), p. 148. Photo courtesy of The Newberry Library, Chicago.

Mariam uses friendship and marital terms to explore: "obedience to a master" who is "in rebellion with himself" makes "all that are his so too" (1.2.350–52). Antigonus's compliance thus "rebels" against a truer, ideal-ized royal self he is both to produce and to obey, as Kent makes powerfully clear in *Lear.* The actions of romance allow Camillo's loyalty to effect, over enormous gaps of space and time, the preservation of Leontes' self, for re-providing his successor perpetuates "his most sovereign name" (5.1.26) in time, and another well-served "other" self returns in Polixenes. Paulina, however (whom Strier aptly describes as Kent's closest counterpart),[43] remains a constant presence within Leontes' court, unlike Camillo and Antigonus. Perhaps gender operates in a manner similar to Kent's self-disguise. Her role as counselor-friend is perhaps the most surprising devel-

43. Strier, "Shakespeare and Disobedience," p. 201.

opment in the play (beyond devouring bears and statues that come to life, that is).

Arguments considering the gender implications of the play's conclusion tend to focus on evaluating Hermione's restoration, construing the return of the "dead" mother in Shakespeare's most unusual finale. Some critics begin to find a foothold for womanhood in the play's arguably softer landing at the end of act 5. Neely has argued that the play's miracles are effected specifically by its female characters, who wield agency "by virtue of their acceptance of 'issue,'" particularly their positive relation to sexuality and childbirth as the ground for "regeneration."[44] She proposes that "manifestations of healthy sexuality" lead to an "easy joyous acceptance of sexuality and procreation which . . . comes to dominate *The Winter's Tale*."[45] While conceding the play's ultimate patriarchalism, Adelman suggests that it uniquely "restores the mother to life and makes the father's generativity and authority contingent on the mother's return."[46] Still focusing on Hermione as the central case, other critics argue that the play's female characters are especially subordinated in the restoration of Leontes' powers. Traub has argued that "the final scene works as wish-fulfillment for Leontes, who not only regains his virtuous wife, . . . but also reassumes his kingly command of all social relations."[47] David Schalwyk has likened the effects of the drama to Prospero's appropriation of the speech of Medea, as an "enactment of both the indispensability and the total appropriation, and thus repression, of the 'lady's word' in all its terrible potency."[48] Both sides here would seem to evaluate Shakespeare's unsurprising preference for restoring "good government" in terms requiring a nonpatriarchal political revision *before* allowing either a less patriarchal construction of gender or a different sense of its role in the process of that restoration to evolve.

The linkage between feminine gender and sexual reproduction *or* eroticism necessary to these arguments is as much a feature of Renaissance gender ideologies as it is a means to explain Shakespeare's establishment of a less misogynistic modus vivendi with "the woman's part" in *The Winter's Tale*. The focus on Hermione as exemplary in this regard, with Paulina figuring secondarily as her attendant and advocate, may unnecessarily di-

44. Neely, "Women and 'Issue,'" pp. 181, 182.
45. Ibid., p. 193.
46. Adelman, *Suffocating Mothers,* pp. 220–36.
47. Traub, "Jewels, Statues and Corpses," p. 45.
48. David Schalwyk, "'A Lady's 'Verily' Is as Potent as a Lord's': Women, Word and Witchcraft in *The Winter's Tale*," *English Literary Renaissance* 22, no. 2 (spring 1992): 242–72, 272.

rect such a result. Contemporary critics, obviously, are not the authors of
such a conflation, which has instances beyond number in the texts of all
periods. But it seems that this play, oddly, may actually trouble this linkage
of women and sex. Rather than resolving itself through an affirmation of
"healthy sexuality," the drama severely limits such expression by crafting
enormous powers for other forms of "regeneration"—friendship, counsel,
and their associated modes of speech and writing all serve to author selves
in other ways, ways that seem freer from the gender determinisms of biological processes. This effort by the play furthers the provocative analogies
and identifications to be made—through friendship's logics—*across* gender, as we have seen in chapter 2.[49]

Despite the clearly overwhelming factors colluding to analogize female
sexuality to female speech and writing in order to regulate both, *The Winter's Tale* declines to maintain that juridical linkage.[50] Against the weight of
an extensive and persistent ideological barrier to free-speaking womanhood, when Paulina boldly determines to admonish the king, she stolidly
announces that "the office / Becomes a woman best" (2.2.30–31). Under
what available logic can this possibly be true? Though Paulina has just been
informed of Perdita's birth and perhaps that announcement could be said
to "become a woman," that is not at all what she has in mind. Perfectly paralleling Kent's diagnosis of Lear's madness, her topic is "these dangerous,
unsafe lunes i'th'king . . . / He must be told on't, and he shall; the office /
Becomes a woman best. I'll take't upon me" (2.2.29–30). Nor does she
plan to implement any suitably feminine or agreeable mode of speech: "If
I prove honey-mouthed, let my tongue blister" (line 32). This is a rich
self-curse, in which a failure to speak acerbic, sharp words will injure the
tongue. But we recognize in her charted action the fully medicalized ways
of Plutarchan friendly counsel.[51] Excoriating the courtiers around Leontes

---

49. For the interest of such crossings, see Eve Kosofsky Sedgwick, "Across Genders,
Across Sexuality: Willa Cather and Others," *South Atlantic Quarterly* 88, no. 1 (winter
1989): 53–72.

50. For a full exploration of the genderings of authorship (for women and men), see
Wendy Wall, *The Imprint of Gender: Authorship and Publication in the English Renaissance*
(Ithaca, N.Y.: Cornell University Press, 1993). As discussed in chapter 2, just this link-
age of chastity and silence as against publicity and voice is explored and protested in *The
Tragedie of Mariam.*

51. Here, Paulina's strategy might usefully be compared with the strategies of Renaissance women authors as Jonathan Goldberg has recently framed them, describing the "complex set of gender identifications that enable [a] writing position" (*Desiring Women Writing:
English Renaissance Examples* [Stanford, Calif.: Stanford University Press, 1997], p. 52 and
passim).

who obsequiously tender his passion ("You / That creep like shadows by
him and do sigh / At each his needless heavings"), Paulina heralds her
arrival with "I do come with words as medicinal as true— / Honest as
either — to purge him of that humour / That presses him from sleep"
(lines 33–39).

Leontes cries out to his attendants against "that audacious lady" and
reprimands them: "I charged thee that she should not come about me; / I
knew she would" (2.3.42–44). Holding her ground, Paulina calls herself
"your physician, / Your most obedient counsellor" (2.3.54–55). Leontes
marshals his best gynophobic vocabulary to resist her offices and dismiss
her words: "a mankind witch," "a most intelligencing bawd," "Dame Part-
let," "crone," and "callet" (lines 67, 68, 75, 76, and 90). Paulina is tainted
with witchcraft, gender-crossing, sexual promiscuity, and the proverbial
talkativeness of the "hen." None of these epithets, which index a whole
range of rationales for why Paulina's speech might *not*, in Renaissance
terms, "become a woman" at all, have any effect.

Why does Shakespeare place the terms of gendered infamy in the
mouth of a raving madman, a madman who happens to be a king reject-
ing the most urgent and valuable form of true counsel? Paulina's violation
of strictures enjoining *female* speech certainly intensifies the politically ex-
igent position of these medicinal words. Her husband, pointedly, is there
to be taunted by Leontes for failing to control his wife ("thou art woman-
tired, unroosted" [2.3.74]), but he, almost jocularly, informs the king that
if he were to "hang all the husbands / That cannot do that feat, you'll leave
yourself / Hardly one subject" (2.3.109–11). This scene represents a major
commingling of domestic and political subjections and insurrections, with
the private and public utterly, overtly entangled. Thus, Paulina's disturbance of the gendered proprieties of marriage as they relate to speech and
governance is related to her role as royal physician and counselor of state.
In a sense, Plutarchan "liberty of speech" in friendship serves to invigorate
both the subject's specifically limited powers of dissent and the wife's narrowly scripted powers to check an errant husband. All three paradigms
evaluate the same question, but it is friendship that gives the rebuker the
greatest scope of "liberty."[52] In gender terms, this convergence raises fasci-
nating re-genderings of a variety of roles: the counselor's role may be seen

52. For suggestive speculation on the relation of this wifely privilege to political rights
of speech and dissent, see Constance Jordan, *Renaissance Feminism: Literary Texts and Political Models* (Ithaca, N.Y.: Cornell University Press, 1990), p. 121, note 54.

as gendered feminine in these lights, as the position of subjects under monarchy may also bear the suggestion of such a gendering.

The gendered complexity of Paulina's technique continues. Charging Leontes to the heart with recriminations upon the "death" of the queen, Paulina finds that her words have wounded him, and she falls back on gendered speech conventions with a pathetic, seeming retraction. But she uses a friendship script also, employing "certain fomentations and lenitive infusions" as Plutarch suggests: "Alas, I have showed too much / The rashness of a woman" and "Sir, royal sir, forgive a foolish woman" (3.2.218–19) His replies, too late, justify her prior speech on the basis of its truth: "thou didst speak but well / When most the truth" (lines 230–31).

And yet we know she lies. For it is Paulina who announces Hermione's "death" with the marked, self-consciously rhetorical "I say she's dead—I'll swear it" (3.2.201). This is not the last we will see of these phrasings, but this act of speech is perhaps Paulina's most "audacious" of all. She—appropriately, as far as the play is concerned—serves well when she lies. When Paulina intervenes this way in Leontes' unfolding narrative, she assumes a responsibility for his moral condition and intellectual knowledge; except for her goodwill, she operates much as Iago does when he perverts the norms of friendship and counsel in *Othello*. Harboring Hermione in the removed custodial spaces of female friendship ("that removed house" [5.2.104–5]), she takes up Leontes as a ward to be tutored. Unlike Bertram in *All's Well That Ends Well*, this male, a king, submits—and to a female authority at that—for sixteen years. Although the final act has the properly schooled Leontes reminiscing and lamenting, "O that ever I / Had squared me to thy counsel" (5.1.51–52), he has, in fact, been "squared"—shaped, framed, and guided—by its fiduciary and falsifying operations.

Counsel's Craft, Friendship's Graft

By the end of act 3, then, Leontes is under the tutelage of Paulina, Hermione is reserved apart under Paulina's care, and Perdita, Polixenes, and Camillo are all safe-harbored in Bohemia in a series of nonbiological or not strictly familial relations. Act 4 takes place in Bohemia, after sixteen years of this regime of entrustment have passed. Its central scene represents a sheep-shearing festival over which Perdita presides, costumed as Flora, for the old shepherd who has been her adoptive father in the pastoral setting of Polixenes' kingdom. Courted by Polixenes' son, Leontes' lost heir plays the role of "mistress o' th' feast" (4.4.68) and will serve as hostess to the

FIGURE 10. Arnold Freitag, *Fictae amicitiae non fidendum*, from *Mythologia Ethica* (Antwerp: Christopher Plantijn, 1579), p. 37. Photo courtesy of The Newberry Library, Chicago.

disguised king and Camillo, who come to discover (and foil) Florizel's courtship. A consideration of the guests hosted at this sheep-shearing suggests additional levels at which paradigms of friendship structure *The Winter's Tale,* and it will provide the basis, finally, for interpreting the political and affective stakes of Camillo and Paulina's agency as counselor-friends.

If the bear figures among the *dramatis animalia* of friendship as the danger from which a true friend gives assistance and protection, the wolf personifies false friendship (fig. 10). His smiling face belies a savage motive, indexed in the proverb "beware the wolf in sheep's clothing." The rogue Autolycus ("the wolf himself," in Orgel's gloss of his entrance at 4.3.1), "littered under Mercury" (4.3.25), approaches the domain of the sheep-shearing singing as he anticipates the ruses he will play on its rustic participants. His behavior directly reflects Camillo's early instruction to Leontes to bear "a countenance" like that which "friendship wears at feasts" (1.2.339–40). Leontes' and Autolycus's mutual abuse of good-faith dealing, indeed, links them as false friends.[53] As further evidence of the noncentrality of the family drama to this play for Renaissance spectators, Orgel observes that while "no reference whatever to the statue scene survives from the seventeenth century," Autolycus seems to have "left the strongest impression, even morally," at least to judge from astrologer Simon Forman's account of the play.[54] For Forman, Autolycus was literally memorable, "the rogue that came in all tattered like colt-pixie." It is from this "wolf himself" that Forman draws the moral message of the play: "Beware of trusting feigned beggars or fawning fellows"[55]—wolves in sheep's clothing or singers of "Placebo." This contemporary gloss on the social and moral meaningfulness of *The Winter's Tale* considers it pithily instructive, reading it to speak in the very cadences of emblem book proverbialism.

On the other hand, when Polixenes and Camillo arrive disguised at the sheep-shearing, they are twice designated "unknown friends," marking them apart from the "false friend" repertoire that Autolycus signals. The old shepherd urges Perdita to "bid / These unknown friends to's welcome, for it is / A way to make us better friends, more known" (4.4.64–66). Perdita's awkward welcome offers them "flowers of winter"—rosemary and rue—and a debate ensues on the appropriateness of this herbal designation of the "unknown friends" as aged. Rosemary, associated with remembrance, was thereby linked to the memory of absent friends by Sir Thomas More: "I have rosemary not just for the bees in my garden, but for absent friends." The old shepherd's hope of making these visitors "better friends, more known," however, must be postponed. The moment at which he asks these "friends unknown [to] bear witness" to the betrothal of the heirs, Polixenes unveils himself with the epithets and curses of enmity instead (4.4.379). Their "better friendship" awaits the last scenes of the play.

Meanwhile, Perdita's exchange with Polixenes at the sheep-shearing offers a classic variant of a perennial Renaissance debate between nature and art.[56] This exchange will also provide the metaphors by which notions of both friendship practice and the counselor's craft may be further speci-

---

53. James Chandler points out to me that the dramatic effect of Leontes and Autolycus equally presiding over their respective portions of the play, especially by means of asides, further situates them as doubles in the drama.

54. Orgel, introduction to *The Winter's Tale,* pp. 63, 50.

55. "Simon Forman's Account of *The Winter's Tale,*" reprinted in Orgel, ed., *The Winter's Tale,* appendix A, p. 233.

56. See Orgel, introduction to *The Winter's Tale,* p. 46 and note on p. 172; see also Howard Felperin, "Our Carver's Excellence: *The Winter's Tale,*" in *Shakespearean Romance* (Princeton, N.J.: Princeton University Press, 1972), pp. 211–45.

fied. In her garden, Perdita declines to cultivate "the fairest flowers o' th' season / . . . carnations and streaked gillyvors, / Which some call nature's bastards"; she has no wish "to get slips of them" (i.e., to cultivate unnaturally by putting stems and cuttings of other plants into use) (4.4.81–83, 85).[57] Her purist rationale "bastardizes" these products of hybridization and the human hand on the grounds that their multicolored blossoms express "an art" which "shares / With great creating nature" (lines 87–88). Horticultural science, interfering with nature's ordinary course, usurps methods and practices reserved to nature itself. Polixenes disagrees. Since the "means" available to art are themselves of nature ("no mean / But nature makes that mean"), the products of art are products of nature too: "so over that art / Which you say adds to nature, is an art / That nature makes" (lines 89–92). Polixenes goes on to detail the process of *grafting,* describing the placement of a branch ("scion" or "bud") into the supporting body of a root ("stock" or "bark")(lines 93–95). This echo of the "rooting" and "branching" friendship of the two kings and of Camillo's being "a grafted servant" retrospectively invigorates those metaphors. Polixenes essentially theorizes the process that results in friendship's "artificial body"—two bodies are literally incorporated by being grafted into one.

But the claim here is also larger than the provision of an expressive conceit for this double-bodied state. It also specifies the practice of intersubjectivity we have considered, through counselorship, to be friendship in action. In his discussion of *The Winter's Tale,* Howard Felperin concisely proposes that "mimesis and poesis are here one and the same," expanding on the various instances of art in the drama to conclude that "the art of the play is romantic and realistic at once. . . . The motto . . . is not art for art's sake . . . but art for life's sake."[58] Moreover, the play does much to specify, in fact, what *kind* of "life forms" are involved here. Situating the much-celebrated place of "art" within a perspective linking friendship to its methods of "artificial" life gives the abstract category "art" both a social and a political context, embodying its agents as counselor-friends.

Grafting represents, first of all, an ongoing mode of regeneration outside or beyond "natural" forms involving the replication of copies;

---

57. For background on these flowers, see William O. Scott, "Seasons and Flowers in *The Winter's Tale," Shakespeare Quarterly* 22 (1971): 87–90; and Stanton J. Linden, "Perdita and the Gillyvors: *The Winter's Tale," Notes and Queries* 26 (1979): 140.

58. Felperin, "Our Carver's Excellence," pp. 229, 244. See also Carol Thomas Neely, who argues that art is subordinated to life (insofar as Hermione's final act of *speech* signifies her fullest emergence from the artifice of the statue) in "*The Winter's Tale:* The Triumph of Speech," *SEL: Studies in English Literature, 1500–1900,* vol. 15 (1975): 321–38.

Polixenes calls it "an art / Which doth *mend* nature—*change* it rather—but / The art itself is nature" (4.4.95–97, emphases mine). Certainly, the graft confounds a notion of individual "life span," as we have seen Bacon construing friendship to do. Even more, grafting specifies friendship's craft as an intersubjective kind of *writing*. For Shakespeare advances a pun on grafting and graphesis, the "graft" and the "graph'd." In Sonnet 37, for example, the poet conscripts the grafting metaphor to describe an intersubjective formation in which another self resupplies the self, itself. Considering the "beauty, birth, or wealth, or wit" of the intimate friend, the poet is "suffficed" and invigorated by means of grafting: "I make my love ingrafted to this store."[59] Sonnet 15 explicitly links this device to writing and to its powerful, perhaps infinite, capacity for the regeneration of the other: "And, all in war with Time for love of you, / As he takes from you, I ingraft you new."[60] The poet's eternizing verse imbues the self, by grafting/graphing, with a new birth of life.

Paulina and Camillo both manage other lives by such writerly means; their illusionistic arts, as Paulina repeatedly insists in the final scene, are "lawful." The twinned crafts of this faithful duo conjointly mend and perpetuate the lives, moral conditions, and posterity of two kings. First, Camillo's intervention in act 4 begins the movement that will reunite all the key figures in Sicilia; it takes the form of theatrical direction and, crucially, *scripting*. When the young Florizel determines to flee his father's kingdom with Perdita by ship, Camillo sees a chance to do what can only be described as "universal" good. He can effect the desires and/or best interests of two heirs, two kings, and himself in addition. He asks Florizel to "embrace but my direction" (4.4.520), and he proceeds to script an entire false plot for Florizel to enact. He will visit Leontes as if on a mission from Polixenes. Camillo directs, *"I'll write you down,"* and instructs Florizel in that "which shall point you forth at every sitting / What you must say" (4.4.557–59, emphasis mine). Camillo is doubly a playwright here, directing the local drama of Florizel's escape as well as the grander scheme of a more universal reunification.

Camillo promises to underwrite Florizel's heirship in Leontes' eyes, even as Polixenes has barred him from succession: "it shall be so my care / To have you royally appointed, as if the scene you play were mine" (4.4.588–90). Perdita picks up the language of theatrical, scripted selves, too, accepting her role in the charade by conceding, "I see the play so

59. Shakespeare, Sonnet 37, lines 5, 11, and 8.
60. Shakespeare, Sonnet 15, lines 13–14.

lies / That I must bear a part" (lines 650–51). Indeed, this play does lie, and continues to do so, until these better-ordered lies replace a disordered reality. When Florizel addresses Camillo in this context, however, he does not name him in the terms of the stage. Echoing the notion of the counselor as physician, not only of the self but of its posterity, he calls him "Preserver of my father, now of me, / The medicine of our house" (lines 584–85). "Pilot," "preserver," "medicine": with an almost religious aura here, Camillo is the sine qua non of three lives, and, ultimately, two dynasties and kingdoms.

For this latter, of course, the complementary theater of Paulina is required. Her staged illusion of Hermione's return to life, complete with curtains, unveiling, and an audience replete with royal blood, takes place in her chapel. The scene, marked by stages of silence, wonder, fear, grief, and amazement, culminates Paulina's script of Leontes' civil repentance: "It is required / You do awake your faith" (5.3.94–95). When Paulina calls Hermione from "Death," claiming "Dear life redeems you," Hermione seems literally redeemed; but it is Leontes, as the object of Paulina's long, therapeutic plot, whose redemption is at stake (line 103). Like Camillo in Bohemia, Paulina is "the medicine of [Leontes's] house." As Camillo had been entrusted with Leontes' "chamber-counsels" and "priest-like . . . cleansed my bosom," so Paulina's succeeding custodial role bears the marks of religious re-authoring and direction. Leontes himself had cast his faithlessness toward Polixenes ("against whose person / So sacred as it is, I have done sin" [5.1.170–71]) as a kind of virtual religion, as we have seen Donne do in his *Letters to Severall Persons*.[61] To invoke Bacon's terms, Paulina's quasi-religious process also finds its place in friendship's register:

> No Receipt openeth the Heart, but a true Frend; To whom you may impart, Griefes, Joyes, Feares, Hopes, Suspicions, Counsels, and whatsoever lieth upon the Heart, to oppresse it, in a kind of Civill Shrift, or confession. (p. 81)

Paulina's script does effect "a kind of Civill Shrift" as she applies the frame of religious awe to essentially secular and emblematically political matters.

As authors of a general amity through the practices of counsel enshrined in friendship doctrine, Paulina and Camillo are, in the strongest sense, the heroes of *The Winter's Tale*. Their faithful deployment of false-

---

61. John Donne, *Letters to Severall Persons of Honour* (London: J. Flesher, 1651), p. 87.

hoods that *should* be true performatively enacts them as "truths." Thus the play's well-attended themes of art and theatricality not only can be specified as writing, but even more, as the writing practices of a custodial friend who scripts the proper self for an errant self. It is not just about writing as an abstract phenomenon, but a much more high-impact, transitive, grafting practice of counselors and friends: *"I write you."* When Paulina and Camillo are paired in "marriage" in the play's last scene, aged and successful, what need have they of the sexual reproduction that most act 5 marriage gestures normally imply? For, as friendly counselors, their artificial forms of regeneration have already written two royal houses, two kingdoms into order, administering "the offices and duties which are beseeming" the selves in their custody. Their proposed "marriage," instead, takes its entire force from Renaissance notions favoring likeness: this "marriage of true minds," the roles of gender having been elided, enacts a union of *likes*.

Friendship's Preternatural Fruits; Political Births

The Winter's Tale, viewed in this light, prefigures the juxtapositioning Derrida makes in *Glas,* in which he situates the Hegelian family and its mechanisms (like the signature) against a reading of Jean Genet that emphasizes a "transformation of [the] proper name," in part through metaphors of grafting and flowers.[62] But while Derrida's exfoliations grow out of Genet's oppositional erotics, Shakespeare (perhaps typically) positions himself apart from *any* sexuality here. This kind of sidelining manages the traumas of sexual reproduction and foregrounds a form of regeneration practiced by and upon both genders. It is by this means that Shakespeare seems able to construct a reunion unlike all his other plays. The contrast between the silenced Imogen still in boy's clothes at the end of *Cymbeline* and the final line of *The Winter's Tale* (in which a king requests a woman to "lead away" [5.3.155]) is enormous. The lens of contemporary heterosexuality and the notions of "family drama" from which it stems have occluded our view of Shakespeare's least gender-exclusive rejoinder to what he seems to have seen as a deterministic biologism, a determinism of just the sort Montaigne tried to escape in the friendship essay. We have seen that contemporary responses to the play, for example, did not necessarily center on Hermione's return. The potentially reproductive plot of Florizel

---

62. Jacques Derrida, *Glas,* trans. John P. Leavey Jr. and Richard Rand (Lincoln: University of Nebraska Press, 1986), p. 5.

and Perdita remains embryonic at best, dwarfed by the magnitude of the custodial preservation of their parents.

While the Hermione scene is enacted before our eyes in 5.3, the preceding scene actually complicates the meaning of our being able to "see" the statue "revive." Three gentlemen discuss the rush of events in Sicilia. Reporting that the court has removed to Paulina's for "some great matter," the First Gentleman agrees that they, too, should attend: "Who would be thence that has the benefit of access? Every wink of an eye, some new grace will be born" (5.2.107–9). A wider circle is flocking to this spectacle of new birth, which is confirmed by the stage direction for 5.3, which lists proper names of speaking characters and adds "Lords, *etc.*"

Presence at *preceding* new births of grace, however, has been explicitly unavailable. The gentlemen's discussion of this echoes the reportedly overwhelming intensity of offstage scenes like the one of Duncan's murder in *Macbeth,* scenes and sights described as unbearable or unrepresentable.[63] Strong language of admiration, wonder, and passion heralds the Second Gentleman's conclusion that "such a deal of wonder is broken out within this hour that ballad-makers cannot be able to express it" (5.2.23–25). The discussion refers to the arrival of Camillo and Polixenes from Bohemia. Asking, "Did you see the meeting of the two kings?" the Third Gentleman avers, "then have you lost a sight which was to be seen, cannot be spoken of" (lines 42–43). He speaks, nevertheless, in friendship's exalted rhetoric. As friendship for Bacon "redoubleth Joyes," in the royal case "one joy crown[s] another," and the odd plurals—"there was casting up of eyes, holding up of hands"—resume (lines 44,46–47). A sense of formality, ceremony, and diplomacy resumes as well, with the claim that "the dignity of this act was worth the audience of kings and princes, for by such was it acted" (lines 78–79). Picking up the language of scripted parts, this assessment also frames the scene as far removed from the ordinary sight of spectators limited by private status. The kings are rescripted into their proper roles and place, and the private persons (of the cast and the audience) are reinterpellated too.

The notion of new births of grace, however, is not limited to the exalted plots of kings. For such matters are also the concerns of the lower-plot, Bohemian pastoral characters, who also find themselves "altered" in Sicilia. As the three gentlemen depart for Paulina's, Autolycus, who has

---

63. In *Macbeth,* Macduff announces the king's murder: "O horror, horror, horror! Tongue nor heart / Cannot conceive nor name thee! / . . . / Approach the chamber and destroy your sight with a new Gorgon" (2.3.64–65, 71–72).

been mainly silent in the scene, remains onstage. He spies the approach of the old shepherd and his son, and he identifies them as "those I have done good to against my will," his wolfish undermining of friendship's good-will having been thwarted (5.2.121). The ensuing discussion represents a hilarious spoof on the Renaissance concept of the "gentleman *born*." Orgel cites *The Booke of Honour and Armes* (1590), which specifies that "in say-ing a gentleman borne, we meane he must be descended from three degrees of gentry, both on the mother's and the father's side."[64] The shepherd and his son have been raised retroactively to "preposterous estate" (malaprop-ism for *prosperous*) by means of their adoptive relation to Perdita, now known to be a princess (5.2.142–45). Autolycus's malapropism also has a perfect correctness, though, since the send-up represents an inversion of temporal order, of pre- and post-, with respect to the social meanings of birth.

The three characters conduct an extensive play on words not only about becoming a gentleman, but also recasting, comically now, what it means to "be born." The son taunts Autolycus: "this other day . . . I was no gentleman born. . . . Give me the lie, do, and try whether I am not now a gentleman born" (5.2.126, 129–30). He requests to be cross-examined to determine whether he is lying. These latter-day births, of course, are noth-ing biological and are entirely social in nature, and the Clown's vocabulary even seems to confound and redefine family names in optative terms:

> I was a gentleman born before my father, for the King's son took me by the hand and called me brother, and then the two Kings called my father brother, and then the prince my brother and the princess my sister called my father father, and so we wept; and there were the first gentlemanlike tears that ever we shed. (5.2.134–40)

Autolycus, naturally, smells an opportunity for a redemptive, new birth of his own. He asks the preposterously raised Clown for a good report to the prince, Autolycus's former master. In *Henry IV, Part 2,* we have seen Davy urge Shallow,

> a knave should have some countenance at his friend's request. An honest man, sir, is able to speak for himself, when a knave is not . . . if I cannot once or twice in a quarter bear out a knave against an honest man, I have but very little credit with your worship. The knave is my honest friend, sir. (5.1.39–44)

---

64. Orgel, ed., *The Winter's Tale,* note on p. 223 to 5.2.124.

In *The Winter's Tale,* the Clown offers to swear to the prince that Autolycus is "as honest a true fellow as any in Bohemia." Precisely echoing Paulina's false avowal of Hermione's death ("I *say* she's dead—I'll *swear* it"), the old father suggests he had better "say it" than "swear it"—lest "it be false." The Clown, however, has the last word, in a preposterously correct deformation of something Cicero, Montaigne, or any proper friendship moralist would refrain from specifying: "If it be never so false, a true gentleman may swear it in the behalf of his friend" (5.2.157–58). Friendship's fruits double as false and true, as preternatural and necessary. Whether we construe them in private or public registers, the practices of friendship turn our sights away from processes like sexual reproduction and toward the far more daily matter of *regeneration.*

Magna Civitas; Magna Solitudo:
Bureaucratic Forms and Civic Conditions

ᕽ

> Luckes, my fair falcon, and your fellows all,
> How well pleasant it were your liberty!
> Ye not forsake me that fair might ye befall.
> But they that sometime liked my company
> Like lice away from dead bodies they crawl.
> Lo! What proof in light adversity!
> But ye, my birds, I swear by all your bells,
> *Ye be my friends and so be but few else.*[1]
> —Thomas Wyatt

In 1541, Thomas Wyatt well knew a subject's experience of embodied monarchy: a swirling pattern of preferment, imprisonment, and exile marks his life under Henry VIII. An esquire of the royal body, he enjoyed important ambassadorial and military appointments—but also endured more than one sojourn in the Tower of London. His satires on retirement to the country make a virtue of the same necessity Falstaff will face in his exile in Gloucestershire. In "Mine Owne John Poyntz," Wyatt reports his decision to "flee the press of courts" rather than "live thrall under the awe / Of lordly looks,"[2] arguing that virtuous autonomy can be sustained only far afield from the contingencies of court life. Instead of dangerously engaging "the friendly foe with his double face" (line 60), Wyatt can meet his hawks, in poetry, under the clear skies of "Kent and Christendom" (line 100). Neither of these two geographies names an "England," and the nation appears here as the place from which friendship is absent.

Wyatt concludes the poem to his hawks by asserting, "Ye be my friends,

---

1. Thomas Wyatt, *The Complete Poems,* ed. R. A. Rebholz (New Haven, Conn.: Yale University Press, 1978), Epigram 68, p. 101. Subsequent references are to this edition.

2. Wyatt, "Mine owne John Poyntz," lines 2–5, p. 186.

and so be but few else." How does this expression compare to the often recirculated one that Montaigne and others attributed to Aristotle, "O my friends, there is no friend"? Both apostrophes address "my friends," but Wyatt's addressees, one feels, are neither his birds nor even the elusive "few else." Instead, Wyatt seems to address someone—is it the king he knew?—who has somehow been "no friend" in a way far more concrete than Aristotle's sense of a philosophical unattainability. While, as Derrida has argued, Aristotle's "no friend" invokes the future possibility of friendship ("Become the friends to whom I aspire"),[3] the lonely Wyatt's friends have already abandoned him.

As Bacon will later argue, however, solitude can take an altogether different form. This solitude lies not in social retreat or abandonment, but in social immersion of a sort. Between Wyatt and Bacon, we see a sea change in the ways they grasp the shapes of government and civic life. While Wyatt's affective plea makes sense of these relational terms by using an intimate and embodied register, Bacon's perspective begins to engage the more systematic question of anonymous public forms. Specifying what true solitude is, Bacon writes, "the Latin Adage meeteth with it a little; *Magna Civitas, Magna Solitudo;* Because in a great Towne, Frends are scattered."[4] Here Bacon disavows any direct analogy between friendship and larger forms of polity. He rebuts, as so many before him had done, the applicability of friendship discourses in the broader schemes of democracy into which they will later be appropriated—schemes that will postdate the demise of "Renaissance friendship."

Generalizing the individuating affect that Renaissance friendship celebrates will take it outside the realm of its own logics. We have seen in chapter 6 that Bacon's sense of "scattered counsels" (always keeping something in reserve and partitioning information among one's auditors) was good wisdom in a king's case, but was the sign of friendship failure for the private person. Against this scattering, Bacon emphasizes that friendship refers to an absolute ascendancy by one person, an other/the same: "I single

3. Jacques Derrida, "The Politics of Friendship," *The Journal of Philosophy* 85, no. 11 (November 1988): 632–44, 635.

4. Francis Bacon, "Of Frendship," in *The Essays or Counsels, Civill and Morall,* ed. Michael Kiernan (Cambridge: Harvard University Press. 1985), pp. 80–87, 81. Subsequent references are to this edition and appear in the text. Here, too, is Robert Burton's paraphrase of one of Cicero's letters to Atticus on this issue: "I live here . . . in a great City, where I have a multitude of acquaintance, but not a man of all that company with whom I dare familiarly breathe." *The Anatomy of Melancholy,* ed. Floyd Dell and Paul Jordan-Smith (New York: Tudor Publishing Co., 1927), p. 472.

him from the generality of those with whom I live" (p. 80, note 1). In a sense, a "national" politics (royal *or* democratic) and absolute friendship each represent the failure of the other. Here we see that an expanding sense of political scale and its resulting processes of institutional compartmentalization run athwart of friendship's rhetorical impulses. Modern bureaucracy—whether idealized as Weberian rationality[5] or defined by its Kafka-esque nightmarish operations—is Renaissance friendship's great opposite.

Friendship's place within the wider phenomenon and theorization of Renaissance polity, then, has nothing to do with an abstractable, generalizable model of political institutions (as it would later serve in representations of the French Revolution or in nineteenth-century U.S. discourses). Instead, it outlines a mythical account of the institution—and maintenance—of political bodies, by means of a sharply differentiated, embodied sense of public and private "personage," a sense that is set by the parameters of "office." While friendship discourses sovereign the private subject, in part, as a compensation for his privation from office, they also detach a form of agency from its origins in monarchical prerogative and authority. In place of a king holding sovereign sway over others, friendship proposes a sovereign self holding title to itself. This self-titled subject exerts two kinds of agency: agency in its greatest utopian extension (imagining a politics of consent) and agency profoundly attentive to its own political constraints (in the pragmatics of counsel). Bacon's voicing of this sovereigned self bespeaks its governmental origin: "If a man have a true Frend, . . . a man hath as it were two Lives in his desires . . . ; where friendship is, all Offices of life, are as it were granted to Him . . . for he may exercise them by his Frend" (p. 86). The language of "offices" here upholds a utopian sense of what we might call capacities insofar as their distinct functions are not yet seen to fragment the subject, but to extend his spheres of operation. In the 1630s, Thomas Browne shows how central the logics of Renaissance sovereignty are to the agentive, multiofficed private self that friendship imagines into being. There, he writes, conflating the place of friendship and the time of dreams, "I can bee a king without a crowne."[6]

While the rhetorical power of Renaissance friendship fades with the onset of republicanism and the renegotiation of monarchy effected by Parliamentary forces in the midseventeenth century, the early modern theory

5. See, for example, Jerry L. Mashaw, *Bureaucratic Justice* (New Haven, Conn.: Yale University Press, 1983).

6. Thomas Browne, *Religio Medici*, in *The Major Works*, ed. C. A. Patrides (London: Penguin, 1977), p. 154, note 104.

of personage it highlights remains significant for contemporary public institutions, their structural challenges, and the quasi-legal norms governing them. Renaissance friendship directed a powerful rhetoric of asceticism at that specific individual who serves as an inaugural experiment in what it means to institute an impartial "public" body. Here we see the beginnings of modern bureaucracy in the affective limits and compartmentalizations required of the individual monarch. These are the exactions that Christopher Marlowe sees (in *Edward II*) when he describes the dilemma of a king longing for privacy whose "enemies" are those who just want him to *be king*. Simply expressed, this differentiated form of public personage begins to conceive what we have since known as "principled," rational bureaucracy—written on the body of one person. In the twentieth century, as Hannah Arendt has so powerfully demonstrated, bureaucracy would chart some further dystopian course and become the rule of "nobody."[7]

Ongoing crises about the legal status of the "private" lives of "public" figures—crises on both sides of the Atlantic—show that our own cultural moment still has roots in these Renaissance logics of "office." In U.S. presidential politics, we still struggle with the conundrum of political personage ("the king's two bodies") and the inevitable practical problems attending an embodied individual (a body natural) who, theoretically, is to emblematize the public good (the body politic). Can an act within the confines of the Oval Office *ever* be "private"? But the public figure's resistance to being cast as virtual public property is an old struggle. Elizabeth I once objected, "I have, . . . during my reign, seen and heard many opprobrious books and pamphlets against me, my realm, and state, accusing me to be a tyrant[;] . . . I pray you give me leave to say somewhat for myself . . . let me acquaint you with my intents."[8] James I repeatedly and haplessly attempted to refute public impressions of him by invoking "a Mirror, or Christall, as through the transparantnesse thereof you may see the heart of your king."[9] Against the presumption of seamless intersubjective commu-

7. Hannah Arendt, *The Human Condition* (Chicago: University of Chicago Press, 1998).

8. Elizabeth I, "Queen Elizabeth's Second Reply to the Parliamentary Petitions Urging the Execution of Mary, Queen of Scots, November 24, 1586, in *Elizabeth I: Collected Works*, ed. Leah Marcus, Janel Mueller, and Mary Beth Rose (Chicago: University of Chicago Press, 2000), pp. 196–204, 201–2.

9. James I, "A Speech to the Lords and Commons of the Parliament," 21 March 1609, in *Political Writings*, ed. Johan P. Somerville (Cambridge: Cambridge University Press, 1994), p. 179.

nication that friendship establishes between friends, the monarch's positioning requires him to be, in a sense, perpetually misunderstood.

While the Renaissance monarch now seems an exotic way to figure the institutions of governance, the tense incommensurability between "person" and "office" remains the insoluble and perhaps signature mark of modern institutional organization. Such civic and corporate institutional forms now overwhelmingly order the world in which we live; the dilemmas of office-holding and the disparate "capacities" it generates (personal, professional, institutional, and otherwise) are a matter of daily observation. These dilemmas bespeak the legacy of the early modern political, legal, and affective mythography that friendship begins to make so visible. Its idioms of "office" and "personage" continue to shape and tangle Anglophone formulations of agency—public *and* private—even at the start of the twenty-first century.

Adelman, Janet. *Suffocating Mothers: Fantasies of Maternal Origin in Shakespeare's Plays, Hamlet to The Tempest*. New York: Routledge, 1992.

Aelred of Rievaulx. *Spiritual Friendship*. Translated by Eugenia Laker, S.S.N.D. Kalamazoo, Mich.: Cistercian Publications, 1974.

Alciati, Andreas. *Omnia Andreae Alciati V.C. emblemata*. Antwerp: Christopher Plantijn, 1577.

Arendt, Hannah. *The Human Condition*. Chicago: University of Chicago Press, 1998.

Aristotle. *Nicomachean Ethics*. Translated by Horace Rackham. Cambridge, Mass.: Harvard University Press, 1926.

Ascham, Roger. *The Scholemaster, Or plaine and perfit way of teachyng children, to understand, write, and speake, in Latin tong*. London: John Day, 1570. Reprint edited by Edward Arber, Westminster: A. Constable and Co., 1897.

Auden, W. H. "The Prince's Dog." In *The Dyer's Hand and Other Essays*. New York: Random House, 1948.

Bacon, Francis. *The Essayes or Counsels, Civill and Morall*. Edited by Michael Kiernan. Cambridge, Mass.: Harvard University Press, 1985.

Baldwin, T. W. *William Shakspere's Smalle Latine & Lesse Greeke*. Urbana: University of Illinois Press, 1944.

Barber, C. L. *Shakespeare's Festive Comedy: A Study of Dramatic Form and Its Relation to Social Custom*. Princeton, N.J.: Princeton University Press, 1959.

Barish, Jonas. "The Turning Away of Prince Hal." *Shakespeare Studies* 1 (1965): 9–17.

Barkan, Leonard. "Diana and acteaon: The Myth as Synthesis." *English Literary Renaissance* (Autumn 1980): 317–59.

Barnes, Barnabe. *Foure Bookes of Offices: enabling privat persons for the speciall service of all good princes and policies*. London: A. Islip, 1606.

Beaumont, Francis, and Fletcher, John. *The Dramatic Works in the Beaumont and Fletcher Canon*. Edited by Fredson Bowers. Cambridge: Cambridge University Press, 1970.

Berry, Philippa. *Of Chastity and Power: Elizabethan Literature and the Unmarried Queen*. London: Routledge, 1989.

Bevington, David. "John Lyly and Queen Elizabeth: Royal Flattery in *Campaspe* and *Sapho and Phao*." *Renaissance Papers* (1966): 57–67.

Blanchot, Maurice. *L'Amitié*. Paris: Gallimard, 1971.

Blank, Paula. "Comparing Sappho to Philaenis: John Donne's 'Homopoetics.'" *PMLA* 10, no. 3 (spring 1995): 358–68, 359.

Boswell, John. "Revolutions, Universals, Categories." *Salmagundi* 58–59 (fall 1982–winter 1983): 89–113.

Bray, Alan. *Homosexuality in Renaissance England*. London: Gay Men's Press, 1982.

———. "Homosexuality and the Signs of Male Friendship in Elizabethan England." *History Workshop*, no. 29 (spring 1990): 1–19.

Breme, Thomas. *The mirrour of friendship: both how to knowe a perfect friend, and how to choose him*. London: Abel Jeffes, 1584.

Browne, Thomas. *Religio Medici*, in *The Major Works*. Edited by C. A. Patrides. London: Penguin, 1977.

Bryant, J. A. "Prince Hal and the Ephesians." *Sewanee Review* 67 (1959): 204–19.

Burton, Robert. *The Anatomy of Melancholy*. Edited by Floyd Dell and Paul Jordan-Smith. New York: Tudor Publishing Co., 1927.

Bushnell, Rebecca. *Tragedies of Tyrants: Political Thought and Theater in the English Renaissance*. Ithaca, N.Y.: Cornell University Press, 1990.

Cary, Elizabeth. *The Tragedy of Mariam, the Fair Queen of Jewry*. Edited by Margaret Ferguson and Barry Weller. Berkeley and Los Angeles: University of California Press, 1994.

Chartier, Roger. "Reading Matter and 'Popular' Reading: From the Renaissance to the Seventeenth Century." In *A History of Reading in the West*, edited by Guglielmo Cavallo and Roger Chartier. Amherst: University of Massachusetts Press, 1999.

Churchyard, Thomas. *A sparke of frendship and warme goodwill, that shewest the effect of true affection and unfoldes the fineness of this world*. London: Thomas Orwin, 1588.

Cicero. *De amicitia*. Translated by John Tiptoft. London: William Caxton, 1481.

———. *Fowre Seuerall Treatises of M. Tullius Cicero, Conteyninge his most learned and Eloquente Discourses of Frendshippe: Oldage: Paradoxes: and Scipio his Dreame*. Translated by Thomas Newton. London: Thomas Marshe, 1577.

———. *De senectute, De amicitia, De divinatione*. Translated by William Falconer. Cambridge, Mass.: Harvard University Press, 1923.

Day, Angel. *The English Secretorie*. London: P. Short, 1599.

Derrida, Jacques. *The Politics of Friendship*. Translated by George Collins. London: Verso, 1997.

———. "The Politics of Friendship." *The Journal of Philosophy* 85, no. 11 (November 1998): 632–44.

Donne, John. *Letters to Severall Persons of Honour*. London: J. Flesher, 1651.

———. *The Complete English Poems*. Edited by C. A. Patrides. London: Dent, 1985.

———. *Poetical Works*. Edited by Herbert Grierson. Oxford: Oxford University Press, 1990.

Dorke, Walter. *A Tipe or Figure of Friendship. Wherein is liuelie, and compendiouslie expressed, the right nature and propertie of a perfect and true friend*. London: Thomas Orwin and Henry Kirkham, 1589.

Elizabeth I. *Elizabeth I: Collected Works*. Edited by Leah Marcus, Janel Mueller, and Mary Beth Rose. Chicago: University of Chicago Press, 2000.

Elyot, Thomas. *The Boke Named the Governour*. Edited by Foster Watson. New York: Everyman, 1907.

Empson, William. "Falstaff and Mr. Dover Wilson." *The Kenyon Review* 15 (spring 1953): 213–62, 220.

———. *Some Versions of Pastoral.* New York: New Directions, 1974.

Erasmus. *Apopthegmes, that is to saie, prompte, quicke, wittie and sentencious saiynges, of certain emperours, kynges, capitaines, philosophiers and orators . . . First gathered and compiled in Latin by the ryght famous clerke Maister Erasmus of Roterodame.* Translated by Nicolas Udall. London: Richard Grafton, 1542. Reprint edited by Robert Roberts, Boston: Lincolnshire, 1877.

———. *The Colloquies of Erasmus.* Translated by N. Bailey. London: Reeves & Turner, 1878.

———. *Adagia.* Vol. 31 of *The Collected Works of Erasmus,* translated by Margaret Mann Phillips. Toronto: University of Toronto Press, 1982.

———. *The Education of a Christian Prince.* Edited by Lisa Jardine. Cambridge: Cambridge University Press, 1997.

Ferguson, Margaret. "Running On with Almost Public Voice: The Case of 'E.C.'" In *Tradition and the Talents of Women,* edited by Florence Henderson. Urbana: University of Illinois Press, 1991.

Ferguson, Margaret, Quilligan, Maureen, and Vickers, Nancy, eds. *Rewriting the Renaissance: The Discourses of Sexual Difference in Early Modern Europe.* Chicago: University of Chicago Press, 1986.

Fish, Stanley. "Authors-Readers: Jonson's Community of the Same." *Representations* 7 (summer 1984): 26–58.

Flesch, William. *The Limits of Generosity: Shakespeare, Herbert, Milton.* Ithaca, N.Y.: Cornell University Press, 1992.

Ford, John. *Perkin Warbeck.* Edited by Donald Anderson. Lincoln: University of Nebraska Press, 1965.

Foucault, Michel. *Foucault Live.* Translated by J. Johnston and edited by Sylvère Lotringer. Columbia University Press, Semiotext(e) Foreign Agents Series. New York, 1989.

Freitag, Arnold. *Mythologia Ethica, hoc est moralis philosophiae per fabulas brutis attributas.* Antwerp: Christopher Plantijn, 1579.

Garrard, Mary D. *Artemisia Gentileschi.* New York: Rizzoli, 1993.

Goldberg, Jonathan. "Sodomy and Society: The Case of Christopher Marlowe." *Southwest Review* 69 (1984): 371–78.

———. *Sodometries: Renaissance Texts, Modern Sexualities.* Stanford, Calif.: Stanford University Press, 1992.

———, ed. *Queering the Renaissance.* Durham, N.C.: Duke University Press, 1994.

Gouge, William. *Of Domesticall Duties.* London: John Haviland and William Bladen, 1622.

Greenblatt, Stephen. *Renaissance Self-Fashioning from More to Shakespeare.* Chicago: University of Chicago Press, 1980.

———. "Fiction and Friction." In *Reconstructing Individualism: Autonomy, Individuality, and the Self in Western Thought.* Edited by Thomas Heller. Stanford, Calif.: Stanford University Press, 1986.

Greene, Robert. *Friar Bacon and Friar Bungay.* Edited by Daniel Seltzer. Lincoln: University of Nebraska Press, 1963.

Greer, Germaine. *Kissing the Rod: An Anthology of Seventeenth-Century Women's Verse.* New York: Farrar Straus Giroux, 1989.

Gutierrez, Nancy. "Valuing *Mariam*: Genre Study and Feminist Analysis." *Tulsa Studies in Women's Literature* (autumn 1991): 233–51.

Guy, John. *Tudor England*. Oxford: Oxford University Press, 1988.

Hall, Edward. *The Triumphant Reigne of Kyng Henry the VIII*. Edited by Charles Whibley. London: 1904.

Hall, Kim F. *Things of Darkness: Economies of Race and Gender in Early Modern England*. Ithaca, N.Y.: Cornell University Press, 1995.

Halpern, Richard. *The Poetics of Primitive Accumulation: English Renaissance Culture and the Genealogy of Capital*. Ithaca, N.Y.: Cornell University Press, 1991.

Holstun, James. "'Will you rent our ancient love asunder?': Lesbian Elegy in Donne, Marvell, and Milton." *English Literary History* 54 (winter 1987): 835–67.

Huizinga, Johan. *Herfsttij der Middeleeuwen: studie over levens en gedachtenvormen der veertiende en vijftiende eeuw in Frankrijk en de Nederlanden*. Harlem: Tjeenk Willink en Zoon, 1921.

Hutson, Lorna. *The Usurer's Daughter: Male Friendship and Fictions of Women in Sixteenth-Century England*. London: Routledge, 1994.

———. "On Not Being Deceived: Rhetoric and the Body in *Twelfth Night*." *Texas Studies in Literature and Language* 38, no. 2 (summer 1996): 140–74.

Irigaray, Luce. *The Sex Which Is Not One*. Translated by Catharine Porter. Ithaca, N.Y.: Cornell University Press, 1985.

James I. *Political Writings*. Edited by Johan P. Somerville. Cambridge: Cambridge University Press, 1994.

Jensen, Kristian. "The Humanist Reform of Latin and Latin Teaching." In *The Cambridge Companion to Renaissance Humanism*, edited by Jill Kraye. Cambridge: Cambridge University Press, 1996.

Jonson, Ben. *Ben Jonson's Plays and Masques*. Edited by Robert Adams. New York: Norton, 1979.

———. *Ben Jonson*. Edited by Ian Donaldson. Oxford: Oxford University Press, 1995.

Jordan, Constance. *Renaissance Feminism: Literary Texts and Political Models*. Ithaca, N.Y.: Cornell University Press, 1990.

Kahn, Coppelia. *Man's Estate: Masculine Identity in Shakespeare*. Berkeley and Los Angeles: University of California Press, 1981.

Kahn, Victoria. "Humanism and the Resistance to Theory." In *Literary Theory/Renaissance Texts*, edited by Patricia Parker and David Quint. Baltimore: Johns Hopkins University Press, 1986.

Kantorowicz, Ernst. *The King's Two Bodies: A Study in Medieval Political Theology*. Princeton, N.J.: Princeton University Press, 1957.

Kastan, David Scott, and Stallybrass, Peter. *Staging the Renaissance: Reinterpretations of Elizabethan and Jacobean Drama*. New York: Routledge, 1991.

Kurland, Stuart. "'We Need No More of Your Advice': Political Realism in *The Winter's Tale*." *Studies in English Literature* 31 (1991): 36–86.

Laqueur, Thomas. *Making Sex: The Body and Gender from the Greeks to Freud*. Cambridge, Mass.: Harvard University Press, 1990.

Latimer, Hugh. "The Sermon of the Plough." In *Sermons by Hugh Latimer*, edited by George Elwes Corrie. New York: Johnson Reprint Corp., 1971.

Lewalski, Barbara Kiefer. *Writing Women in Jacobean England*. Cambridge, Mass.: Harvard University Press, 1993.

Lewicke, Edwarde. *The most Wonderful and pleasaunt History of Titus and Gisippus, whereby is fully declared the figure of perfect frendshyp, drawen into English metre.* London: 1562.

Lyly, John. *The Complete Works of John Lyly.* Edited by R. Warwick Bond. Oxford: Clarendon Press, 1902.

MacCaffrey, Wallace. *Elizabeth I.* London: Edward Arnold, 1993.

Maclean, Ian. *The Renaissance Notion of Woman: A Study in the Fortunes of Scholasticism and European Intellectual Life.* Cambridge: Cambridge University Press, 1980.

Machiavelli, Niccolò. *The Prince.* Edited by Quentin Skinner and Russell Price. Cambridge: Cambridge University Press, 1988.

Masten, Jeffrey. *Textual Intercourse: Collaboration, Authorship, and Sexualities in Renaissance Drama.* Cambridge: Cambridge University Press, 1997.

Middleton, Thomas. *The Second Maiden's Tragedy.* London: 1611.

Mills, Laurens. "The Meaning of *Edward II.*" *Modern Philology* 32 (1934–35): 11–31.

———. *One Soul in Bodies Twain: Friendship in Tudor and Stuart Literature.* Bloomington, Ind.: The Principia Press, 1937.

Milton, John. *The Doctrine and Discipline of Divorce Restored to the Good of Both Sexes.* In *John Milton,* edited by Stephen Orgel and Jonathan Goldberg. Oxford: Oxford University Press, 1990.

Montaigne, Michel de. *The Essayes of Montaigne: John Florio's Translation.* Edited by J. I. M. Stewart. New York: Modern Library, 1933.

———. *Essais.* Edited by Pierre Villey. Paris: Presses Universitaires de France, 1988.

Montrose, Louis. "The Elizabethan Subject and the Spenserian Text." In *Literary Theory/ Renaissance Texts,* edited by Patricia Parker and David Quint. Baltimore: Johns Hopkins University Press, 1986.

Mueller, Janel. "Troping Utopia: Donne's Brief for Lesbianism in 'Sappho to Philaenis.'" In *Sexuality and Gender in Early Modern Europe,* edited by James Grantham Turner. Cambridge: Cambridge University Press, 1993.

Mulcaster, Richard. *Positions concerning the Training Up of Children.* Edited by William Barker. Toronto: University of Toronto Press, 1994.

Nashe, Thomas. *The Unfortunate Traveller.* In *An Anthology of Elizabethan Prose Fiction,* edited by Paul Salzman. Oxford: Oxford University Press, 1987.

Neely, Carol Thomas. "Women and 'Issue' in *The Winter's Tale.*" *Philological Quarterly* 57 (1978): 181–94.

Norton, Thomas, and Sackville, Thomas. *The Tragedie of Gorboduc.* London: William Griffith, 1565.

Ong, Walter. *Rhetoric, Romance, and Technology: Studies in the Interaction of Expression and Culture.* Ithaca: Cornell University Press, 1971.

Orgel, Stephen. *Impersonations: The Performance of Gender in Shakespeare's England.* Cambridge: Cambridge University Press, 1996.

Ovid. *The Metamorphoses.* Translated by Frank Justus Miller. Cambridge: Harvard University Press, 1916.

Parker, Patricia. "Gender Ideology, Gender Change: The Case of Marie Germain." *Critical Inquiry* 19 (1993): 337–64.

Patterson, Annabel. *Early Modern Liberalism.* Cambridge: Cambridge University Press, 1997.

Peacham, Henry. *Minerva Britanna or a Garden of Heroical Devises.* London: W. Dight, 1612.

Pearson, D'Orsay. "Unkinde Theseus: A Study in Renaissance Mythography." *English Literary Renaissance* (spring 1974): 276–98.

Plutarch. *The philosophie commonlie called, the morals, written by the learned philosopher Plutarch of Chaeronea. Translated out of Greeke into English, and conferred with the Latin translations and the French.* Translated by Philemon Holland. London: Arnold Hatfield, 1603.

Pye, Christopher. *The Regal Phantasm: Shakespeare and the Politics of Spectacle.* London: Routledge, 1990.

Rich, Adrienne. "Compulsory Heterosexuality and Lesbian Existence." *Signs: A Journal of Women in Culture and Society* 5, no. 4 (summer 1980): 631–60.

Ripa, Cesare. *Nova Iconologia.* Padua: Pietro Paolo Tozzi, 1618.

Roberts, Jeanne. "Crises of Male Self-Definition in The Two Noble Kinsmen." In *Shakespeare, Fletcher, and The Two Noble Kinsmen,* edited by Charles H. Frey. Columbia: University of Missouri Press, 1989.

Rollins, Hyder Edward, ed. *Tottel's Miscellany (1557–1587).* Cambridge, Mass.: Harvard University Press, 1956.

Rose, Mary Beth. *The Expense of Spirit: Love and Sexuality in English Renaissance Drama.* Ithaca, N.Y.: Cornell University Press, 1988.

Roper, William. *The Life of Sir Thomas More.* In *Two Early Tudor Lives,* edited by Richard Sylvester and Davis Harding. New Haven, Conn.: Yale University Press, 1962.

Rosen, Barbara, ed. *Witchcraft.* London: Edward Arnold, 1969.

Rigolot, Francois. "Reviving Harmodius and Aristogiton in the Renaissance: Friendship and Tyranny as Voluntary Servitude." *Montaigne Studies* 11 (1999): 107–19.

Schwarz, Kathryn. *Tough Love: Amazon Encounters in the English Renaissance.* Durham, N.C.: Duke University Press, 2000.

Sedgwick, Eve Kosofsky. *Between Men: English Literature and Male Homosocial Desire.* New York: Columbia University Press, 1985.

Shakespeare, William. *The Winter's Tale.* Edited by Stephen Orgel. Oxford: Oxford University Press, 1996.

———. *The Complete Works of Shakespeare.* Edited by David Bevington. New York: Longman, 1997.

Shakespeare, William, and Fletcher, John. *The Two Noble Kinsmen.* Edited by Eugene Waith. Oxford: Clarendon Press, 1989.

Shannon, Laurie. "Nature's Bias: Renaissance Homonormativity and Elizabethan Comic Likeness." *Modern Philology* 98, no. 2 (November 2000): 183–210.

Skinner, Quentin. *Liberty before Liberalism.* Cambridge: Cambridge University Press, 1999.

Smith, Bruce. *Homosexual Desire in Shakespeare's England: A Cultural Poetics.* Chicago: University of Chicago Press, 1991.

Smith, Thomas. *De Republica Anglorum.* Edited by Mary Dewar. Cambridge: Cambridge University Press, 1982.

Spenser, Edmund. *The Poetical Works of Edmund Spenser.* Edited by J. C. Smith and E. de Selincourt. Oxford: Oxford University Press, 1912.

———. *The Faerie Queene.* Edited by A. C. Hamilton. London: Longman, 1977.

Stallybrass, Peter. "Patriarchal Territories: The Body Enclosed." In *Rewriting the Renaissance: The Discourses of Sexual Difference in Early Modern Europe,* edited by Margaret Ferguson, Maureen Quilligan, and Nancy Vickers, pp. 123–42. Chicago: University of Chicago Press, 1986.

Starkey, David. *The English Court: From the Wars of the Roses to the Civil War.* London: Longman, 1987.

Strier, Richard. *Resistant Structures: Particularity, Radicalism, and Renaissance Texts.* Berkeley and Los Angeles: University of California Press, 1995.

Summers, Claude. "Homosexuality and Renaissance Literature, or The Anxieties of Anachronism." *South Central Review* 9, no. 1 (spring 1992): 2–23.

Taverner, Richard. *The Garden of Wysdom.* London: Richard Bankes, 1539.

Thomas à Kempis. *The Imitation of Christ.* Translated by Leo Shirley-Price. London: Penguin, 1952.

Tillyard, E. M. W. *Shakespeare's History Plays.* London: Chatto & Windus, 1944.

Tilney, Edmund. *The Flower of Friendship: A Renaissance Dialogue Contesting Marriage.* Ed. Valerie Wayne. Ithaca, N.Y.: Cornell University Press, 1992.

Traub, Valerie. *Desire and Anxiety: Circulations of Sexuality in Shakespearian Drama.* New York: Routledge, 1992.

———. "The (In)significance of Lesbian Desire." In *Queering the Renaissance,* edited by Jonathan Goldberg. Durham, N.C.: Duke University Press, 1994.

Trumbull, H. Clay. *Friendship: The Master-Passion.* Philadelphia: John Wattles, 1894.

Twain, Mark. *The Innocents Abroad.* Hartford, Conn.: American Publishing Co., 1869.

Vickers, Nancy. "Diana Described: Scattered Woman and Scattered Rhyme." *Critical Inquiry* (winter 1981): 265–79.

Weller, Barry. "The Rhetoric of Friendship in Montaigne's *Essais.*" *New Literary History* 9 (spring 1978): 503–23.

———. "*The Two Noble Kinsmen,* the Friendship Tradition, and the Flight from Eros." In *Shakespeare, Fletcher, and The Two Noble Kinsmen,* edited by Charles H. Frey. Columbia: University of Missouri Press, 1989.

Wilson, John Dover. "The Falstaff Myth." In *Henry IV: Critical Essays,* edited by David Bevington. New York: Garland Press, 1986.

Wither, George. *A Collection of Emblemes, Ancient and Modern.* London: A. Mathewes, 1635.

Wyatt, Thomas. *The Complete Poems,* edited by R. A. Rebholz. New Haven, Conn.: Yale University Press, 1978.

Zeigler, Georgiana. "My Lady's Chamber: Female Space, Female Chastity in Shakespeare." *Textual Practice* (spring 1980).

INDEX

Act in Restraint of Appeals, 31–32
Adelman, Janet, 66 n.33, 168 n.29, 190, 210
Aesop, 208
affect, 1, 19, 50, 90–95. *See also* homonorma-
    tivity; love
agency, 31–34, 53, 97, 225. *See also* legal per-
    sonage; sovereignty, private
Alciati, Andreas, 36, 199
Amazons, 96, 96 n.21, 109, 112, 121–22
Arendt, Hannah, 226
Aristotle, 1, 40, 42, 58, 136, 224, passim
Ascham, Roger, 23–24, 27
Auden, W. H., 169
autonomy, 30-38. *See also* sovereignty, private
aversion, 46–47; hetero-, 55–56, 62, 64–68

Bacon, Francis, 98 n.32, 143, 183, 194–99,
    224–25
Baldwin, T. W., 27–28
Barber, C. L., 182
Barnes, Barnabe, 10
Berry, Philippa, 62, 69, 80–81
Bevington, David, 138 n.30
Blank, Paula, 20, 101 n.40
Boswell, John, 97 n.23
Bray, Alan, 94, 133, 160–61
Breme, Thomas, 5, 18, 28, 32–33
Browne, Thomas, 34, 225
bureaucracy, 148, 225–26
Burton, Robert, 34–35, 194–96
Bushnell, Rebecca, 57 n.3, 64 n.28, 142 n.39, 158

Cary, Elizabeth, 70–71, 73, chap. 2, passim
chastity: associative, 57, 69–70, 80–89, 92,

115–16; female, 56–58, 68–70, 75–79,
    122; and friendship, 56–58, 69–70, 79–80,
    121–22; male, 56, 57; seclusion, 83–84,
    119–20
Chandler, James, 215 n.53
Chartier, Roger, 26 n.22, 29
Chaucer, 102–3
Churchyard, Thomas, 5, 28, 32–33
Cicero, 3, 23–31, 40–41, 47, 52, 58–59, 61,
    90–91, 105, 202, passim; Newton's 1577
    translation of, 28, 32, 41, 48; Tiptoft's 1481
    translation of, 3, 6–7, 24–26, 31, 40–41,
    58, 67, 90, 128
class. *See* likeness of station
Clinton, Bill, 226
closet drama, 70–71, 162
concord, 36–38
consent, 7, 22–23, 38–44, 61
contract, 38–40, 43–44, 46
corporatism. *See* incorporation
counsel: and friendship, 23, 46–51, 189–90,
    197–99, chap. 6 passim; and the humanists,
    22–23, 47–51, 110, 142; and gender, 110,
    209–13; and virtuous falsehoods, 213–19.
    See also Plutarch; Bacon; "liberty of speech"

Day, Angel, 129
degree. *See* likeness of station
democracy. *See* political thought; bureaucracy
Derrida, Jacques, 18, 44, 125, 219, 224
Diana, 63, 69–70, 81–83, 85–86, 96, 100,
    117
difference, 2, 10, 91, 126. *See also* legal person-
    age; likeness

237

93–94; of sex, 2–3, 55, 65 n.29, 66, 98, 115–16; of station, 2–3, 98, 128–36, 141–47; virtual, 21, 39–40
love, 64–68, 106–7, 111, 158
Lyly, John, 65–67, 138–40

Machiavelli, Niccolò, 139
Maclean, Ian, 58
Marlowe, Christopher, 135, 144, 159–65
marriage, 54–64, 74–75, 91, 101–2, 111, 113, 212, 219
Masten, Jeffrey, 2, 20 n.8, 22 n.14, 91 n.4, 201 n.28
Melancthon, Philip, 28
Middleton, Thomas, 74
mignonnerie. See kingship
Mills, Laurens, 2 n.2, 160–61
Milton, John, 61, 153
monarchy. *See* kingship
Montaigne, Michel de, 4, 7, 17–18, 32, 43–44, 54–55, 58–60, 65, 92, 104–5, 115, 133, 187, passim
Montrose, Louis, 96 n.21, 148
More, Thomas, 57, 215
Mueller, Janel, 94, 101, 138 n.31
Mulcaster, Richard, 27

Nashe, Thomas, 135–36
Neely, Carol Thomas, 206, 210

obedience, 56–60, 63, 71, 80
offices/office holding, 11, 19, 125–26, 225–27
Ong, Walter, 26, 28
Orgel, Stephen, 63, 215
Ovid, 82–83

Parliamentary power, 52, 61, 148
Patterson, Annabel, 18 n.3
Peacham, Henry, 35–36, 188–89, 208
pedagogy, 5, 23–24, 30, 45
Petrarchism, 88–89, 113–15
Plato, 1 n.1, 60 n.13
Plowden, Edmund, 150
Plutarch, 47–52, 191–94
political thought: democracy, 9, 18–19, 23, 46, 52, 224–25; and friendship, 7–8, 17–19, 23, 46, 64; orthodox, 126–28, 136, 142–43, 148–55; republicanism, 126, 191, 225–26; resistance, 8, 71; sedition, 44, 142–43, 164–65, 142 n.38; utopian, 3, 7, 17, 22, 43–45, 101–2, 113

popularization of classical friendship ideas, 4, 28–29, 34, 208–9
Pye, Christopher, 148

reading and readership, 5, 25–30, 52–53
regeneration, 190, 210, 216, 222. *See also* grafting
Rich, Adrienne, 61 n.18, 100
rights vs. friendship discourses, 18–19
Rigolot, François, 3 n.4, 38 n.52
Ripa, Cesare, 35
Rose, Mary Beth, 67, 100, chap. 3 passim

Schwarz, Kathryn, 96 n.21
Sedgwick, Eve Kosofsky, 8–9, 66, 67 n.35, 211 n.49
self-fashioning, 5–6, 22, 24–25, 29, 30–34
sexual reproduction vs. friendship, 43, 190, 198, 201, 210–11, 219–22
sexuality: and friendship, 54–56, 90–99, 120–22; heterosexuality, 8–9, 55–56, 64–68, 90–99, 100, 107, 116, 190, 210–11; historical, 1, 90–99, 146, 200, 215; homosexuality, 91–99, 146 n.49; homosexuality, female, 92–99, 101–2, 116, 118–22, 186–87
Shakespeare, William: sonnets of, 2, 8–9, 91, 148; *All's Well that Ends Well*, 55, 66; *As You Like It*, 4; *Hamlet*, 31, 32; *Henry IV, Parts One and Two*, chap. 5, passim; *Henry V*, 10, 183; *Henry VIII*, 146 n.47; *King Lear*, 205, 209; *The Merchant of Venice*, 54; *A Midsummer Night's Dream*, 68–69, 109, 185; *Othello*, 206, 213; *Romeo and Juliet*, 67; *Troilus and Cressida*, 129; *Twelfth Night*, 43; *Two Gentlemen of Verona*, 106 n.53; *The Two Noble Kinsmen*, chap. 3 passim; *The Winter's Tale*, chap. 5 passim
Shannon, Laurie, 71 n.46, 91 n.3
Sidney, Philip, 169
Skinner, Quentin, 18 n.3
Smith, Thomas, 96 n.19, 154
sodomy, 91–93, 98 n.31, 133, 161
solitude, 155, 223–24
sovereign (as adjective), 6–7, 32
sovereignty, private, 2, 9, 18–19, 22, 30–38, 45–46, 53, 96–97, 102, 116–17, 125, 196–97, 225; sovereignty, private, and gender, 56, 102, 113
sovereignty, public, 9–10, 31–32, 126–28, 147–55, 198–99, 225–27
speech. *See* liberty of speech
Spenser, Edmund, 57 n.4, 62, 83, 132

Printed in Great Britain
by Amazon